The Labor Market in Japan

The Labor Market in Japan

Selected Readings

Edited by
Shunsaku Nishikawa

Translated by
Ross Mouer

UNIVERSITY OF TOKYO PRESS

2δ0695

The essays in this book were originally
published in the Japanese-language
versions listed on the opening pages of each.

English translation © 1980 by
THE JAPAN FOUNDATION

UTP 3036–57085–5149
ISBN 0–86008–262–8

Printed in Japan

Contents

v

Translator's Preface

Since the late 1960s the interest of Western social scientists in Japanese society has increased markedly. One major concern has been the mechanism which brings the human individual into economic production. On the one hand, by the late 1960s the focus of development economists had already shifted; a narrower concern with simply the accumulation of physical capital had given way to an interest in the larger social setting, and particularly the contribution to the development of human capital and the role of education.[1] On the other hand, because Japan was seen as the first non-Western nation to industrialize, sociologists interested in social change and the processes of "modernization" increasingly had come to consider Japan as an important case study for examining issues raised in the debate on convergence and divergence.

From these perspectives, the Japanese approach to industrial relations has attracted the attention of both economists and sociologists. Much of the Western research in this area has been interdisciplinary and within the framework of area studies. Behind this flowering of research has been economic growth itself (a phenomenon which no doubt stirred people politically, shifted the flow of financial support toward research projects related to Japan, and opened up new channels of cultural contact).

Although research on comparative occupational structures, employment practices, and values in the mid-1950s set the tenor of the debate

---

[1] For a brief discussion of this research in Japan, see Nakayama Ichirō, *Industrialism and Labor-Management Relations in Japan* (Tokyo: Japan Institute of Labour, 1975), pp. 93–101.

vii

regarding the nature of work in Japan for years to come,[2] it was really in the late 1960s that concern about Japan's "miraculous" economic growth focused attention on the unique facets of Japanese economic behavior. The term "Japanology", which came to describe a massive effort in institutionalized research, also contained, like the words "Kremlinology" and "Sinology", the connotation that a foreign society can best be understood by deciphering the secret codes that uniquely define behavior within that society.

Much of the English literature about the labor market in Japan, though not all of it, similarly stresses the uniqueness of Japan's employment practices,[3] with attention being focused on the practices of career (lifetime) employment, seniority wages, and enterprise unionism. Unfortunately, much that is written in this area has relied on individual case studies, participant observation, and personal anecdotes. While these basically anthropological methods have yielded numerous

[2] An article suggesting the similarity of the occupational structure in Japan and other industrial societies by Peter M. Rossi and Alex Inkles is "National Comparisons of Occupation Prestige," *American Journal of Sociology* (vol. 61, no. 4: January 1956), pp. 329–339. The major argument stressing Japan's cultural uniqueness appeared in James Abegglen's *The Japanese Factory: Aspects of Its Social Organization* (Glencoe: The Free Press, 1958), pp. 1–10 and 122–142. On values, see Robert N. Bellah, *Tokugawa Religion: The Values of Pre-Industrial Japan* (New York: The Free Press, 1957). These works remain the point of departure (though not necessarily agreement) for many later works appearing over the next two decades. See, for example, Robert Cole, *Japanese Blue Collar: The Changing Tradition* (Berkeley: University of California Press, 1971), p. 1, or Thomas P. Rohlen, *For Harmony and Strength: Japanese White-Collar Organization in Anthropological Perspective* (Berkeley: University of California Press, 1974), p. 2. Both books give brief summaries of the issues in the debate and bring in a broader range of literature.

[3] Volumes tending to stress the uniqueness of Japanese tradition in personnel management include James C. Abegglen, *Management and Worker: The Japanese Solution* (Tokyo: Sophia University in co-operation with Kodansha International Ltd., 1973); Robert J. Ballon, ed., *The Japanese Employee* (Tokyo: Sophia University in co-operation with the Charles E. Tuttle Company, 1969); Thomas P. Rohlen, *For Harmony and Strength;* Ronald P. Dore, *British Factory–Japanese Factory: The Origins of National Diversity in Industrial Relations* (Berkeley: University of California Press, 1973); and Ezra Vogel, ed., *Modern Japanese Organization and Decision-Making* (Berkeley: University of California Press, 1975). Many articles in the following volume tend to take a similar stance: Kazuo Okochi, Bernard Karsh and Solomon B. Levine, *Workers and Employers in Japan: The Japanese Employment Relations System* (Tokyo: University of Tokyo Press, 1973). Koji Taira's *Economic Development and the Labor Market in Japan* (New York: Columbia University Press, 1970) uses quantitative data on wage rates and other variables to build a careful refutation of the above approach. Though less assertive, Robert Cole also tends to suggest that some form of convergence—perhaps a synthesis of traditional norms and industrial logic—is taking place. See his *Japanese Blue Collar*. Finally, one should mention Robert Evans's *The Labor Economics of Japan and the United States* (New York: Praeger Publishers, 1971).

insights, their value has been diminished by the failure to consider carefully the problems of inference and of variation within Japanese society.

Given such methodological problems in the English literature, the essays in this volume would seem to have a particular value in providing a counterbalance: most offer a broader view of behavior in the Japanese labor market and utilize broadly based statistical data. While explanation and interpretation remain the core of enlightened social science, one must begin with an accurate assessment of the facts about the actual behavior which is to be explained. Most of the essays in this volume are behavioral in approach; many utilize quantitative analysis.

However, the essays are not just descriptive of Japanese behavior in the labor market; many are also written on three other levels. The first concerns the analysis of Japanese phenomena. On this level, the essays make known the abundance of good quality statistical data which is available in Japan. Although most data are collected from surveys by the government, a variety of semi-official and private organizations also compile reliable statistical data. The effective use of such quantitative data underlines their importance for planning in modern, information-oriented industrial societies. A second concern involves methodology. Although some of the methodologies reflect peculiarities of the Japanese data, much of the methodological discussion concerns more general issues relevant to the promotion of fruitful comparative research abroad. Finally, there are the policy implications. A feature of Japanese academic life is participation in governmental bodies and involvement in semi-official study groups. Consequently, many essays seek to tie the analysis of past phenomena not to some abstract literature but to a projection of future developments which will help people make more informed decisions, thereby adding a dynamic element to Japan's use of "indicative planning" and improving competition within the Japanese economy. These three levels are interrelated: the need for new methodologies reflects the fact that changes in the labor market often involve broader changes in society and the economy, which in some cases have resulted from the publication of earlier research.

Herein lies a major problem in translating a volume of this type. Many of the interconnections which make the articles significant are taken for granted by the authors. Originally written for a Japanese audience with a more-or-less common awareness of the major facets of the labor market and the broader social and historical setting in which it functions, the articles are defined by the particular points in time at which they appear. In other words, they tend to assume an appreciation of the situational linkage. The dates of original publication are important and should be kept in mind.

In the translation I have taken the liberty of elaborating on the more significant interconnections while deleting a few of the more involved but generally unnecessary digressions, repetitions, and expositions on very specialized and narrowly defined interconnections which were so abstract or compact as to require extended explanation for the non-Japanese reader. Certain terms, such as *"kyūjinbairitsu"* (literally, "the multiple of labor demand") or *"shoninkyū"* (starting salaries), do need to be defined in terms of a specific setting which requires a whole phrase rather than a single word. I am also aware of the tendency to prepare volumes about Japanese society for overseas audiences in a manner which "talks down" to the reader. Pains have been taken to minimize the occurrence of such irritating passages.

In the process of adding needed general explanation and deleting excessively specific explanation, each article no doubt has gone through a transformation. Indeed, translation itself is an interpretation. The translator seldom transposes that which he does not understand; rather, he interjects his own understandings into each set of meanings. As separate intellectual entities, translators are bound to see things in a way which is different from that of the author. To some extent the translator can learn his "subject" and come to feel empathy with the author. Nevertheless, although I have read several other articles or books by each of the authors in this volume, my ability to approach fifteen different authors remains limited. Accordingly, because I often had some of the author's other work in mind when translating that person's chapter, as well as a larger body of literature on the subject, it was easier to see certain continuities develop whereas the identification of new elements was more difficult. This is no doubt an important source of divergence from the original texts.

For these kinds of reasons, the translation is not simply a verbatim translation. It seeks to be an interpretative translation which focuses first on the major themes of the authors, and only secondarily on their personal vocabularies. Although this approach may be an anathema to some of the "purists", I feel that emphasis on themes and readability should have top priority in order to produce a volume which speaks not only to those generally interested in Japan but unfamiliar with the technical vocabulary on the economics of the labor market, but also to those who have a specialized knowledge of the theoretical literature on labor economics but little knowledge of Japan per se.

Finally, a number of editorial changes should be mentioned. Where practical, tables have been updated. Although American English usage has been followed throughout, a number of anomalies remain. For example, the American spelling of "labor" is used in the text, although the British spelling of "labour" has been used to maintain the officially designated spelling for the title of certain agencies including the Ministry of Labour and the Japan Institute of Labour.[4] An effort was also made with a modicum of success to standardize the footnoting. Japanese academicians often assume a familiarity with government statistics and other common sources of data and abbreviate references to them in a non-standardized fashion. This is often true of their citations of other literature as well. Although the lacunae were in many cases filled, smaller holes remain in a more-or-less random fashion. In the transliteration of Japanese words, elongated vowels are indicated except in commonly used place names such as "Tokyo" or "Osaka". Finally, Japanese names are presented in the order accepted in Japan, with the family name being followed by the given name.[5]

One of the questions with which I grappled was whether to include numerous Japanese words and phrases when they were used, however loosely, to represent a rather specific (though sometimes vague) concept for which no precise English equivalent exists. While their inclusion added precision for those familiar with Japanese, as well as heuristic value for those now learning the language, their presence tended to encumber the reading; consequently, many were omitted from the final draft, although the Japanese words were left behind in parentheses when they seemed crucial in distinguishing among several related concepts.

A number of stylistic changes were made. The fifteen essays in this volume originally appeared in a variety of magazines and journals ranging from *Shūkan Tōyō Keizai* (The Weekly Oriental Economist) for the general reader to *Kikan Riron Keizaigaku* (The Journal of the Association of Quantitative and Theoretical Economics) for a particular brand of specialized economists. Accordingly, there was a need to find a middle ground between stilted prose which is extremely tightly woven and the looser, sometimes repetitious style characterizing the more popular periodicals. There are also certain dictates of the English language. For example, the criteria for paragraphs in English and Japanese seem to differ. In many of the original manuscripts twenty-or

[4] On this point it is interesting to note that the Japan Institute of Labour publishes the *Japan Labor Bulletin*.

[5] *Publisher's note:* The only exception to this practice is that the editor's name appears in western order (family name last) on the jacket and title page, in order to avoid mistakes in catalogues and bibiliographies.

thirty-sentence paragraphs were interspersed with one-sentence paragraphs. Some effort has been made to construct fairly standardized paragraphs by connecting shorter paragraphs and dividing excessively long ones. Nevertheless, care has also been exercised to preserve individual personalities, philosophical bents, and intellectual approaches to scholarship, although such considerations have had lower priority and some of the personal color is lost. To some extent the old adage still holds: literature is best read in the original.

Finally, I must express appreciation to a number of persons. Although translations are often viewed as "closet jobs", with translators simply sitting down and mechanically transcribing the story from one script into another, the process is more complex. Translations require a modicum of financial support and the pooling of a great many heads to answer seemingly trivial questions and to ferret out meanings hidden deep in oblique rhetorical prose. Indeed, it is this meeting with other people to play the intellectual game of pursuing all inferences (ambiguous and otherwise but usually unintended) to their logical, though often absurd, conclusions that provides some measure of joy in doing translations. The list of those bothered or otherwise inconvenienced is never short. Moreover, public expressions of indebtedness are always fraught with the danger of omissions. Yet the fact remains that little of the translation could have been completed without the kind assistance of a great many people. Although there is not space here to list all who have assisted with the translation, I am most grateful for their kind and untiring support.

One hopes this translation will assist in having Japanese scholarship more fully appreciated abroad. Too many English-language studies on Japan have been prefaced by comments to the effect that very little work has been done in the field to be dealt with, where in fact a sizeable literature exists, and the foreign researcher goes about his merry way without relating his study to this literature. This small translation cannot eradicate this tendency; that will occur only when all researchers do their own homework on the Japanese literature available. It can, I hope, make people more aware of the rich literature available in Japanese. Although Japanese scholarship is often criticized as being too descriptive and methodologically sloppy, it is time to take another look at a literature which is very sensitive to ideological pluralism in a society so often treated as a homogeneous whole.

Brisbane   Ross Mouer

Editor's Preface

In order to understand fully the labor market in a given country, it is useful—indeed necessary—for one to have a basic knowledge of that country's society and economy. It is within this larger framework that the labor market functions. Although this volume cannot supply that background, it does bring together a number of essays which place the labor market in its broader socio-economic setting. It has been compiled for specialists and researchers who wish to learn more about the labor market in Japan but who do not have easy access to the literature in Japanese. Care has been taken to avoid impressionistic descriptions which simply scratch the surface or merely sketch in the so-called Japanese peculiarities.

My aim has been to present empirical research which uses statistical data to examine observable phenomena and to test hypotheses and models which are of theoretical importance to economists. Many of the papers have appeared in leading academic journals, and the authors include persons who have been or now are employed by the Ministry of Labour. All adhere to the same high standard, and represent important contributions in their given fields. Hopefully, the reader will gain from the variety of perspectives, the different methods of observation, the discovery of previously unknown phenomena, and the policy implications built into this collection of papers. Finally, the papers which are presented allow the reader to go beyond the specifics of the Japanese situation and to formulate broader theoretical propositions relevant to the understanding of labor markets in general.

The idea for the present selections arose out of a volume which I edited some years ago, *Nihon Keizai Riidingusu (III): Rōdō Shijō* [Readings on the Japanese Economy (III): The Labor Market]. The volume was originally published in 1971 by Nihon Keizai Shimbun Sha and contained twenty-three selections. Five of the selections in this volume are from that original set of readings; nine are more recent publications (three of the nine by authors who made different contributions in the original set). Several considerations have resulted in these revisions. First, Japan has experienced extensive socio-economic changes since the first publication. In particular, the "Nixon shocks" and the oil crisis had a great impact on the Japanese economy. One result has been a continuing discussion concerning the various social ramifications of the shift from "high" to "low" rates of economic growth. Accordingly, the contributions of Horiuchi, Kaneko, Nishikawa and Shimada, Nakamura, Kōshiro, and Sano have been added. Second, the original volume included some items of doubtful interest to the foreign reader. Moreover, some of the original selections have previously appeared in English. Finally, a number of the original selections have been omitted due to time and space limitations.

The old and the new in this volume have been mixed together. The chapters have been organized around two major themes: the labor market and wage determination. In the remaining paragraphs, I wish briefly to discuss the significance and interrelationship of the selections herein presented, looking first at those related to the labor market and then focusing on those related to wage determination.

A. The Labor Market

The national census taken in 1955 indicated that nearly 40 percent of Japan's forty-one million workers were employed in primary industry. That portion of the work force, along with family members who comprised the unemployed part of the agricultural population, served as the major source of labor for the industrial sectors which came to be the major driving force behind Japan's rapid economic growth over the next two decades. In the 1950s, the research of Namiki Masayoshi suggested that in the prewar Shōwa years (1925–1940) the inflow of labor to industry from the agricultural sector had been roughly equal to the natural increase in the agricultural population and was responsive to that increase rather than to other economic forces. Soon afterwards, Minami Ryōshin and Ono Akira came to entertain certain doubts about the thoroughness of Namiki's research. They retabulated the original data on the number of agricultural households and presented their own figures, arguing that the net outflow of labor from the agricultural sector was indeed quite sensitive to the business cycle. Out of these findings was born a spirited debate. The first selection in this volume appraises both positions and underlines the danger of arguing too strongly for one position without viewing the merits of the other. Previously at the same research institute with Namiki, Hatai Yoshitaka is in a unique position to synthesize the contributions made by both sides in the debate.

Over time the agricultural population has continued to decline; it was recorded as being just under 14 percent of the total labor force by the national census taken in 1975. During the interim Ichino Shōzō used data from the national census and other relevant surveys to examine closely the sources of labor supply and the reasons for attrition in both the agricultural and non-agricultural sectors. Closely examining inter-sectoral flows, Ichino's presentation shows a meticulous concern for detail, and his work provides both a framework and a factual background for a realistic picture of how labor is actually supplied in the postwar economy.

Although the percentage of workers in the agricultural sector steadily dropped throughout the 1960s, the percentage remained quite high in comparison with the corresponding figures for the other highly industrialized nations of the world. In addition, we should also be aware of the large numbers in the non-agricultural industries who either are self-employed or are "family workers". Indeed, the importance of considering these two groups in terms of measuring labor's share is discussed by Ono Akira in his essay in Part II. For these and other reasons it would be desirable to consider extending Ichino's analysis to the present.

A major change in the labor market which began to appear in the late 1960s was the contraction of the workweek. The average number of days and hours worked per month dropped substantially from 24.2 days and 207 hours in 1960 to 20.8 days and 167.8 hours by 1975. This can be attributed partially to the increase in national holidays after 1966, an increase in the actual utilization of paid vacation leave, and the appearance of the two-day weekend. One might go further and perhaps argue that these changes are in turn due to the rapid improvement in the overall standard of living resulting from the remarkable economic growth experienced during the 1960s. The empirical findings of Paul Douglas in the United States and Arisawa Hiromi in Japan demonstrated that the behavior of the individual needs to be viewed in terms of the household. Certain shortcomings were apparent in the labor supply functions commonly used in macro-economic models which had merely summed the number of seemingly uniform individuals as interchangeable units, in line with the labor force behavior ascribed by traditional microeconomic theory to that mythical individual known as "economic man". Traditional theory did not throw much light on shifts in labor supply behavior, nor did it yield very useful predictions. Obi Keiichirō's major contribution has been the articulation of a comprehensive theoretical framework which makes the major unit of analysis the household rather than the individual. From that perspective it is impossible to consider the behavior of different types of individuals separately in terms of their relationship to the household.

Tsujimura Kōtarō maintains that working time was reduced during the 1960s in order to attract and keep a work force at the workshop. He emphasizes that the reduction in working time cannot be explained correctly without taking into account increases in productivity and improvements in the standard of living during the period. He further calls our attention to the fact that a failure to shorten working time can even stimulate criticism from abroad against the "workaholism" of Japanese workers.

Increases in leisure time so far have been only sluggish, however, in spite of the increasingly strong desire of workers for it. This is because, on the one hand, management worries about increases in costs, reductions in international competitiveness, and a slowing down of economic growth, and, on the other hand, unions are not as enthusiastic as they are in wage negotiations. He asserts that these worries and attitudes are mistaken. He recommends that we ought to reach a consensus on a shortening of working time and thereby restore a desirable balance between leisure and income as quickly as possible. Tsujimura's research was originally undertaken in order to allay the fears of both management and the government that a decrease in the number of hours of work would automatically be translated into higher costs and lower productivity. Indeed, the empirical findings suggested that the decrease in hours of work and, in particular, the introduction of the two-day weekend *increased* productivity. The results suggested that offsetting increases in productivity would be promoted not only by improved techniques developed by industrial engineers and personnel managers, but also, quite independently, by the impact shorter workweeks would have on the home life of the individuals involved. For example, an exhaustive survey made by NHK's research institute on the use of time shows that the drop in the average workday of adult males from 8.1 to 7.15 hours between 1960 and 1975 was partially canceled by an increase from 37 minutes to 59 minutes in the average time daily spent commuting. The increase in commuting time is a result of the suburban sprawl, but certainly underlines the need for shorter hours of work, two-day weekends, and more vacations.

The 1976 White Paper on Labor projected two important changes in the composition of the labor force between 1975 and 1985. One is a sharp rise in the average level of education associated with those in the work force as an increasingly large number of young people enter tertiary institutions; the other is a rise in the average age of those in the work force. Presenting a variety of statistical evidence, the 1976 White Paper on Labor attracted the attention of many people. Although both trends have already been evident, it seems likely that the pace at which these changes occur will dramatically quicken in the coming decades and create a number of problems in the labor market on both the supply and the demand sides of the employment equation. The papers by Kaneko Yoshio and Horiuchi Akiyoshi appeared earlier in time, but anticipated the 1976 White Paper. Each focused on one of these problems, Kaneko dealing with the problem of forced retirement[1] and Horiuchi with the costs and benefits of tertiary education. Both papers discuss the central importance of value judgments about desirable levels of inequality: Horiuchi suggests that education involves a regressive redistribution of income, and Kaneko argues that in reorganizing the system of retirement care must be taken so as not to redistribute elsewhere the foregone income due the middle-aged worker for his past labor. The Kaneko paper also analyzes the ramifications of various proposals for structural change, particularly with regard to the older worker's opportunities for meaningful reemployment, and concludes with Kaneko's own proposal.

As the recession which began in 1974 continued into 1976 and 1977, the number of job separations increased for middle-aged males, and the trend toward extending the retirement age seemed to slacken. Moreover, the market for graduates of colleges and universities shifted from a seller's market to a buyer's market. A major consequence was a drop in the percentage of high school graduates going on to tertiary education in 1977. Only the future will show the full effects of the past explosion in education. For example, will older persons with higher educations be able to find work which is appropriate to their qualifications? The answers to such questions contain serious implications for the future development of Japanese society.

Going back a bit further to the oil crisis in late 1973, Shimada

---

[1] Retirement is usually compulsory at the age of 55. During the 1960s, the age was extended slightly, but it is still short of 60. Since the social security pension is not available until the age of 65, most workers are compelled to spend the years after retirement at 55 working in small enterprises or at odd jobs; others try to start their own businesses. Some are reemployed by their old firms, but at considerably lower wages than those they received before "retirement".

Haruo and I attempt to trace some of the structural changes which have occurred in the labor market. In 1974, the number of dismissals increased sharply, but they largely involved females who were employed on a part-time basis. Since many of these persons did not remain in the work force nor actively look for work once they were laid off, the statistics on unemployment did not register the spectacular increase which many had anticipated. Our short review also touches upon the new legislation which came into effect in 1975 to facilitate the adjustment of employment levels within the firm.

By late 1975, exports of electrical goods and automobiles had picked up, and employment levels also improved; women flowed back into the labor force. Inflation was also brought under control, and many judged that the economy had finally recovered from the initial setback attributable to the oil crisis. Unfortunately, however, in order to control prices it was necessary to restrain wage hikes. Because the real increase in disposable income was held at close to zero, consumer demand was slow to rise, and this in turn slowed down the rate of recovery. The years 1976 and 1977 have thus been referred to as a period of "structural" recession *(kōzō fukyō)*. The number of separations increased for both males and females, and the unemployment rate rose above 2 percent. Although international pressure on the value of the yen increased considerably late in 1977, I believe that excessive wage restraint, the maintenance of lower levels of effective demand, and the failure of the government's policy on exchange rates were largely responsible for the downturn in 1976 and 1977. It will take a considerable effort and an extended period of time before the resultant level of unemployment can be appreciably reduced.

B.   Wage Determination

The second part of this volume contains seven chapters on the structure of wage rates and the mechanism determining wages. The chapter by Ono Tsuneo surveys changes in the wage system over the postwar period, considering wage determination within the framework of collective bargaining and focusing on the wage policies proposed by labor, management, and the government. This serves as a terse summary of developments in this field. In his summary, Ono poses the question: "How has the seniority-merit wage curve changed?" This has certainly been a central concern of anyone discussing the wage system in Japan. Indeed, the next three chapters all deal in one way or another with this issue.

Umemura Mataji identifies the major themes appearing in the

literature on the seniority wage system, a literature which is itself extremely complex, and from a strong grounding in economic theory adds his cogent critique of the validity of many of the arguments associated with the seniority wage system. Umemura clearly stands in opposition to those who overemphasize the uniquely Japanese features. While recognizing the merits of an approach which stresses the acquisition of skills,[2] he goes on to point out that Japan's particular approach to job training was a necessary but not sufficient condition accounting for the wage differential between large and small firms. Related to this is the last paper in this volume, in which Ono Akira discusses labor's share and the large differentials by firm size, partially in terms of technological change.

Also writing during the period of rapid economic growth, Tanaka Hirohide uses data from local offices of the Public Employment Security Agency on the placement of middle-school and high-school graduates to examine variation in the starting wages for new graduates. Industry and firm size are also underlined as important sources of variation. This was a period when employers felt overall shortages in the supply of new graduates and competed fiercely to obtain their services. Tanaka uncovered a paradoxical situation in which there was greater variation in the actual starting wages than in the projected wage rates initially offered by firms when they were just beginning their recruitment operations.

Nakamura Atsushi uses the Ministry of Labour's Basic Survey on the Wage Structure to analyze wage rates for two distinct groups of employees: those who are employed upon graduation and remain with the same firm until retirement at 55 (the standard employee) and those who do not spend their whole working lives with the same employer (the non-standard employee). Clearly demonstrating the continued significance of age and years of continuous employment with the same firm, his analysis provides ample evidence that the seniority-merit wage system has survived. On this point, one needs to remember that the sharp increase in starting wages in 1973 has flattened the age profiles. Working within the framework of internal labor markets, Nakamura suggests that the framework provides ample explanations of the seniority-merit wage curve. Moreover, because the supposedly peculiar Japanese approach to improving the skill level of the work force is a rather straightforward variant of the human capital approach, a chain of recent developments in labor economics

---

[2] The theory cited by Umemura has been expounded by Ujihara Shōjirō, Tsuda Masumi, and others.

now opens for us the possibility of formulating a general theory of seniority wage systems.[3]

The procedure of settling wage increases each spring through the unions' annual spring wage offensive is generally well known. Since the large majority of unions are enterprise unions, the unions in each industry develop a joint, industry-wide strategy under the aegis of a central coordinating body for all industries. Although unions in a given industry generally enter negotiations *en masse*, each enterprise union tends to carry out its own negotiations with management somewhat independent of negotiations at the other firms. Nevertheless, in addition to gauging the ability of each individual firm to pay and other factors affecting the firm's recent performance, labor and management frequently observe the behavior of labor unions and management at other firms both within and without the industry. Sano Yōko has undertaken a wide range of studies focusing on the nature of the spring wage offensive and the patterns of wage negotiations.[4] Citing data gathered in 1966 (from a nation-wide sample) and 1969 (from a sample in Nagano Prefecture), Sano summarizes the manner in which a quantitative wage model was constructed and concludes with an evaluation of the model's performance.

In the thirteenth essay, Kōshiro Kazutoshi examines the impact and social cost of strikes in the public sector, concluding that they contribute significantly to the bargaining power of unions in the private sector. Kōshiro also presents the first published estimates of the costs imposed upon the national economy by such strikes. His study has been referred to frequently since the fall of 1975, when the question of the right to strike for employees in the public sector became a national issue.[5]

The final contribution on labor's share by Ono Akira differs from the other studies in two ways: it analyzes long-term trends, and it makes explicit use of international comparisons. Moreover, to the extent that it deals with the structure of the labor force and the role of the

---

[3] On this point, see Tachibanaki Toshiaki, "Quality Change in Labor Input: Japanese Manufacturing," *The Review of Economics and Statistics* (vol. 58, no. 3: August 1976). For a comparative analysis of data for Japan and the United States, see Shimada Haruo, *The Structure of Earnings and Investment in Human Capital: A Comparison Between the United States and Japan*, a doctoral dissertation presented to the University of Wisconsin (Madison, Wisconsin) in 1974.

[4] See, for example, the items cited in footnotes 2 and 10 in the article by Sano Yōko in this volume.

[5] Legislation prohibits public servants and employees in the five national enterprises and three public corporations from striking. Arguing that ILO conventions support their demands, public employees have adamantly campaigned for the right to strike. Major transport strikes have occurred as part of that struggle.

self-employed, it provides a link between the discussion of wages and the chapters in the first half of the volume. Briefly summarized, Ono concludes that the relatively low wage level in Japan results from the fact that Japan was rather late in starting on the road to industrialization and the fact that excessive labor existed in the self-employed sector. The result was a rather low share for labor. During the postwar years the Japanese economy grew rapidly with "borrowed" technology, and labor productivity soared while wages grew at a steady but slower pace. Consequently, labor's share decreased.

The essays in this volume very closely reflect the changing times in Japan. Indeed, they cannot be fully understood apart from a knowledge of how Japan's economy has developed over the past two decades. With that background in mind, I hope the chapters in this volume will give the reader some idea of the breadth and depth of work being done by Japanese scholars on the labor economy in Japan.

Mita, Tokyo   NISHIKAWA SHUNSAKU

The Labor Market in Japan

PART I

The Labor Market

Business Cycles and the Outflow of Labor From the Agricultural Sector

Some Comments on Namiki's Debate with Minami and Ono

Hatai Yoshitaka

1. Introduction

Until Namiki Masayoshi published his studies on the behavior of agricultural households in the prewar Showa period, scholars had for some time believed that the mobility of labor from agricultural households adjusted itself to fluctuations in the business cycle. Namiki argued that the outflow of labor from agricultural households to the other sectors of the economy tended to be fixed, with the volume being determined by the natural increase in the agricultural population, not by the business cycle.[1] Recently,* however, Minami Ryōshin and Ono Akira presented their own empirical data showing net movements of the population in agricultural households. Their data showed a high correlation between their index of mobility and the rate of economic growth (which served as their proxy for the business cycle).[2]

This paper first appeared as "Nōka Jinkō Idō to Keiki Hendō—Minami-Ono·Namiki Ronsō ni Tsuite," *Kikan Riron Keizaigaku* (vol. 14, no. 1: September 1963), pp. 28–32. The author is Professor of Economics at Meiji Gakuin University.

[1] Namiki Masayoshi, "Nōka Jinkō no Idō Keitai to Shūgyō Kōzō" [The Employment Structure and Types of Mobility of the Population in Agricultural Households], in *Nōgyō ni Okeru Senzai Shitsugyō* [Disguised Unemployment in Agriculture], ed. by Tōhata Seiichi (Tokyo: Nihon Hyōron Shin Sha, 1956), pp. 195–214.

[2] See, for example, Minami Ryōshin and Ono Akira, "Nōka Jinkō Idō to Keiki Hendō to no Kankei ni Tsuite no Oboegaki" [A Note on the Relationship of Business Cycles and the Mobility of the Population in Agricultural Households], *Kikan Riron Keizaigaku* (vol. 4, no. 3: June 1962), pp. 64–67.

* *Editor's note:* The reader should note that this paper was written in 1963.

They thus argued that at least the net flow of the labor force was very sensitive to fluctuations in the business cycle.

In response to the criticism of Minami and Ono, Namiki underlined some of the weaknesses in their method of estimating the net mobility of the population in agricultural households.[3] For example, he pointed to the way in which the increase in the agricultural population was estimated by multiplying the increase in the number of agricultural households by the average number of household members. He further argued that the increase in the number of households was due to the formation of new agricultural households out of older households which were much larger in size, not to changes in the overall size of the population living in agricultural households, which remained rather constant throughout this period. He thereby dismissed the evidence of Minami and Ono.

This paper examines the mobility of labor in agricultural households in light of the arguments put forth by Namiki, on the one hand, and Minami and Ono, on the other. Other writers have shown great interest in these issues as they relate to economic growth,[4] but I will seek to evaluate the debate in terms of the literature on demography. Part of the problem lies in the data used by both parties to the debate. At the same time, however, it is also necessary for us to rethink the entire theoretical framework in which the debate emerged.

2. Some Problems in Namiki's Theory

Namiki's theory of a fixed supply of labor from agricultural households no doubt emerged from his interest in applying to Japan the theory that movements in the agricultural population are sensitive to the business cycle, a proposition which can be found in the work of Theodore W. Schultz.[5] In the highly developed capitalist countries the depression of the 1930s was severely felt at all levels of society, and

---

[3] See, for example, Namiki Masayoshi, "Minami-Ono Shi no Hihan ni Kotaeru" [An Answer to the Criticism of Minami and Ono], *Kikan Riron Keizaigaku* (vol. 12, no. 3: June 1962), pp. 67–69.

[4] In particular, see Shinohara Miyohei, "Sangyō Kōzō Nyūmon (9): Nōgyō to Rōdōryoku Idō" [An Introduction to Industrial Structure (IX): Agriculture and Labor Mobility], *Kin-yū Jānaru* (vol. 4, no. 2: February 1963), pp. 16–20; and his "Nōgyō to Rōdōryoku Idō" [Agriculture and Labor Mobility], which appeared as one part of a series in *Nihon Keizai Shimbun* (March 12–17, 1963), on p. 12 each day.

[5] See his *Agriculture in an Unstable Economy* (New York: McGraw-Hill Book Company, 1945), p. 100.

the rural-to-urban flow of the population stopped during this time. In countries like prewar Japan which were only partially developed, however, the effects of depression were not so pervasive, and the rural areas continued to push out excess population caused by natural increases in the agricultural population.

Namiki used the population figures developed by Takagi Naofumi for towns and villages with populations below ten thousand to support his views (see Table 1). The estimates were for 1925, 1930, and 1935. Considering the fact that the net outflow from rural areas between 1925 and 1930 (1,811,000) was nearly the same as that for the following five-year period of 1930–1935 (2,030,000), he reasoned that there was little change over time. Namiki himself stated that the five-year data were too spread out and recognized the need for the more precise annual figures. Therefore, as supportive evidence for his case, he presented statistics on levels of employment in small factories with five to nine employees. Since a large proportion of those leaving the agricultural population found work in small firms of this size, he

Table 1: Namiki's Figures on the Population Outflow from Agricultural Villages: 1920–1940

(Unit 1000 persons)

		Villages with a population of less than 5,000	Villages with a population of 5,000–10,000	Total for all villages with populations at or below 10,000
1920–1925	Net increase	230	481	711
	Natural increase	1,775	875	2,650
	Outflow	−1,544	−394	−1,938
1925–1930	Net increase	602	633	1,235
	Natural increase	2,022	1,023	3,046
	Outflow	−1,420	−390	−1,811
1930–1935	Net increase	345	646	991
	Natural increase	1,983	1,045	3,030
	Outflow	−1,640	−399	−2,039
1935–1940	Net increase	338	410	748
	Natural increase	2,000	1,000	3,000
	Outflow	−1,662	−590	−2,232
1920–1940	Net increase	1,515	2,170	3,685
	Natural increase	7,782	3,943	10,725
	Outflow	−6,266	−1,773	−8,039

Source: Namiki Masayoshi, "Sangyō Rōdōsha no Keisei to Nōka Jinkō" [The Agricultural Population and the Formation of the Industrial Work Force], in *Nihon Shihonshugi to Nōgyō* [Japanese Capitalism and Agriculture], ed. by Tōhata Seiichi and Uno Kōzō (Tokyo: Iwanami Shoten, 1959) p. 152.

claimed that the absence of any marked shift in employment levels in these firms reflected the fact that the outflow from the rural areas was not much affected by the depression.

The core of Namiki's theory is his explanation of the behavior of the agricultural household. Second and younger sons (who were not to become successors to the household head) were considered surplus labor, and had to face the fate of being pushed out of the agricultural household. Moreover, the Japanese economy was such that there was always a place where this surplus labor could be absorbed. Finally, bceause the annual amount of surplus population produced by agricultural households was fixed, the amount of labor supplied by the rural sector remained constant since the mechanism described above worked to channel out such labor as soon as it became marketable.

The major thrust of Namiki's argument is set forth in very clear terms. One area, however, needs elaboration. It concerns the extent to which economic institutions adapted to maintain given levels of employment. First, the outflow of population from rural Japan was not limited to young men just out of school. It also included second and third sons who were much older. It is hard to believe that these persons did not feel the effects of the depression. In the textile industry, for example, the number of employees dropped by 130,000, or 12 percent. A survey by Watanabe Shin'ichi suggests that an average of five persons (including family members) returned to each village as a result of the depression.[6] Accordingly, even if we accept the fact that the actual numbers returning to rural Japan were very small, it is nevertheless rather difficult to deny the fact that the net effect of the depression was a decrease in the outflow of persons from agricultural households.

Returning to the data which Namiki used as primary evidence to support his theory, we must emphasize the fact that data gathered at five-year intervals are insufficient for close correlation with the business cycle. This basic fact was stressed by Minami and Ono, and was also acknowledged by Namiki himself. However, Minami and Ono constructed their own data (Tables 2 and 3 and Figure 1), which gave them different results, and therein the debate was born. Similarly, despite the fact that the secondary evidence may also be correct, data on the work force in small factories with five to nine employees are in themselves not sufficient proof. If we consider the figures for all

[6] Namiki Masayoshi, "Sangyō Rōdōsha no Keisei to Nōka Jinkō" [The Agricultural Population and the Formation of an Industrial Work Force], in *Nihon Shihonshugi to Nōgyō* [Japanese Capitalism and Agriculture], ed. by Tōhata Seiichi and Uno Kōzō (Tokyo: Iwanami Shoten, 1959), p. 157.

Table 2: The Estimated Net Outflow of the Population from Agricultural Households: 1926–1940

(Unit: 1,000 persons)

Year	Net Outflow
1926	490
1927	436
1928	411
1929	443
1930	360
1931	285
1932	472
1933	603
1934	441
1935	554
1936	504
1937	595
1938	615
1939	444
1940	481

Source: Minami Ryōshin and Ono Akira, "Nōka Jinkō Idō to Keiki Hendō to no Kankei ni Tsuite no Oboegaki" [A Note on the Relationship of Business Cycles and the Mobility of the Population in Agricultural Households], *Kikan Riron Keizaigaku* (vol. 12, no. 3: June 1962), p. 64.

Table 3: Annual Number of Agricultural Households in Yamanashi Prefecture: 1928–1932

Year	Survey of the Ministry of Agriculture and Forestry	Survey of Yamanashi Prefectural Office
1928	78,440	80,101
1929	67,125	80,432
1930	67,945	81,550
1931	82,992	82,992
1932	83,845	83,845

Note: The survey of the Ministry of Agriculture and Forestry was contracted to the Japan Agricultural Association (Teikoku Nōkai).

Source: The surveys of the Ministry of Agriculture and Forestry as reported in *Nōrin Shō Tōkei Hyō* [Statistical Yearbook of the Ministry of Agriculture and Forestry] and the surveys of the Yamanashi Prefectural Office as reported in *Yamanashi Ken Tōkei* [Statistical Yearbook of Yamanashi Prefecture].

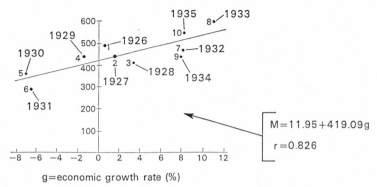

g=economic growth rate (%)

Figure 1: The Relationship of Economic Growth Rates and the Net Outflow
of Population from Agricultural Households during the Ten Years
around the Shōwa Depression: 1926–1935.
M=net outflow (unit 1,000 persons)

Source: See, for example, Minami Ryōshin and Ono Akira, "Nōka Jinkō Idō
to Keiki Hendō to no Kankei ni Tsuite no Oboegaki" [A Note on the
Relationship of Business Cycles and the Mobility of the Population in
Agricultural Households], *Kikan Riron Keizaigaku* (vol. 12, no. 3:
June 1962), p. 65.

factories, there was a decline of 390,000 in the number of employees.
Accordingly, it seems somewhat out of place to argue as Namiki does
that "in any case each person would have a chance to work in one way
or another."[7] It is quite likely that the smaller-sized firms were more
involved in producing consumer goods, and therefore less affected
by the business cycle. As a result, the number of smaller-sized firms
tended to increase along with the Japanese population. Many of the
persons laid off by the larger firms no doubt found their way into
these smaller firms. The fact that unemployment did not become conspicuous is no doubt due to the absorptive capacity of the urban sector
of the Japanese economy, which consisted largely of these small
family-run firms. It would seem probable that agricultural households
also served as part of this family-based system of economic production
which mitigated the effects of unemployment.

Here we can identify a contradiction in the Namiki theory. While
arguing that there is a more-or-less fixed flow of second and third sons
out of agriculture, Namiki also claims that the number of those staying
behind to work the family farm is affected by the business cycle.
According to Namiki's linear regression analysis ($r=0.9567$), the rate
of decline in the work force retention rate of the agricultural popula-

[7] Namiki, "Sangyō Rōdōsha no Keisei to Nōka Jinkō," p. 157.

tion (R) was related to the economic growth rate (G) in the following way:

$$R = -5.48 + 1.264G.$$

Namiki's contribution lies in his having drawn forth a more general "law" of economic behavior based upon his observation of the behavior of new graduates. However, there remains the fact that this contradicts his general views concerning the sensitivity of the labor market to the cycle.

Using Namiki's formulation, the work force retention rate of the agricultural population is defined by the following fraction:

$$\frac{\text{the number of new male graduates entering the agricultural labor force}}{\text{the number of such graduates needed to maintain the number of agricultural households.}}$$

Since the denominator is fixed at about 200,000, and is equal to the agricultural population (5.5 million agricultural households) divided by the average number of years spent in the work force (about 30 years), changes in the work force retention rate occur only when the value of the numerator changes. However, the numerator (the number of new graduates entering the agricultural labor force) depends on (1) the business cycle and (2) the total number of new graduates.

The results of the regression analysis suggest that the rate of retention will rise as the rate of economic growth falls. This means that the number of persons employed in agriculture rises whenever a recession occurs. Namiki's equation suggests that even the new graduates entering the agricultural labor force are in some respects sensitive to fluctuations in the business cycle; it would seem obvious that the number of those leaving the agricultural work force to join the urban or industrial work force will respond even more sensitively to the fluctuation. However, the statistics suggest that there has not actually been such a conspicuous change in the number of graduates entering the agricultural labor force. Namiki defends his position against the criticism that the behavior of new graduates is not so sensitive to the fluctuation by saying that the coincidental change in the total number of graduates just happened to occur in such a way as to weaken the correlation between R and G. In other words, he holds, if this chance occurrence were removed, the correlation would be clear.[8]

[8] Namiki Masayoshi, "Saikin ni Okeru Nōgyō Jinkō no Hojū Keikō" [Recent Trends in the Rate of Retention in the Agricultural Population], *Keizai Kenkyū* (vol. 11, no. 4: October 1960), pp. 417–420.

3.   Some Problems in Namiki's Rebuttal

As the debate continued, a number of difficulties became apparent in the arguments of both sides.[9] First Namiki's rebuttals will be studied. Namiki criticized the work of Minami and Ono on two counts: errors in methodology and inconclusiveness of statistical evidence. The following paragraphs examine each of these criticisms in turn.

A.   Methodological Problems

Namiki sharply criticized the way in which Minami and Ono used the number of agricultural households as the basic measure of the agricultural population. He argued that the effect of the economic cycle must be shown in terms of changes in the population engaged in agriculture, the rural population, or the population in agricultural households, not in the number of households *per se*. Although nobody would argue against the need to use figures for the actual population in the agricultural work force, the real question is whether the number of agricultural households can be used as a proxy. Before denying the validity of this procedure, Namiki should prove that movements in the number of agricultural households are unrelated to the business cycle. Without such proof it is difficult to accept Namiki's argument at face value. Preconceptions are a barrier to the development of science, and it would seem wise to invite as many experiments as possible, regardless of their ultimate success or failure.

Namiki argued that the most important shortcoming in the Minami-Ono research is the attempt to estimate the increase in the population in agricultural households by multiplying the increase in the number of households by the average number of household members in existing agricultural households. He claimed that the increase in the number of agricultural households in the prewar period was due to the establishment of branch households and not to the return of labor from the urban sector to agriculture. Accordingly, he argued that although the number of households did increase, the population did not. Although the process of establishing branch households in prewar Japan can be accepted at face value, we must also realize that the structure of rural society and the composition of the agricultural population are more complex. In addition to the core group of households, consisting of

---

[9] All references to the respective arguments come from the articles in notes 2 and 3 unless otherwise indicated.

main and branch households which own land, there were other agricultural households which owned very small parcels of land or did not own any land at all, including the households of tenant farmers. This latter group was unable to establish branch households in the traditional fashion. Nevertheless, it is clear that these households also supported a surplus population despite the fact that it meant a lower standard of living for the other members. It would seem that this latter set of households continued to support a surplus population even while the number of agricultural households increased or branch households were being established. This process, then, very likely contributed to a rise in the average size of all agricultural households.

On the other hand, when the number of agricultural households diminishes, the surplus population declines, the number of branch households falls, and the average size of each household also decreases. In other words, the number of households and the average size of all households move together. Therefore, the total shift in the population is in the same direction but of even greater proportions than estimated. This no doubt is how the population mechanism really works.

The validity of this assertion can be demonstrated statistically. Although there are unfortunately no figures for the prewar period, postwar figures are available except for the period immediately after the war when people were returning to the rural areas in great numbers to take up farming (Table 4). The parallel movements in columns A and B of Table 4 should be observed. It is probably safe to assume that movements in household size accompanied similar changes in

Table 4: The Number and Average Size of Households: 1948–1960

Year	A Total number of households engaged in rice cultivation	B Total population in households engaged in rice cultivation	C Average size of households engaged rice cultivation (B/A)
1948	5,325	32,075	6.023
1949	5,443	33,378	6.133
1950	5,488	33,700	6.141
1951	5,485	33,599	6.126
1952	5,456	33,492	6.138
1953	5,413	33,208	6.135
1960	5,320	31,325	5.888

Note: The average size of households in 1951 is underestimated due to an error in doing the survey or the tabulations.

Source: Shokuryō Chō (Food Agency), *Shokuryō Kanri Tōkei Nenpō* [Statistical Yearbook of Food Administration] (Tokyo: Shokuryō Chō, annual), figures taken from appropriate pages in each volume.

the number of households. In other words, the pressure of excessively large households resulted in an increase in the number of households. That increase was made possible by the establishment of branch households, the reclamation and exploitation of new land, and geographic mobility. One can also imagine situations in which older branch households not previously engaged in agriculture received land and became active in agriculture. Given these facts, the estimates of Minami and Ono are not at all unreasonable.

The above relationships can also be expressed mathematically. Let $i+1$ represent the year in which a recession occurs; N_{i+1}, the total number of persons in agricultural households in that year; n, the average size of such households; and F, the number of such households. We can then express the above-described relationships as follows:

$$N_{i+1} > n_i,$$
$$N_{i+1} > n_i,$$
and $$F_{i+1} > F_i.$$

Accordingly, the change in the population $(N_{i+1} - N_i)$ may be expressed as follows:

$$(N_{i+1} - N_i) = (F_{i+1} \cdot n_{i+1}) - (F_i \cdot n_i)$$
$$\Delta N = (F_i + \Delta F)(n_i + \Delta n) - (F_i \cdot n_i)$$
$$\Delta N = (\Delta F \cdot n_i) + (F \cdot \Delta n) + (\Delta F \cdot \Delta n).$$

The mathematical presentation makes it clear that Minami and Ono have underestimated the amount of change in the population, as their calculation takes into consideration only the first $(\Delta F \cdot n_i)$ of the three components representing the total amount of change in the last equation. If we accept that average household size and the total number of households move together in the same direction, Namiki's criticism is without support.

B.   Problems with the Statistics Used for Estimating Household Size

Namiki's second criticism concerns a certain carelessness in the use of statistical data (see Table 3). He claims that the official statistics on agricultural households contain a number of discrepancies and that, accordingly, the tabulated results of Minami and Ono do not represent reality. As proof he cites the strange fluctuations in the total number of agricultural households in Yamanashi Prefecture, which must have affected the total number of agricultural households in Japan. Nevertheless, even if their estimates for the total number of agricultural households in Japan in 1929 and 1930 were too low, their overall framework of analysis and findings should not be significantly disturbed by that error. Even after the necessary corrections were made in the data, similar results were derived from their regression analysis.

In this regard Namiki suggests that the figures used by Minami and Ono for the number of agricultural households in Yamanashi Prefecture in 1931 were artificially adjusted in order to obtain a certain continuity over time in the figures for 1928 and afterwards. He thus argues that the increase in the number of households in Yamanashi Prefecture in 1931 was a result of these adjustments rather than of fluctuations in the business cycle. Namiki's criticism was backed up by the assertion that the Survey of Agricultural Activities (Nōji Tōkei) used in 1929 followed a method at variance with that used in earlier surveys. Namiki justifies his criticism by pointing out that the results used for 1929 were from the Agricultural Survey (Nōgyō Chōsa). However, Namiki is incorrect on this point. The number of households used by the Ministry of Agriculture and Forestry in 1929 did not come from the Agricultural Survey. Accordingly, the number of agricultural households estimated for 1929 is considerably below the figures taken from the Survey on Agricultural Activities used for the years up to and including 1928. Accordingly, the pronounced decrease in the number of houses in 1929 comes in part from the changeover in surveys. However, this does not substantiate the assertion that the statistics for 1931 were derived from a census-type survey.

The second type of criticism voiced by Namiki involves the fact that the number of households in Hokkaidō continued to grow throughout the period of observation due to the movement of people into that region, while the corresponding figures for the Tōhoku region and southern Kyushu rose steadily from about 1910 and the beginning of the Taishō period onwards. Namiki thus claims that the use of such figures is clearly precluded by the presence of other overwhelming factors which would make it difficult to single out trends related to the business cycle. However, such a problem occurs only when the master trend in each geographic region is not stabilized and fluctuates erratically from year to year during the period of observation. In reality, the master trends are stabilized, and short-term fluctuations caused by other factors can be detected as the master trend is accelerated or retarded. Accordingly, we must dismiss this objection to the study by Minami and Ono.

4. Problems in the Work of Minami and Ono

The discussion in the preceding two sections would tend to suggest that Minami and Ono have been vindicated on most points. However, it must be noted that they were not as thorough as they should have been in their use of the statistical data. As Namiki has pointed out, there are some strange curiosities in the prefectural data, and these should have been examined before the analysis was run. Although the revised calculations did not seriously alter their findings,[10] Minami and Ono should feel some chagrin at having tried to cut corners in their research.

A second problem is their reliance on a fixed figure to express the average size of households. They used a figure from the census results for 1930. One wonders whether they might not have been a bit more imaginative. For example, using the data presented above in Table 1, a few simple assumptions could be introduced to interpolate for the prewar data. In addition, there is a need to allow for the fact that the 1930 census excluded both one-person agricultural households and agricultural households in which the household head was not engaged in agriculture. Moreover, the 1930 census also included Okinawa. When these factors are also taken into consideration, the desirability of treating the average family size as a variable rather than a constant becomes clear.

5. Conclusion

To what extent have the points of difference been reconciled? Minami and Ono were forced by Namiki's criticism to redo their whole analysis. However, the revised calculations still supported their original conclusions, and we are forced to recognize that, as they assert, the flow of population from rural agricultural households to the urban areas in the prewar years was sensitive to the business cycle. Coefficients for both correlation and significance clearly warrant that conclusion.

The position of Namiki is unfortunately unclear. In one place he seems to soundly refute the theory that the movement of the popula-

[10] Minami Ryōshin and Ono Akira, "Nōka Jinkō Idō to Keiki Hendō—Namiki Masayoshi Shi no Hanhihan ni Tsuite" [Business Cycles and the Mobility of the Population in Agricultural Households: Some Comments on Namiki Masayoshi's Rejoinder to Criticism], *Kikan Riron Keizaigaku* (vol. 14, no. 1: September 1963), pp. 64–66.

tion in agricultural households is sensitive to the business cycle by stating that "the criticism just does not stand up." Elsewhere he takes a softer stance, suggesting that Minami and Ono have tried to set up a straw man by portraying him as taking an extreme stance in exclusive support of the constant supply theory. He goes on to state that "this is nothing more than a misreading of what I have written." To be sure, Namiki does not necessarily deny the validity of the theory that movements in the population in agricultural households are sensitive to the business cycle. Rather, while recognizing that fact, he argues that the amount of fluctuation owing to the business cycle is small; consequently he tends to lay considerable emphasis on the importance of the more-or-less constant outflow from agricultural to urban areas. In the process of stressing the constant flow, however, it is likely that he simply overlooked the fact that the size of the flow was to a significant extent influenced by the business cycle. This no doubt was one factor stimulating the debate. Indeed, he went so far in one paper as to write that "our analysis proves that the outflow of the population in agricultural households over the long run tended to equal the natural increase in that population, with the outflow remaining fairly constant over the short run."[11] It is thus difficult to see how he can claim that he was "set up" as a straw man; he seems to have quite fairly defined his own position.

The debate was not without its fruits: more reliable estimates of the population in agricultural households and of the correlation between net outflow and economic growth rates. Accordingly, rather than stressing the points of difference, it is important that we emphasize the points of agreement. One is that there continued to be a net flow of population from agricultural households to urban areas despite the great depression. Namiki's contribution is that he proved that there was not a net flow back into agricultural households as had previously been thought. The importance of this contribution is not diminished by the fact that the size of the net outflow was shown to be affected by the business cycle.

The debate has not, however, in any way served to determine whether the drop in the net size of the outflow during the great depression was due simply to a drop in the number leaving agricultural households or whether it was the result of substantial increases in the number returning to that sector. It would seem likely that the flow back into agricultural households increased somewhat as the outflow contracted. Watanabe's figure of five persons per village returning to agriculture

---

[11] Namiki, "Sangyō Rōdōsha no Keisei to Nōka Jinkō," p. 156.

in northern Japan during the depression seems quite reasonable. It is now time for us to direct our energies to a thorough study of the mechanism which explains how this flow back to agriculture and a greater hesitancy among the resident population to leave the agricultural villages worked together to produce a lower net outflow during the depression.

The Structure of the Labor Force and Patterns of Mobility: 1950–1965

Ichino Shōzō

1. Introduction

Since 1950, when a measure of economic stability was established, the Japanese economy has grown at an average annual rate of approximately 10 percent, accelerating slightly in the 1960s.* During this period the average annual rate of increase in the labor force has been about 2 percent. However, productivity has grown at an annual rate of about 8 percent, considerably above the rate of 2 to 4 percent found in most other industrialized countries. This tremendous growth is due to a number of factors. One is the improvement in productivity in each individual sector of the economy. Another is the shift of labor from sectors with low productivity to sectors with high productivity. Table 1 shows that a large portion of the labor force has shifted in a short time from agriculture and forestry, where the productivity of labor is relatively low, to other industries where it is higher. In the early 1960s the labor market began to tighten, and in July 1967 the total number of persons looking for work fell below the total number of job openings. Manpower policy and the efficient utilization of existing manpower thus became a major economic issue, equal in

This paper first appeared as "Shūgyō Kōzō no Chōki Hendō," *Rōdō Tōkei Chōsa Geppō* (Monthly Labour Statistics and Research Bulletin) (vol. 20, no. 3: March 1968), pp. 1–9. The author is employed at the Ministry of Labour's Statistics and Information Department, Minister's Secretariat.

* *Editor's note:* This and the figures which follow refer to the period up to 1968, when this paper was written. Beginning in 1974, of course, the rate of growth dropped substantially.

Table 1: Changes in the

Sector	Gainfully employed (1000s of persons)			
	1950	1955	1960	1965
1. *Males and females*				
A. Gainfully employed in agriculture and forestry	16,478	15,409	13,686	11,116
B. Employees in all industries other than agriculture and forestry	13,237	17,307	22,981	28,753
C. Self-employed and family workers in all other industries than agriculture and forestry	5,776	6,546	7,040	7,760
D. Gainfully employed in all industries	35,491	39,262	43,707	47,629
E. Persons aged 15 or over but not in the labor force	18,217	20,215	21,618	25,507
F. Population aged 15 or older	53,708	59,477	65,324	73,136
2. *Females*				
A. Gainfully employed in agriculture and forestry	8,342	7,932	7,296	5,910
B. Employees in all industries other than agriculture and forestry	3,377	4,910	6,934	9,039
C. Self-employed and family workers in all industries other than agriculture and forestry	2,005	2,535	2,867	3,569
D. Gainfully employed in all industries	13,724	15,368	17,097	18,572
E. Persons aged 15 or over but not in the labor force	14,163	14,427	16,577	19,154
F. Population aged 15 or older	27,887	30,795	33,774	37,726

Note: In 1950 the age breakdown is for persons aged 14 or older.

Source: Sōrifu Tōkei Kyoku (Bureau of Statistics, The Prime Minister's Office), *Kokusei Chōsa Kekka* [The Results of the National Census] (Tokyo:

importance to the international balance of payments and consumer price inflation.

This study provides basic data for the development of a positive policy to deal with the labor shortage. It begins by considering changes

Composition of the Labor Force

Index of change			Percentage composition			
1950	1955	1960	1950	1955	1960	1965
95.5	88.8	81.2	30.68	25.91	20.95	15.20
130.7	132.8	125.1	24.65	29.10	35.18	39.31
113.3	107.5	110.2	10.75	11.01	10.78	10.61
110.6	111.3	109.0	66.08	66.01	66.91	65.12
111.0	106.9	118.0	33.92	33.99	33.09	34.88
110.7	109.8	112.0	100.00	100.00	100.00	100.00
95.0	92.1	81.0	29.91	25.73	21.60	15.67
145.4	141.2	131.1	12.11	15.94	20.53	24.10
126.4	113.1	124.5	7.19	8.23	8.49	9.46
112.0	111.3	108.6	49.21	49.90	50.62	49.23
108.9	108.1	114.9	50.79	50.10	49.38	50.77
110.4	109.7	111.7	100.0	100.00	100.00	100.00

Okura Shō Insatsu Kyoku, published every five years), appropriate pages in the volumes for each census.

in three successive five-year periods: 1950–1955 (period I), 1955–1960 (period II), and 1960–1965 (period III). On the macro level changes in the size and employment status of the work force can best be understood by examining changes in the various categories set out in Table 1.

Moreover, a number of factors influencing the overall size of the labor force need to be considered: the death rate, the inflow of new graduates, trends in the student population, and openness to the "foreign sector" (primarily Okinawa) as a supply source. Finally, it is important to consider differences in the behavior of men and women. In order to gain an overview of changes in the structure of the labor force preceding the present labor shortage, it is useful to construct an inflow-outflow table showing the movement of labor to and from the various sectors listed above. Unfortunately, limited space does not allow for a detailed analysis of each sector. Accordingly, attention is focused on the basic factors affecting mobility into and out of (1) the ranks of the gainfully employed and, more specifically, (2) the large stratum of employees in industries other than agriculture and forestry. Although increases in the number of female entrepreneurs and family workers have aroused considerable interest in recent years, space does not permit an analysis of such developments in this paper.

2. Changes in the Number of Gainfully Employed

The gainfully employed labor force grew 10.6 percent from 1950 to 1955, 11.3 percent from 1955 to 1960, and 9.0 percent from 1960 to 1965 (Table 1). The rate of growth rose slightly in the late 1950s and then fell dramatically in the early 1960s. The variables accounting for these changes are shown in Table 2. The net increase of 3.99 million in the number of gainfully employed between 1960 and 1965, for example, can be attributed to the fact that the gross outflow of persons—due to death (1.24 million), retirement, marriage (1.72 million), and so on—was more than offset by the gross inflow of new graduates fresh out of school (6.85 million) and a few workers from Okinawa (31,000).

A closer look at the aggregate figures shows a great difference in the labor force behavior of men and women. Although there is little difference in the inflow of new graduates entering the labor force, with each sex contributing roughly 3.4 million persons, the number of women (2.95 million) entering the labor force from the nonengaged population aged over 15 is nearly 30 percent above the number of men (2.32 million). This reflects the fact that men tend to enter the labor force permanently upon graduation, whereas women enter for a short time, drop out to get married and raise children, and then rejoin the labor force at a later date. On the other side of this same coin, almost twice as many women (4.61 million) are leaving the ranks of the gainfully employed as are men (2.38 million). This means that 27.0 percent of the gainfully employed women leave the work force each year as compared with only 8.9 percent of their male counterparts. Due to their higher average age, 3.6 percent of all men in the work force die before retiring, compared with 1.7 percent of their female counterparts. The next few paragraphs look more carefully at each type of flow over time.

A. The Supply of New Graduates

The number of new graduates entering the labor force rose quickly during the 1950s but then leveled off in the early 1960s. There are two major factors which explain these trends. The first is the overall increase in the number of students going on to higher education. This trend was especially pronounced in the late 1950s. As Table 3 shows, the number of high school graduates entering the labor force immediately after graduation has declined. Consequently, the labor force grew at a slower rate than was expected.

Second, there was a drop, particularly in the mid-1950s, in the number of graduates neither going on for a higher education nor entering the labor force. Such persons include those who marry upon graduation, persons studying on their own to enter a tertiary institution, the unemployed, and those learning the domestic arts (often in preparation for marriage). The percentage of high school graduates entering the labor force rose from an average of 69.6 percent in the first five-year period to 80.0 percent and then 81.8 percent in the succeeding two periods. There thus seems to have been a change in attitudes toward work among these graduates. The rise in the percentage of women entering the work force is particularly noticeable, and by the third period the percentage was nearly the same as that for men. This partially offset the overall rise in the number of high school graduates going on for tertiary education.

B. The Inflow of Labor from the Nonengaged Population

The number of persons aged 15 or over who left the nonengaged population and joined the labor force increased. The pattern was similar for both men and women. However, their relative importance in terms of the size of the labor force has decreased over time (with the exception of males in the mid-1950s).

Table 2: Sources of Change

Employment category	1950–1955		
	Actual number	Percentage gainfully employed at the beginning of the period	Percentage of the change in actual numbers during the period
Total (males and females)			
A. Number gainfully employed at the beginning of the period ($A_t = I_{t-1}$)	35,491	100.0	—
B. Net increase in the number employed during the period ($B = -C + F - G + H$)	3,771	10.6	100.0
C. Change in the number of persons not in the work force aged over 15 (except for the entrance of new graduates) ($C = E - D$)	663	1.9	17.6
D. Persons entering the work force from category (C)	(4,508)	(12.7)	—
E. Persons entering category (C) from the work force	(5,171)	(14.6)	—
F. New graduates entering the labor force	5,540	15.6	146.9
G. Deaths among those in the labor force	1,106	3.1	29.3
H. Movement of workers to and from Okinawa	—	—	—
I. Number gainfully employed at the end of the period ($I_t = A_{t+1}$)	39,262	10.6	—
Total (males and females)			
A. Number gainfully employed of the beginning of the period ($A_t = I_{t-1}$)	13,724	100.0	—
B. Net increase in the number employed during the period ($B = -C + F - G + H$).	1,644	12.0	100.0
C. Change in the number of persons not in the work force aged over 15 (except for the entrance of new graduates) ($C = E - D$)	705	5.1	42.9
D. Persons entering the work force from category (C).	(2,569)	(18.7)	—
E. Persons entering category (C) from the work force	(3,274)	(23.9)	—
F. New graduates entering the labor force	2,632	19.2	160.1
G. Deaths among those in the labor force	283	2.1	17.2
H. Movement of workers to and from Okinawa	—	—	—
I. Number gainfully employed at the end the period ($I_t = A_{t+1}$)	15,368	112.0	—

in the Size of the Work Force

Time period examined					
1955–1960			1960–1965		
Actual number	Percentage gainfully employed at the begin- ning of the period	Percentage of the change in actual numbers during the period	Actual number	Percentage gainfully employed at the begin- ning of the period	Percentage of the change in actual numbers during the period
39,262	100.0	—	43,707	100.0	—
4,445	11.3	100.0	3,992	9.0	100.0
999	2.5	22.5	1,717	3.9	43.8
(5,001)	(12.7)	—	(5,273)	(12.1)	—
(6,000)	(15.3)	—	(6,990)	(16.0)	—
6,711	17.1	151.0	6,845	15.7	174.5
1,274	3.2	28.7	1,237	2.8	31.5
5	—	0.2	31	0.1	0.8
43,707	111.4	—	47,629	109.0	—
15,368	100.0	—	17,097	100.0	—
1,129	11.3	100.0	1,475	8.6	100.0
1,192	7.8	68.9	1,669	9.7	112.5
(2,731)	(17.8)	—	(2,953)	(17.3)	—
(3,923)	(25.5)	—	(4,612)	(27.0)	—
3,239	21.1	187.3	3,404	19.9	230.8
319	2.1	18.4	283	1.7	19.2
2	—	0.1	11	0.1	0.7
17,097	111.3	—	18,572	108.6	—

Table 3:   The Number of Graduates Entering the Labor Force

Category	Sex	Period		
		1950–1955	1955–1960	1960–1965
A. The number of students available to enter the work force if the same percentage of students aged 16 or over continues on for more education at each level	Both sexes	8,730.5	8,921.2	10,931.9
	Male	4,388.9	4,486.5	5,524.4
	Female	4,341.6	4,434.7	5,407.5
B. The actual increase in the number of tertiary students	Both sexes	769.3	531.5	2,560.8
	Male	362.2	243.0	1,343.2
	Female	407.1	288.5	1,127.6
C. The actual number of students available to enter the work force (C=A−B)	Both sexes	7,961.2	8,389.7	8,371.1
	Male	4,026.7	4,243.5	4,181.2
	Female	3,934.5	4,146.2	4,189.9
D. The actual number entering the labor force	Both sexes	5,540.2	6,711.1	6,844.9
	Male	2,908.5	3,473.4	3,440.2
	Female	2,631.7	3,237.8	3,404.7
E. The employment rate of students leaving school (E=D/C)	Both sexes	69.6	80.0	81.8
	Male	72.2	81.9	82.3
	Female	66.9	78.1	81.3

Source: Mombu Daijin Kanbō Chōsa Tōkei Ka (Research and Statistics Division, Minister's Secretariat, Ministry of Education), *Gakkō Kihon Chōsa* [The Basic Survey of Schools] (Tokyo: Okura Shō Insatsu Kyoku, published annually).

C.   The Outflow of Labor to the Nonengaged Population

The percentage of the work force leaving to join the nonengaged sector increased from 14.6 percent in the first five-year period to 15.3 and 16.0 percent respectively in the next two periods. This trend is even more noticeable among women (23.9, 25.5, and 27.0 percent respectively).

Some additional differences in the behavior of men and women are brought to light when we break down the labor force into different age groups. Unfortunately, since comparable data were not gathered in the 1950 census, the analysis must be limited to the second and third periods. Table 4 gives a breakdown of male and female labor force participation rates by age group for each of three major categories of employment. Two trends are evident in these data.

(1)   *The rise in labor force participation for middle-aged women.*   Labor force participation rates have risen for males aged between 25 and

Table 4: Labor Force Participation Rate by Age Groups and Major Employment Categories

Age	A Labor force participation rate			B Percentage in primary industry			C Percentage employed in secondary and tertiary industries			D Percentage self-employed and family workers in secondary and tertiary industries		
	1955	1960	1965	1955	1960	1965	1955	1960	1965	1955	1960	1965
Males												
All age												
groups	83.5	84.3	82.0	28.2	21.9	16.1	42.0	50.1	54.8	13.3	12.3	11.0
15–19	52.1	50.6	37.0	17.3	8.8	3.8	31.0	38.7	31.6	3.8	3.1	1.6
20–24	85.3	86.8	85.4	23.9	14.3	6.7	53.2	65.2	72.7	8.2	7.3	6.0
25–29	93.9	96.1	96.4	25.5	18.4	10.1	57.8	66.6	76.5	10.6	11.1	9.8
30–34	95.1	97.2	97.3	26.1	21.5	14.9	55.2	63.7	70.0	13.8	12.0	12.4
35–39	95.8	97.2	97.3	27.1	22.9	18.8	51.3	59.8	66.2	17.4	14.5	12.3
40–44	95.8	97.2	97.2	27.0	24.6	20.5	48.1	54.6	62.3	20.7	18.0	14.4
45–49	95.5	96.7	97.0	30.6	25.3	22.4	43.3	51.4	57.2	21.6	20.0	17.4
50–54	93.9	95.4	96.3	37.2	29.0	23.9	36.1	45.9	52.9	20.5	20.5	19.5
55–59	89.1	89.6	91.5	42.5	35.3	28.1	26.4	34.7	43.6	20.2	19.4	19.8
60–64	81.3	82.1	83.6	45.3	39.4	34.2	18.4	23.8	31.8	17.6	18.9	17.6
65–69	56.1	70.0	71.7	38.7	39.8	35.5	7.6	15.0	21.0	9.8	15.2	15.2
70–	56.1	41.9	40.7	38.7	28.7	23.0	7.6	5.7	8.8	9.8	7.5	8.9
Females												
All age												
groups	49.8	50.5	49.2	26.2	22.1	16.0	15.9	20.4	24.0	7.7	8.0	9.2
15–19	48.4	48.9	37.0	16.2	8.3	2.5	29.2	38.4	33.2	3.0	2.2	1.3
20–24	66.7	68.7	68.3	25.3	17.1	7.1	34.9	45.8	55.3	6.5	5.8	5.9
25–29	51.1	49.7	45.7	26.5	21.0	12.8	17.3	21.4	24.0	7.3	7.3	8.9
30–34	49.0	51.0	47.5	27.8	26.0	18.2	11.8	15.9	18.6	9.4	9.1	10.7
35–39	52.9	54.8	57.8	29.5	27.2	23.2	11.7	15.6	22.3	11.7	12.0	12.3
40–44	55.1	56.5	61.6	31.4	28.3	24.4	11.2	15.1	22.6	12.5	13.8	14.6
45–49	54.1	56.6	62.1	33.0	29.8	25.7	9.8	13.7	20.8	11.3	13.1	15.6
50–54	51.1	51.5	56.9	33.8	29.4	25.9	6.9	10.4	16.8	10.4	11.7	14.2
55–59	45.5	46.5	49.8	31.9	29.7	25.6	4.7	6.9	12.0	8.9	9.9	12.2
60–64	38.4	39.0	39.1	28.8	26.9	23.0	2.9	4.2	6.5	6.7	7.9	9.6
65–69	20.6	30.6	28.2	16.3	22.7	17.3	1.2	2.6	3.8	3.1	5.3	7.1
70—	20.6	15.2	10.7	16.3	11.9	6.6	1.2	0.7	1.2	3.1	2.6	2.9

Source: Sōrifu Tōkei Kyoku (Bureau of Statistics, The Prime Minister's Office), *Kokusei Chōsa Kekka* [The Results of the National Census] (Tokyo: Ōkura Shō Insatsu Kyoku, published every five years).

70 and for females between 35 and 65. Over 97 percent of all males in their thirties and forties were in the work force, suggesting that full employment had been achieved for males in these age groups.

Looking at changes over time in the labor force participation rates for cohort groups (Table 5), it would seem that the increase in the labor force participation rate occurred largely in the late 1950s.

The labor force participation behavior of women differs in three respects. First, there is a large drop in the labor force participation rate of women as they move through their twenties and into their early thirties. Second, the labor force participation rate then rises rapidly as they enter their late thirties and early forties. Third, there is a recent trend toward higher participation rates among women, whereas among men there has been little change since nearly full participation is achieved by the age of 25. A closer look (in Table 6) shows that the participation rate for women in primary industry drops steadily for all age groups. This trend was accelerated in the third period. In secondary and tertiary industries, the propensity for middle-aged women to enter the labor force as employees has increased for all age groups over 30. The same trend can also be seen among women becoming self-employed or taking up work at home in a family enterprise. These trends no doubt appear for two reasons.

Table 5:   Changes in the Labor Force Participation Rates for Age Cohorts

Age cohort group at the beginning of the five-year period	Males				Females			
	For all industries		For secondary and tertiary industries (employees only)		For all industries		For secondary and tertiary industries (employees only)	
	1955–1960	1960–1965	1955–1960	1960–1965	1955–1960	1960–1965	1955–1960	1960–1965
20–24	10.8	9.6	3.4	11.3	−17.0	−23.0	−13.5	−21.8
25–29	3.3	1.2	5.9	3.4	−0.1	−2.2	−1.4	−2.8
30–34	2.1	0.1	4.6	2.5	5.8	6.8	3.8	6.4
35–39	1.4	0	3.3	2.5	3.6	6.6	3.4	7.0
40–44	0.9	−0.2	3.3	2.6	1.5	5.6	2.5	5.7
45–49	−0.1	−0.4	2.6	1.5	−2.6	0.3	0.6	3.1
50–54	4.3	3.9	−1.4	−2.3	−4.6	−1.7	0	1.6
55–59	7.0	6.0	−2.6	−2.9	−6.5	−7.4	−0.5	−0.4
60–64	11.4	10.4	−3.4	−2.8	−7.8	−10.8	−0.3	−0.4
65–					−5.4	−10.2		

Note: The change in percentage is calculated in the following way (with the sample figures for males in all industries between 1955 and 1960 in the 30–40 age bracket):

$$\begin{pmatrix} \text{The labor participation} \\ \text{rate for those aged 35–} \\ \text{39 in 1960} \end{pmatrix} - \begin{pmatrix} \text{The labor participation} \\ \text{rate for those aged 30–} \\ \text{34 in 1955} \end{pmatrix} = \begin{pmatrix} \text{Amount of change} \\ \text{recorded in this} \\ \text{table} \end{pmatrix}$$

$$97.2\% \quad - \quad 95.1\% \quad = \quad 2.1$$

Source: This table is tabulated from the data in Table 4.

Table 6: Changes in the Labor Participation Rate for Female Cohorts by Industry and Age Group: 1955–1965

Age cohort group at the beginning of the period	Industry and five-year period					
	Primary industry		Secondary and tertiary industries			
			Employees		Self-employed and family employees	
	1955–1960	1960–1965	1955–1960	1960–1965	1955–1960	1960–1965
25–29	−0.5	−2.8	−1.4	−2.8	1.8	3.4
30–34	−0.6	−2.8	3.8	6.4	2.6	3.2
35–39	−1.2	−2.8	3.4	7.0	1.4	2.6
40–44	−1.6	−2.6	2.5	5.7	0.6	2.5
45–49	−3.6	−3.9	0.6	3.1	0.4	1.1

Note: The same procedure for calculation was used as for Table 5.
Source: Data in Table 4.

First, as the labor shortage became more pronounced, many wives of small entrepreneurs began to work in the family business. Between 1955 and 1965 the increase in the number of women employed as family workers was most pronounced in textiles (with a jump from 75,000 to 102,000), wholesaling (from 66,000 to 119,000), retailing (from 851,000 to 1,092,000), individual services (from 168,000 to 220,000), entertainment (from 6,000 to 10,000), and medicine and insurance (from 24,000 to 51,000). This trend toward employment in family-run businesses is present even among those in their late twenties, while in the same age group there is a net outflow of women from the labor force in primary industry and among employees in secondary and tertiary industries. Moreover, these differences have become more pronounced over time. It might be hypothesized that many women leave work as employees in order to marry, and then reenter the labor force again afterwards as family workers.

A second reason for these trends is the rapid improvement in the standard of living which has resulted in various new consumer demands for a variety of services. The increase in female entrepreneurs is particularly pronounced in the third period among women aged between 20 and 35. Much of the increase is concentrated in the service industry where the number of female entrepreneurs increased from 460,000 to 517,000 between 1960 and 1965. Many of these women work as piano teachers, home tutors, poster artists, and designers. These trends contribute to the fact that the labor force participation rates for Japanese women are high by international standards (Table 7).

(2) *The drop in labor force participation for women in the youngest and*

Table 7: International Comparisons of Work Force Participation
Rates for Middle-aged Women

| Age group | Japan (1965) | | U.S.A. (1960) | France (1962) |
	For all industries	For secondary and tertiary industries		
30–34	47.5	35.9	35.5	38.7
35–39	57.8	45.1	40.3	39.6
40–44	61.6	49.2	45.3	41.2
45–49	62.1	49.0	47.4	45.0

Note: Since part-time employment is handled differently in the statistics of the various countries, the comparisons are not precise. The second column for Japan represents an attempt to avoid the bias introduced by the fact that, in comparison with the other two countries, a large percentage of Japan's labor force is in agriculture. The labor force participation rate for women in secondary and tertiary industries in Japan is calculated as follows:

$$\begin{Bmatrix} \text{Labor force participa-} \\ \text{tion rate for women in} \\ \text{secondary and} \\ \text{tertiary industries} \end{Bmatrix} = \frac{\begin{pmatrix} \text{All gainfully} \\ \text{employed} \end{pmatrix} - \begin{pmatrix} \text{Gainfully employed in} \\ \text{primary industry} \end{pmatrix}}{\begin{pmatrix} \text{Population aged} \\ \text{over 14} \end{pmatrix} - \begin{pmatrix} \text{Gainfully employed in} \\ \text{primary industry} \end{pmatrix}}$$

Source: Figures for the United States and France are from statistics supplied by the individual governments. Figures for Japan are from Table 4.

oldest age groups. Partially offsetting the increase in the labor force participation rate of middle-aged women is the drop in the rate for women in their late twenties and for those over 60 (Table 5). Among those in their late twenties this no doubt reflects a decline in the need for married women to work as the standard of living improves and a greater willingness to consider housework and child rearing as a specialized function. Among those aged over 60 this trend likely reflects the improved financial position of older people, due perhaps to improved pensions and income transfers from their children. In the youngest age bracket (ages 15–19), the drop in the labor force participation rate is marked because of the increase in the number of girls going on for further education at the secondary and tertiary level. This trend started earlier for boys and, consequently, the rate at which their labor force participation rate drops off is not so noticeable. Among the oldest age groups a similar pattern prevails for men and women.

To summarize the two trends discussed above, changes in patterns of labor force participation are most noticeable among women who tend to play a supplementary role in terms of household income. The propensity to work has dropped among those in the younger and older age groups, and has risen among the middle-aged. The overall trend showed a slight rise in the labor force participation rate for both males and females in the late 1950s and then a slightly greater drop in the early 1960s. The overall impression gained from a study of the various inflows and outflows suggests that employment patterns have stabilized as the economy has reasserted itself. This is partially reflected in the average length of continuous employment with the same firm. Table 8 shows that the average number of years with the same firm has increased for women over 30, whereas it has declined for those under 30. The trend toward higher education has shortened the time between graduation and marriage, and largely accounts for the drop in the average length of employment with the same firm for women in their twenties.

D.   Changes in the Mortality Rate

Finally, there has been a drop in the rate at which losses to the work force occur as a result of death. In the respective five-year periods, 3.1, 3.2, and 2.8 respectively of those in the labor force died. This reflects the overall drop in the mortality rate and the fact that fewer of the aged are now in the labor force.

The net rates of attrition for men and women for each of the five-year periods are given in Table 9. They are considerably below the

Table 8: Average Number of Years with the Same Firm by Age Group for Men and Women: 1958, 1961, and 1966

Age	Women			Men		
	1958	1961	1966	1958	1961	1966
Average for all age groups	3.9	3.8	4.0	7.4	7.5	8.0
–17	1.3	1.3	1.4	1.3	1.2	1.4
18–19	1.8	1.7	1.7	1.7	1.7	1.7
20–24	3.5	3.3	3.3	3.1	3.0	3.5
25–29	6.3	5.7	4.8	6.0	5.4	5.5
30–34	5.9	6.9	6.1	8.5	8.9	8.0
35–39	5.9	5.7	6.5	10.0	10.9	11.7
40–49	6.1	5.7	6.1	12.2	12.8	14.0
50–59	6.1	6.8	7.0	12.8	13.6	14.0
60–	6.1	7.3	7.6	12.8	9.1	9.2

Source: Rōdō Daijin Kanbō Tōkei Jōhō Bu (Statistics and Information Department, Minister's Secretariat, Ministry of Labour), *Chingin Kōzō Kihon Tōkei Chōsa Kekka* [Results of the Basic Survey of the Wage Structure].

Table 9:   The Average Annual Rate of Attrition from the Work Force by Sex: 1950–1965

(percentages)

Sex	Time period		
	1950–1955	1955–1960	1960–1965
Males	0.7	0.7	0.7
Females	1.3	2.0	2.2

Note:

$$\left\{\begin{array}{c}\text{The rate}\\\text{of}\\\text{attrition}\end{array}\right\} = \left\{\dfrac{\left(\begin{array}{c}\text{Those leaving the}\\\text{labor force to enter}\\\text{the nonengaged}\\\text{population}\end{array}\right) + \left(\begin{array}{c}\text{Those dying}\\\text{while still}\\\text{in the labor}\\\text{force}\end{array}\right) - \left(\begin{array}{c}\text{Those entering}\\\text{the labor force}\\\text{from the rest of}\\\text{the population}\end{array}\right)}{\text{(The labor force)}}\right\} \times 100$$

rates of 2.5 percent for men and 4.0 percent for women which would result if we assumed the average length of time spent in the work force to be 40 years for men and 25 years for women. This no doubt reflects the net flow into the labor force from the nonengaged population and the gradual extension of the average length of time spent in the labor force.

E.   Other Sectors

The inflow of workers from Okinawa increased from 5000 persons in the second period to 31,000 in the third period.

3.   Employees in Industries Other than Agriculture and Forestry

Looking only at the sector of employees in industries other than agriculture and forestry (hereafter referred to simply as "employees"), it is clear from Table 1 that the rate of increase, whether in absolute numbers or in percentages, has been greater than that for the work force as a whole. In addition to the inflow of new graduates and others from the nonengaged population, there has been considerable mobility from other sectors into the ranks of employees. These sources of labor supply are shown in Table 10.

During the third five-year period, the number of employees registered a gross increase of 53.8 percent. The figures show that the largest inflow was from new graduates (26.5 percent), followed by the nonengaged population (excluding students) aged 15 or older (18.4 percent), those employed in agriculture and forestry (5.6 percent), the

Table 10: The Inflow and Outflow of Employees in Non-agricultural and Non-forestry Industries: 1950–1965

Time period	Sex	Number of employees at the beginning of the period	Direction of flow											Total number of employees at the end of the period
			Inflow						Outflow					
			From the nonengaged or unemployed population	From new graduates	From Okinawa	From agriculture & forestry	From the self-employed and family workers not engaged in agriculture or forestry	Total inflow	Those joining the nonengaged or unemployed population	Deaths	Those going to agriculture or forestry	Those becoming self-employed or working as family workers	Total outflow	
1950–1960	Both sexes	13,237	3,171	3,421	—	1,304	624	8,520	2,813	320	693	623	4,449	17,307
	Male	9,860	1,502	1,929	—	707	434	4,572	1,174	289	186	386	2,035	12,397
	Female	3,377	1,669	1,492	—	597	190	3,948	1,639	31	507	238	2,415	4,910
1955–1960	Both sexes	17,307	3,747	5,493	5	1,464	713	11,422	3,744	380	851	774	5,749	11,981
	Male	12,397	1,823	2,921	3	929	456	6,137	1,455	344	222	461	2,482	16,047
	Female	4,924	1,924	2,573	2	536	258	5,293	2,289	36	629	313	3,267	6,934
1960–1965	Both sexes	22,981	4,229	6,079	31	1,298	731	12,368	4,399	444	561	1,191	6,595	28,753
	Male	16,046	1,993	3,077	20	750	463	6,303	1,532	399	266	483	2,690	19,660
	Female	6,934	2,235	3,002	11	548	268	6,064	2,867	45	295	698	3,905	9,093

self-employed in industries other than agriculture and forestry (3.2 percent), and workers from Okinawa (0.13 percent). During the same period, 28.7 percent of those who were employees at the beginning of the period left for other sectors, 19.1 percent leaving the work force altogether, 5.2 percent becoming entrepreneurs or family workers, 2.4 percent moving into agriculture, and 1.9 percent dying. The net increase in the number of employees was 5.77 million, or 25.1 percent, in the third five-year period.

The net flows for each category are given in Table 11. In contrast to the net inflows from the nonengaged population and urban entrepreneurs in the early 1950s (totaling 8.8 percent), net outflows were registered by the early 1960s (totaling 10.9 percent). This alone accounts for a 19.7 percent difference in the number of employees. However, this is offset by the net inflow of graduates, which accounted for 84.0 percent of the net increase in the number of employees in the early 1950s and 105.3 percent by the early 1960s (meaning that 5.3 percent of what was a net outflow in other categories was covered by the incoming graduates). Net inflows were also registered from agriculture and forestry and from Okinawa. Finally, the net loss due to death remained constant.

Considering the trends for males and females separately, one immediately notices the high net outflow to the nonengaged population of 29.3 percent for women in the third period, whereas there is a net inflow of 12.8 percent for men. The net outflow registered to the self-employed and family workers during the same period was also due largely to the behavior of women (with a net outflow of 19.9 percent); the net outflow for men was only 0.8 percent. Deaths accounted for the loss of more male employees (7 percent) than female employees (2.1 percent). The following subsections will briefly examine changes over time in the individual flows within each sector.

A.   Graduates

The number of new graduates becoming employees increased rapidly from 3.42 million in the first period to 6.08 million in the third period, a 77.7 percent increase. The increase was particularly marked for women (see Table 11). In addition to the increase in the absolute number of persons graduating, the percentage of graduates seeking employment in non-agricultural industries as employees increased from 63.1 percent to 90.8 percent (see Table 12). The relative elasticity of the supply of graduates as defined in Table 12 was 1.73 for employees

Table 11:   Sources of the Increase in the Number of Employees in Non-agricultural and Non-forestry Industries

Category	Time period					
	1950–1955		1955–1960		1960–1965	
	1000s of persons	Percent	1000s of persons	Percent	1000s of persons	Percent
Both sexes						
Net increase in the nonengaged or unemployed population	359	(8.8)	3	(0.1)	−170	(−2.9)
New graduates	3,421	(84.0)	5,493	(96.8)	6,079	(105.3)
Gainfully employed workers in agriculture and forestry	611	(15.0)	613	(10.8)	737	(12.8)
Self-employed and family workers in non-agricultural and non-forestry industries	1	(—)	−61	(−1.1)	−460	(−8.0)
Workers from Okinawa	—	(—)	5	(0.1)	31	(0.5)
Deaths	−320	(−7.9)	−380	(−6.7)	−444	(−7.7)
Net increase in employees	4,071	(100.0)	5,637	(100.0)	5,773	(100.0)
Females						
Net increase in the nonengaged or unemployed population	30	(2.0)	−365	(−18.0)	−632	(−29.3)
New graduates	1,492	(97.3)	2,573	(127.0)	3,002	(139.1)
Gainfully employed workers in agriculture and forestry	90	(5.9)	93	(−4.6)	253	(11.7)
Self-employed and family workers in non-agricultural and non-forestry industries	−48	(−3.1)	−55	(−2.7)	−430	(−19.9)
Workers from Okinawa	—	(—)	2	(0.1)	11	(0.5)
Deaths	− 31	(−2.0)	−36	(−1.8)	−45	(−2.1)
Net increase in employees	1,533	(100.0)	2,026	(100.0)	2,159	(100.0)

in industries other than agriculture and forestry, 0.23 for self-employed workers in industries other than agriculture and forestry, and 0.18 for those in agriculture or forestry. This pattern is even more pronounced among females.

By the late 1960s, however, the postwar boom babies will have graduated and entered the labor force, and the delayed entry of those going on for a higher education will also have occurred. Moreover, the

Table 12:   The Employment Patterns of New Graduates

Time period	Both sexes				Males				Females			
	Number of new graduates (1000s of persons)	Percentage composition			Number of new graduates (1000s of persons)	Percentage composition			Number of graduates (1000s of persons)	Percentage composition		
		Agriculture and forestry	All other industries			Agriculture and forestry	All other industries			Agriculture and forestry	All other industries	
			Employees	Self-employed or family workers			Employees	Self-employed or family workers			Employees	Self-employed or family workers
A. 1950–1955	5,540	31.1	63.1	5.8	2,909	29.2	64.1	6.7	2,632	33.7	61.7	4.6
B. 1955–1960	6,711	14.7	80.8	4.5	3,473	15.3	79.4	5.4	3,238	14.0	82.5	3.5
C. 1960–1965	6,845	5.5	90.8	3.7	3,440	6.6	88.9	4.6	3,405	4.2	93.1	2.7
D. Total number of persons gainfully employed in 1960	—	31.3	52.6	16.1	—	24.0	60.3	15.7	—	42.6	40.6	16.8
E. Elasticity of new graduates relative to percent allocation of total work force (C/D)	—	0.18	1.73	0.23	—	0.28	1.47	0.29	—	0.10	2.29	0.16

percentage of high school graduates going on for further education will have leveled off. Consequently, it is unlikely that any further increase in the number of employees will come from that sector. As a percentage of all employees at the beginning of each five-year period, the number of incoming graduates equaled 25.8 percent in the first period, 31.7 percent in the second, and 26.5 percent in the third. In the future, employers will find it increasingly difficult to rely on this source of labor.

B. The Nonengaged Adult Population

Although there was a net inflow from the nonengaged adult population in the early 1950s as the economy began to recover and pick up momentum, the early 1960s were characterized by a net outflow (Table 11). Nonengaged males continued to register a net inflow throughout the three periods, although the importance of that inflow diminished over time. On the other hand, the small net inflow registered by women in the first period had changed to an increasingly large net outflow by the early 1960s.

Looking at these trends by age groups (Table 5), the increase in the labor participation rate due to males becoming employees occurs largely among those in their twenties and (to a lesser degree) their thirties. Most of those who enter the labor force were previously unemployed. For women the shift from nonengagement to employment occurs most frequently in their thirties and (to a lesser extent) their forties. Women in their twenties and members of both sexes over 55 register a net dropout from the employee sector.

The change from a sizeable net inflow to a small net outflow is due largely to the fact that the absolute figures for the outflow grew more rapidly than those for the inflow (see Tables 10 and 13). The gradual drop in the amount of movement back and forth between employees and the nonengaged population suggests that the economy has stabilized itself.

C. Deaths

Deaths did not greatly affect the total number of employees. Nevertheless, the death rate did drop from 0.45 percent of all employees in the first period to 0.38 and 0.35 percent in the successive pentads. These are considerably below the rates registered for the work force as a whole (3.1, 3.2, and 2.8 percent, respectively) (Table 2). This reflects the fact that retirement comes earliest in this sector (Table 4),

Table 13:   The Annual Rate of Labor Force Entry and Exit

Category	Sex	Time period		
		1950–1955	1955–1960	1960–1965
Rate of	Both	4.0	3.6	3.2
entry	Male	2.6	2.5	2.2
	Female	7.8	6.3	5.4
Rate of	Both	3.8	3.8	3.5
exit	Male	2.2	2.1	1.8
	Female	8.2	8.0	7.4

Note:

$$\text{Rate of entry} = \frac{\text{Annual average number entering the labor force (excluding new graduates)}}{\text{Average size of the labor force}}$$

$$\text{Rate of exit} = \frac{\text{Annual average number leaving the labor force (excluding deaths)}}{\text{Average size of the labor force}}$$

Source: The figures in this table have been calculated from the figures in Table 10.

and also perhaps the fact that the standard of living of employees is higher than that of workers in the other sectors.

D.   Agriculture and Forestry

Next to the student sector (which supplied the new graduates), agriculture and forestry was the most important source of new employees. Although the absolute number becoming employees increases from 1.3 million in the early 1950s to 1.46 million in the late 1950s and then drops back to 1.3 million in the early 1960s, the percentage of people in agriculture and forestry who make the shift increases from an annual rate of 1.6 percent in the early 1950s to 2 percent and 2.1 percent in successive pentads as the reserves in that sector are gradually drawn out (Table 14). The movement out of the employee sector to agriculture and forestry follows a similar pattern in terms of the increase and subsequent decrease in the absolute size of the gross outflow (Table 10). Although three-fourths of those moving to agriculture in the first pentad were women, the numbers had become about the same for both sexes by the third period. The net flow into the employee sector of about 610,000 workers in each of the first two periods rose to nearly 740,000 in the last pentad. Males registered a net inflow to the employee sector, whereas women represented a net inflow only in the first and third periods and a net outflow in the middle pentad.

The inconsistency in the behavior of women is perhaps due to the

Table 14:   Mobility Rates for Labor Moving between Agriculture and Forestry and the Employee Sector for All Other Industries

Mobility rate	Sex	Time period		
		1950–1955	1955–1960	1960–1965
Persons leaving agriculture and forestry to become employees in other industries ÷ Persons gainfully employed in agriculture or forestry	Both	1.6	2.0	2.1
Persons quitting as employees in other industries to enter agriculture or forestry ÷ Employees in non-agricultural and non-forestry industries	Both	0.9	1.2	0.9
	Male	0.5	0.7	0.9
	Female	1.3	1.7	0.9

Source: The figures in this table have been calculated from the figures in Table 10.

fact that many women from farming households found employment as employees after graduating in the first period but then returned to agriculture in the second period. Looking at cohort behavior, 16.2 percent of those aged 15–29 in 1955 were employed in primary industry, and 17.2 percent of those aged 20–24 were so employed in 1960. By 1965, however, an examination of cohorts (Table 4) suggests that there was a drop in the percentage of young women employed in primary industry. By this time it would seem likely that rather than returning to agriculture, many simply dropped out of the work force.

E.   Self-employed and Family Workers in Industries Other than Agriculture and Forestry

In the early 1950s the inflow and outflow of persons between the employee sector and the self-employed and family workers' sectors in industries other than agriculture and forestry were balanced. However, the outflow from the employee sector increased very rapidly (by 90.5 percent) in the following decade, with a net outflow of 460,000 in the third pentad. The net outflow from the employee sector thus rose from zero to about 8 percent by the early 1960s. This trend is largely accounted for by the accelerated outflow of women (Tables 10 and 11). However, the figures for the cohorts aged 25–29 in Table 4 and the net flows in Table 15 suggest that a certain percentage of the young women who gave up their status as employees to get married ended up employed as entrepreneurs or family workers.

Table 15:   The Percentage Composition of the Outflow of Female Employees from Industries Other than Agriculture and Forestry

Direction of outflow		Time period		
		1950–1955	1955–1960	1960–1965
A.	Agriculture and forestry	2.5	2.2	0.8
B.	Self-employment or family work in industries other than agriculture and forestry	1.2	1.1	1.8
C.	The unengaged or unemployed population	8.2	8.0	7.3
D.	Death	0.2	0.1	0.1
E.	Persons remaining as employees in industries other than agriculture and forestry	87.9	88.9	90.0
	Total	100.0	100.0	100.0

Source: The figures in this table have been calculated from the figures in Table 10.

F. Okinawa

The number of new employees from Okinawa rose sharply in the early 1960s, but the impact on the total number of employees was very small.

4. Conclusions

The above analysis shows that the reservoir of unutilized labor has been tapped as much as possible. This is particularly true for the sector composed of employees. Moreover, considering the drop in the size of the student population and the continuing rise in levels of education in the years to come, the labor market will continue to tighten. It is for this reason that attention must be given to developing a new approach to manpower planning in the near future. Existing supplies of labor will have to be used more effectively in the near future; this will require improved efficiency at all levels and further reallocation of existing labor from industries with low productivity to those with high productivity.

The Theory of Labor Supply
Some New Perspectives and Some Implications

Obi Keiichirō

1. The Revival of Labor Supply Analysis

For ten years beginning in the late 1930s, economists seemed to be preoccupied with Keynesian models of income determination, and concern with labor supply seemed to wane. The Keynesian theory of income determination lacked a theory of value or price determination relevant to the behavior of households, firms, and other such actors in the economy; accordingly, the popularity of Keynesian doctrine resulted in the behavioral factors determining labor supply being overlooked. Indeed, it was argued that the level of employment in the national economy could be determined without regard to the supply curve for labor if the economic system were left to function by itself. They seemed to imply that the supply curve for labor was of minor importance in determining the overall level of employment and wage differentials. However, the great concern with economic development during the 1960s served to rekindle an interest in the labor supply mechanism.

The process of economic development begins when a new, highly productive technology is introduced to a national economy otherwise characterized by "traditional" industries with low productivity. Economic growth occurs as the sector using the newer technology expands. In this process, labor employed in the traditional sector becomes the supply source of labor for the new sector. To attract labor from the

This paper first appeared as "Rōdō Kyōkyū no Riron: Sono Kadai Oyobi Kiketsu no Gan'i" in *Mita Gakkai Zasshi* (vol. 61, no. 1: January 1968), pp. 1–25. The author is Professor of Economics at Keio University.

traditional sector, firms in the new sector must offer a sufficiently high wage, which may be paid either in cash or through other forms of economic inducement. The minimum supply price of labor is defined as the lowest wage rate which will draw to the new sector a sufficient supply of labor from the traditional sector. The student of economic development, then, is interested in knowing the factors which determine the minimum supply price of labor and, thereby, the factors which partially control the rate at which the new sector can expand. This in turn requires an understanding of the labor supply of households in the traditional sector (including those engaged in farming, cottage industries, and traditional services).

In the context of theories on economic development, the theory labor supply follows closely the guidelines developed by traditional of economics, with the focus being on the determination of wages and employment. However, considerable advances were made in empirical research as improved experimental design allowed for rather abstract theories to be applied to the exploration of observable phenomena. In the purely theoretical framework of the neoclassical school, it was assumed that the basic behavioral unit determining labor supply was the individual. In the process of operationalization, an empirical counterpart for the "theoretical individual" was left unspecified. Theorists interested in economic development, on the other hand, redefined the behavioral unit determining labor supply to the modern sector. No longer was it seen as being the abstracted, uniform "economic man". Rather, the behavioral units were seen as the members of households engaged in farming or small-scale manufacturing in the traditional sector. This development meant that the empirical counterpart of "the individual" in pure neoclassical theory could be regarded as the household in the traditional sector.

This brings us back to the important but difficult question which is the key to understanding the labor supply mechanism: What factors determine or regulate the supply price of labor? Although considerable doubt has been thrown on Malthus's formulation which suggests that wages will remain at a subsistence level (at least in those countries where some measure of economic growth has been achieved), it can still be posited that in many societies a minimum subsistence standard exists not only in terms of physical or biological needs, but also in terms of certain social and psychological needs which must be met. In referring to the total reproduction costs of the labor force, the concept of a minimum level of subsistence loses much of its precision. The complexities of reality leave us with a concept that actually defies empirical measurement. To be sure, we can still argue that the subsistence wage is that rate which is associated with the kink in the supply curve. However, unless we can explain how the kink is determined, the assertion is nothing more than a tautology. Nevertheless, our understanding of the whole developmental process depends largely upon our ability to explain the mechanism which determines the minimum supply price of labor—the minimum value at which labor in the traditional sector will make itself available to entrepreneurs in the new sector.

In this fashion, then, the concern with economic growth has revived our interest in the theory of labor supply while at the same time awakening us to the need to go beyond the abstracted framework used to explain labor supply by the neoclassical economists. Indeed, the model of development presented by Fei and Ranis suggests that the mechanism determining the minimum supply price of labor is of particular importance in explaining the early stages of economic growth.[1] This does not mean, however, that we can gain a full understanding of the whole developmental process simply by applying our understanding of the minimum supply price of labor to only the first stages of growth. For an example, we can look at wages in Japan's textile industry during the 1930s. Even within the textile industry there were many subdivisions. Beginning with the manufacturing of silk thread, where the lowest wage rates could be found, there were different wage rates in cotton spinning, silk spinning, wool spinning, and wool weaving. These groupings were pretty much stratified according to their respective (average) wage rates, and the order in which they were arrayed from low-wage to high-wage sectors follows closely the listing given above. Moreover, although silk thread manufacturing paid the lowest wage rates, even these rates varied from year to year, and a close look reveals differentials even within the silk thread manufacturing industry. The Labor Statistics Survey (Rōdō Tōkei Jitchi Chōsa) for 1927, 1930, 1933, and 1936 shows a set relationship between hours of work and the hourly wage rates. In each of the above years and for each sector the highest hourly wage rates were paid to workers with either the most or the fewest hours of work. The lowest hourly rates were paid to workers with a medium work load. This fact suggests that there existed a minimum level below which wages could not go.

The heavy dependence of silk thread manufacturers on the labor supply from agricultural households is well known. For this reason the lower wage rates in silk thread manufacturing tended to serve as an index of the lowest wage rates which would siphon labor from

[1] J. C. H. Fei and G. Ranis, *Development of the Labor Surplus Economy* (Homewood: Richard D. Irwin, Inc., 1964).

agriculture to industry. Given this basic framework, attention is focused on (1) the factors which caused the minimum supply price of labor from agricultural households to vary from year to year and (2) the source of the differentials among the different sectors of the textile industry. While referring the reader elsewhere on the second question,[2] I can briefly state in partial answer to the first that the minimum wage rates in any given year were closely related to the level of income earned by tenant farmers during the previous years.[3] These two variables clearly move in the same direction. Although this fact will be discussed again below, here it is important to note the broader significance of those questions that have emerged from an initial concern with the early stages of economic growth. Indeed, upon these very basic facts is built our understanding of wage structures even in economies which are fully developed and industrialized.

2. Issues in the Theory of Labor Supply

A. The Decision to Work

In discussing the supply of labor, three components of the supply must be considered: the size of the labor force, the hours worked, and the quality of the work performed. The size of the labor force depends upon the size of the population and the rate at which persons participate in the labor force. Malthus and the classical economists accepting his theory regarded population as an endogenous variable which would be determined by the differential between the actual wage and the minimum amount necessary for subsistence. However, they failed to distinguish clearly between the size of the population (or at least that part of the population of an age suitable for participating in the work force) and the size of the actual labor force. While the neoclassical economists, beginning with Jevons[4] and progressing

---

[2] Obi Keiichirō, "Chingin to Rōdō Jikan no Kakusa" [Differentials in Wages and Working Hours], in *Chingin Mondai to Chingin Seisaku* [Wage Problems and Wage Policy], ed. by Nakayama Ichirō (Tokyo: Tōyō Keizai Shimpō Sha, 1959), Chapter Three, pp. 65–134.

[3] On the relationship between marginal productivity in agriculture and wage rates, see Torii Yasuhiko, "Keizai Hatten Riron to Rōdō Kyōkyū Shutai no Kinkō Zushiki" [The Theory of Economic Development and Equilibrium Analysis in Terms of the Supply of Labor], *Keizaigaku Nenpō*, the annual review of economics published by Keio University (no. 9: 1965), pp. 73–162.

[4] W. S. Jevons, *The Theory of Political Economy* (London: Macmillan, 1871). The Japanese version was translated by Koizumi Shinzō, Terao Takuma, and Nagata Kiyoshi and appeared as *Keizaigaku no Riron* (Tokyo: Nihon Hyōron Sha, 1944).

through Hicks,[5] made population an exogenous variable, a clear distinction was made between the employable population of working age and the actual size of the labor force.

Following the publication of Jevons's *The Theory of Political Economy*, neoclassical economists developed a theory whereby the individual would optimize the number of hours he worked. This framework was derived from principles of utility maximization. However, the link between labor force participation and the notion of an individual's optimal hours of work has never been clearly demonstrated. Looking at the development of labor supply theory, then, we can say that the classical economists and those dealing with economic development focused their attention on the actual number of people in the labor force, whereas the neoclassical theorists spoke of man-hours in referring to the total supply of labor. Nevertheless, neither group came up with any clear-cut theory about the relationship between the mechanism determining the number of persons supplied for the work force and the mechanism determining the number of hours that given individuals were actually willing to work.

With regard to the behavioral unit which makes the decision to supply labor, classical economists focused primarily on the household. The neoclassical thinkers, on the other hand, frequently referred to abstracted invididuals, but with few exceptions the household as an economic unit was not mentioned. Among those dealing with economic development, however, the labor supply for the emerging modern sector was conceived primarily in terms of workers and families existing in the traditional sector. Although each of the schools of thought was concerned with the determination of levels of wages and employment, generally speaking there was little agreement as to (1) how the behavioral unit should be identified and (2) how to measure the quantity of labor supplied. Consequently, there was considerable variation in sophistication with regard to the way in which they spoke about the potentially available supply of labor. It is thus necessary to consider more recent developments along these lines.

B. The Douglas-Long-Arisawa Findings and the Origins of Modern Labor Supply Theory

Quantitative studies on the supply of labor began in the 1930s with

---

[5] John R. Hicks, *The Theory of Wages* (New York: Macmillan, 1932). The Japanese translation by Uchida Tadahisa appeared as *Chingin no Riron* (Tokyo: Tōyō Keizai Shimpō Sha, 1963).

the pioneering work of Paul Douglas.[6] Briefly summarized, Douglas used cross-sectional data for thirty-eight cities in the United States and found that the labor force participation rates for males during their prime working years were unrelated to intercity variations in the wage rates for male adults. However, the participation rates of young males and females, older males, and middle-aged and older females varied closely, but in a negative fashion, with the wage rates for male adults. In other words, in cities where the income of males in the prime age groups was high, the labor force participation rate for young males and females, older males, and middle-aged and older females was comparatively low. Cities with low wage rates for males in the prime age groups showed the opposite pattern. The labor force participation rate of males during their prime working years was, however, high in all the cities studied and did not seem to be affected by shifts in the wage rate.

The extensive statistical analysis of Long in the 1950s is another important milestone.[7] Using data collected over a twenty-year period (primarily census data), Long's probing investigation gives further support to Douglas's major conclusions regarding the relationship between the earnings of adult males and the variations in labor force participation by sex and age.

The importance of these findings is twofold. First, the decision of individuals to participate in the labor force is not an independent act. Rather, there is a relationship of mutual interdependence. Moreover, it can reasonably be hypothesized that this kind of mutual interdependence occurs within the social unit known as the household. Second, the male at his prime working age (when his labor force participation rate is insensitive to earnings) is usually the primary earner or, more colloquially, "the breadwinner". Accordingly, the extent to which other household members participate in the labor force as secondary earners will vary inversely with the income of the primary earner. The labor force participation rate of youth is no doubt affected by the fact that students' tendency to continue their education is closely related to the income of the primary earner. Females in the middle and upper age brackets normally base their decision to work upon the need for secondary income to supplement that of the primary earner, who is usually the husband.

Arisawa's examination of the households of employees shows that

---

[6] Paul H. Douglas, *The Theory of Wages* (New York: Macmillan, 1934).
[7] C. D. Long, *Labor Force Under Changing Income and Employment* (Princeton: Princeton University Press, 1958).

the same relationship also exists in Japan.[8] Arisawa used a statistical source which had just become available in Japan, the special tabulations made from the September 1954 returns for the Family Income and Expenditure Survey (Kakei Chōsa Tokubetsu Shūkei Kekka). The data, which are classified by the income of the household head, show clearly the strong negative correlation between the participation rate of the household (here calculated as the number of working persons divided by the total number of household members) and the income of the household head.

The observations of Douglas, Long, and Arisawa provide a new basis for quantitative research on the supply of labor. The research of these three scholars takes us beyond the abstracted individual of the neoclassical school, who acts as though he were in a vacuum. Their empirical findings indicate that the individual's decision to participate in the labor force is made only after considering his relationship to others in the same social unit known as the household. One must therefore conclude that it is instructive to think of the household rather than the individual as the behavioral unit which makes decisions about participation in the labor force.

Two further issues immediately come to mind. First, the investigations of Douglas, Long, and Arisawa focused on behavior in the households of employees working primarily in the industrial sector. Can the same effect be found in the households of the self-employed which are concentrated in the traditional sector? A related question concerns the transformation which occurs with economic development as households headed by self-employed individuals are replaced by households whose heads are employees. Second, how is the labor force behavior of the primary earner in employee households determined?

With regard to the first question, it is commonly known that the supply of labor for the modern sector comes from two sources during the early stages of development: (a) family workers in the households of the self-employed in the traditional sector, and (b) the households of employees who depend primarily on wage income in the modern sector. The fact that these two sources of labor exist side by side is partly indicative of the complicated institutional arrangements carried over from the past, and this coexistence markedly affects the economic,

---

[8] Arisawa Hiromi, "Chingin Kōzō to Keizai Kōzō—Teichingin to ngi to Haikei" [Wage Differentials and the Structure of the Economy: Some Background Factors and the Meaning of Low Wages], in *Chingin Kihon Chōsa* [A Study of Wages], ed. by Nakayama Ichirō (Tokyo: Tōyō Keizai Shimpō Sha, 1955), Chapter One, pp. 40–57.

social, and psychological predilections of the actors. Given the form of participation in the labor force (self-employment or hired labor) and the general earning power of the primary earner (the rate of productivity for the self-employed and the wage rate for the employee), the decision of other (mainly female) household members (a) to work in the family business, (b) to seek employment outside, or (c) not to participate at all will affect the structure of the labor force (the percentage employed and the percentage self-employed) in the next generation. Accordingly, two major concerns of those studying the labor force are (1) the decision of household members other than the primary earner, based upon their appraisal of the primary earner's present or future earning capacity, to participate or not to participate in the labor force and (2) the form which such participation takes when it does occur.

In the household of the self-employed, primary income will depend upon the household's financial assets, its productive technology, and the demand for that which it can produce. In the household of the employee, primary income will depend upon the wage or salary of the primary earner. Families which depend wholly on entrepreneurial income and those which depend wholly on wage earnings are two distinct types. In between, many intermediate combinations with mixed income are possible. One can arbitrarily classify a household according to the income of the primary earner. However, in households where the primary earner (the household head) has chosen to be self-employed, the decision of other household members to find "secondary" employment outside the home can mean that the largest amount of income in such households often comes from employment.

The factors explaining this kind of transition are numerous and intricately interwoven; they no doubt include many "non-economic" considerations. At present, we have only the most rudimentary information on this process. However, one fact has been uncovered through the retabulation of the Survey of Entrepreneurial Firms (Kojin Kigyō Keizai Chōsa). We classified non-agricultural entrepreneurial households into the following three groups: those in which someone from the next generation will continue the family business, those in which it is anticipated that the next generation will shift wholly to outside employment, and those for which the future is unclear. Although the three classifications are very simple and there may be some error in placement, the percentage of households with the second generation shifting over to employment income seems to vary inversely with the amount of entrepreneurial income.[9]

[9] Obi Keiichirō, "Chōki Keikaku to Rōdō Kyōkyū Jōken" [Long-term Planning and the Supply of Labor], *Sekai Keizai* (no. 132: August 1967), pp. 2–7.

This observation is certainly consistent with the findings of Douglas, Long, and Arisawa. Indeed, by simply imagining that entrepreneurial income plays the same role as primary income for employee households, it could be said that this transfer effect is nothing more than a natural corollary to their formulation. If the presence of this effect can be ascertained through the examination of a wide variety of other kinds of data as well, then perhaps one could conclude that economic considerations are of primary importance in the process of transition from entrepreneurial household to employee household and are not canceled by other forces. At this stage, however, we are not prepared to say anything more definite about the effect.

Turning to the second question raised above, what can be said about the behavior of the primary earner in the employee household? Few would argue that the motivation of the employee who quits his job and sets out on his own as an entrepreneur is not an interaction of extremely complex psychological, social, and institutional factors. However, here again we do not have the kinds of empirical survey data necessary for making further judgments. At present we will have to consider the labor force participation and consequent income of the primary earner as given, and focus our attention instead on the labor force behavior of the other household members.

By definition, the major source of income in the employee household is that which comes from employment, and the Family Income and Expenditure Survey defines the household head as the major source of income. These data show that, as Douglas indicated, the decision of the household head to work has very little to do with the amount of income he can earn. It is therefore most appropriate to regard his behavior as being rather strictly determined by various institutional constraints. Accordingly, our discussion will focus on the factors which affect the opportunities of other household members who seek employment, with the income of the household head being considered a given. If the mechanism which supplies secondary earners to the labor force from employee households can be explained in this fashion, the assumption that the income of the household head (which is determined by efficiency and financial assets) in entrepreneurial households plays a role similar to that of the wage income of the household head who is an employee allows us to explain the labor supply behavior of other household members in the entrepreneurial households as well.[10]

[10] Since this paper was written, the author has developed his own scheme for estimating the general supply of labor which includes this "entrepreneurial household transfer effect". See his "Kakei no Rōdō Kyōkyū no Riron ni Tsuite" [A General Theory of the Labor Supply Behavior of Households], *Mita Gakkai Zasshi* (vol. 72, no. 6: August, 1980) pp. 58–83.

C.   Some Empirical Findings

A careful analysis of the long-term trends in the overall labor force participation rates for employee households yields some interesting findings. For example, the labor force participation rate has been increasing for women in the United States. Long's research suggests that this trend is also present in the countries he studied. However, at the same time the number of hours worked has been declining.

We are thus presented with two problems. First, how does the long-term increase in the female participation rate square with Douglas's formulation which suggests that female participation should go down as primary income goes up? Second, why is the number of persons in the work force increasing while the number of hours per participant is decreasing?

On the first point, one would expect higher levels of primary income over time to result in a lower participation rate for women. According to Japanese census data for 1950, 1955, and 1965, the increase in the percentage receiving further education among those in the youngest age bracket (aged 15–19) resulted in a drop in the female participation rate. However, among older females (aged 30–59), a steady rise in the participation rate can be seen. The overall trend in the participation rate for women, then, shows a very slight decline or no change at all. The desire for further education is reflected in the fact that the decrease in the participation rate for young girls is correlated with successive increments in the income of the household head in a manner consistent with Douglas's formulation. However, women aged between 20 and 25 and those aged over thirty have shown an increased propensity to work, a finding consistent with the pattern found by Long in Europe and the United States. Long explains this trend in terms of the improvements in both the quantity and quality of opportunities for women in the work force.

Long's interpretation seeems to be given further support by an examination of labor force participation rates for households categorized by the income of the household head as available in the special tabulations for the Family Income and Expenditure Survey[11] (which are available for the years 1955 through 1958 only for families with three adults and an unspecified number of younger members). Since the income of the household head seems to have grown at more or less the same rate for

[11] Tsujimura Kōtarō, Sasaki Takao, and Nakamura Atsushi, "Kakei ni Okeru Rōdō Kyōkyū no Bunseki Shiryō" [Analytical Materials on the Labor Supply Behavior of Households], *Keizai Bunseki*, a research bulletin published by the Economic Research Institute of the Economic Planning Agency (no. 3: 1961).

each household, the participation rates corresponding to a fixed percentile point on the head's income distribution may be regarded as the trace of the changes in the participation rate of the specific group of households over the four years. Looking at the traces corresponding to different percentile points, we observe the following salient features. First, the absolute amount of increase in the income of the household head from 1955 to 1958 was smallest in the bottom group of households, whereas the increase in the labor force participation rate was most noticeable in this group. Second, at higher income levels the amount of increase in the income of household heads was larger, whereas rates of increase in labor participation were much smaller. Third, the absolute increase in the income of household heads in the group next to the top was the largest, and the participation rate remained unchanged or even dropped. Fourth, the increase in the participation rates even for the lowest groups was relatively small between 1957 and 1958 as the economy experienced a slight recession.

Considering these findings, we might conclude that two effects coexist simultaneously. Increases in the income of the household head tend to lower the participation rate as hypothesized by Douglas. At the same time, however, the quality and quantity of employment opportunities, as indicated by the change in business conditions, are also important. Accordingly, the participation rate is influenced by both effects, each seeming to offset the other. In households where primary income is low, the increase in employment opportunities during periods of economic expansion seems to have more than offset the propensity to drop out of the labor force as the income of the household head increases over time. At the other end of the income scale, the increase in the propensity for other household members to work during periods of economic expansion is canceled by the decision to refrain from working as the head's income increases. In the second income group from the top, the increase in the income of the primary earner seems to have been a major consideration as the participation rate decreased slightly. From 1957 to 1958 we see the effect of a slow-down in economic activity as employment opportunities drop.[12] These same phenomena can be seen in similar data for the years 1961 through 1964 with regard to the behavior of wives in households with a husband, wife, and children under age 15.

The above findings can be summarized as follows. Two factors seem to affect the decision of household members other than the household

---

[12] Ozaki Iwao and Obi Keiichirō, "Kinrō Kakei ni Okeru Yūgyōritsu no Kenkyū" [Research on the Employment Participation Rate of Employee Households], *Keizai Bunseki* (no. 6: 1961).

head to work. One is the income of the household head. An increase in primary income tends to lower the work force participation rate, when job opportunities are given. The second is the number and attractiveness of job openings, particularly as reflected in wage rates and hours of work. Accordingly, we can also postulate that, other things being equal, the participation rate for households in the same income bracket will increase as employment opportunities expand. The first effect means that, given the number and attractiveness of job openings, the larger the size of the household head's income is, the lower the household participation rate is. These two effects are, as discussed above, quite consistent with the findings of Douglas, Long, and Arisawa and accordingly are referred to below as the first and second DLA effects.[13] The first effect suggests a curve dropping as it moves from left to right, with the participation rate being shown on the vertical axis and the income of the household head being shown on the horizontal axis. Once this curve is given or defined according to the first DLA effect that has been observed in cross-sectional data at some fixed point in time, we can conceive of the curve moving up or down over time according to fluctuations in economic activity and thereby in employment opportunities. The second effect allows us to explain the long-term rise in labor force participation rates for women in a manner consistent with the first DLA effect.

These two effects tell us much about the labor supply phenomenon in terms of numbers of persons, and provide us with a base upon which to build a more comprehensive theory about the supply of labor. An awareness of how the two effects interact also underlines our need to reexamine the schematic approach of the neoclassical theorists who focused on the hours of work done by an abstracted individual known as "economic man" but failed to link this with the number of persons supplied to the labor market. However, there is still no synthetic theory which fully integrates these two elements, optimal hours of individual work and number of persons supplied, as closely inter-dependent variables. Clearly stated, we need a theory which will allow us to derive both of the DLA effects from the traditional framework of utility maximization and an analysis of indifference curves for income and leisure, which has not advanced much since Jevons's work many years ago.

---

[13] The compound reference to the "Douglas-Long-Arisawa Effect" was first made by Tsujimura Kōtarō in *Keiki Hendō to Shūgyō Kōzō* [Business Cycles and the Structure of the Labor Force], No. 2 in the monograph series of the Economic Research Institute of the Economic Planning Agency (Tokyo: Ōkura Shō Insatsu Kyoku, 1960).

3. Toward a Synthetic Theory of Labor Supply

A. Some Theoretical Issues

The preceding discussion leads us to focus on two issues central to labor supply theory. First, how are the optimal hours of work related to a given wage rate? Second, how is the decision made to accept or refuse a given employment opportunity?

The first point concerns the mechanism which relates the *optimal hours of work potentially supplied by an individual at a given wage rate* to the total number of hours *actually* worked. The explanation given by earlier theorists for the total number of hours actually worked assumed that the individual could regulate the number of hours he worked. In the case of the entrepreneurs who tend to predominate in the traditional sectors of the economy (where the agricultural household is the basic economic unit), the individual's hours of work may be set in this fashion. However, a fundamental change accompanies industrialization. In the "modern" sectors of the economy, the labor market organized primarily around entrepreneurs is gradually replaced by one in which most laborers are hired as employees. As a result, the offer of employment to the potential employee comes to involve not just a wage rate to which the employee can freely respond, but a wage rate which is tied to a fixed number of hours to be worked.

The offer of employment with the requirement that a fixed number of hours be worked at specified times is no doubt closely related to the demands of modern industrial technology. The important point, however, is that the behavior of the person entering the labor market is not based on a calculation which views the number of hours as a variable that can be adjusted to meet income needs once the hourly wage rate is known. Rather, one responds to a package deal: so many hours at so much per hour. Having accepted employment on such terms, the employee is no longer free to decide his own working hours. Of course, he still often has some minimal leeway as he can reduce or increase the number of hours by being late to work, leaving early, being absent altogether, or working overtime. However, a complex array of social, psychological, and institutional factors usually produces a situation where excessive tardiness or absenteeism will result in dismissal. At the same time, there are clearly limits to the amount of overtime which is either physically or institutionally possible. Accordingly, we can say that the decision to enter the labor market depends on one's willingness to accept a given wage rate and a given number of hours as a package deal. The room for personal discretion is minimal.

Continuing along this line, we can construct a schema comparing acceptances and refusals of given employment opportunities as responses to given combinations of wage rates and working hours. Moreover, if we hold the number of hours assigned by firms constant, we can see the effect of changes in the wage rate on the number of prospective employees who accept employment. Finally, we can see how the assigned hours of work cause the wage-employment curve to shift.

We are now ready to consider the circumstances under which one might refuse or accept a given offer of employment. The choice will be between two combinations of income and leisure. Rejection of the employment offer means that the household has less income and that the drop in income must be weighed against the utility associated with an increase in leisure and the way in which it will be used to alter domestic arrangements which will in turn affect the total income which other members of the household can earn. The member of an entrepreneurial household has several options: (1) to accept outside employment with a fixed income and a fixed number of hours or (2) to stay at home and either (a) be satisfied with the income earned by other members of his household or (b) work in the family business the number of hours which will maximize the member's utility in terms of the trade-off expressed by indifference curve analysis. In the employee's household, the decison of other household members to work is simple: take the entire employment package with a fixed wage rate and a given set of hours, or be content with no work and the monetary income of the household head. Which alternative is chosen will in turn depend upon three factors: first, the attractiveness of the employment opportunity (the wage-and-hour package deal); second, the total amount of household income should the offer be turned down; and third, the shape of the indifference map of the household for income and leisure. In the absence of that additional, secondary source of income, the household's income can best be thought of as being the employment income of the household head in the household of an employee and the entrepreneurial income (which, to repeat, is dependent on assets, technology, and product demand) of the entrepreneurial household.

In order to explain the supply of labor in terms of number of persons, it is important to consider more fully the third factor mentioned above. Providing us with an important pioneering work in this area, Ragner Frisch sought to quantify the preference of household members for work and income.[14] However, Frisch focused upon the way in which

[14] Ragner Frisch, *New Methods of Measuring Utility* (Tübingen: J. C. B. Mohr, 1932).

changes in the wage rate would affect the individual's choice of optimal work hours. He did not analyze the response to fixed combinations of wages and hours. But in order to understand more fully the decision to work, particularly in the case of secondary earners, it is necessary to generalize the neoclassical concept of labor supply.

B. The Overlooked Connection between Hours of Work and Participation Rate

There are two major reasons why, in the past, research on the number of persons in the work force and research on working hours were carried out separately. First was the failure to appreciate fully the fact that employment in industrial societies is a package deal involving a set combination of assigned hours of work and wage rates that cannot be altered very much. Second, the reasons why job offers are accepted or rejected were not well understood. This second shortcoming not only made it inevitable that research on these two dimensions would be carried out separately, but also retarded the application of quantitative methods to the empirical study of labor supply.

A number of comprehensive studies of working hours using regression analysis have been completed in recent years.[15] However, studies which approach the problem with the household as the major behavioral unit are few even in the United States. Well-known studies of this type include the regression analyses of Richard Rosett and Jacob Mincer. Their household budget survey contains a wealth of information on families at each primary income level as originally set out by Douglas, Long, and Arisawa, supplying more information than is usually available in aggregated time series data. Considering the husband's income as the independent variable and an index of the wife's hours of work as the dependent variable, Rosett uses regression analysis to formulate a labor supply function.[16] Because the family income and expenditure surveys of the Bureau of Labor Statistics in the United States do not make a clear distinction between the income of the primary earner and that of secondary earners, Rosett used the Survey of Consumer Finance and Saving conducted by the Survey Research Center at the University of Michigan to obtain a breakdown of household income by earner. However, this survey, like those in Japan, does not report the number of working hours. As a second-best

[15] One recent example of this kind of work is John D. Owen, *The Price of Leisure* (Rotterdam: Rotterdam University Press, 1969). The Japanese translation by Saitō Seiichirō appeared as *Rēja no Keizaigaku* (Tokyo: Nihon Keizai Shimbun Sha, 1971).
[16] Richard N. Rosett, *Working Wives: Studies in Household Economic Behavior*, Yale Studies in Economics No. 9 (New Haven: Yale University Press, 1958).

solution Rosett assumes that the volume of labor supplied by each wife is proportionate to her income measured as a percentage of her husband's income. However, to proceed in this fashion Rosett had to assume first that the ratio of the wife's hourly wage rate to the husband's was the same for all wives and second that the number of hours worked by all husbands was the same. Mincer uses the labor force participation rate to approximate the total number of hours worked throughout the wives' lifetimes in a specified set of households.[17] However, in order for the participation rate to be accepted as a good index of total hours, one has to assume that the working hours of wives are distributed randomly over their lifetimes, and this assumption is difficult to accept.

While the above examples all illustrate the difficulties of obtaining adequate data, they also underline the importance of using a well-designed analytical framework to attack the problem. The problems inherent in such assumptions can also be seen in using data on household expenditures during a period of official rationing (such as World War II or the immediate postwar years) as a basis for speculating about the rationale behind patterns of consumption of households when there is a free market. To study the relationships between the demand for goods and prices, data gathered under free-market conditions are most appropriate. Data on consumer behavior which have been gathered only during a period of wartime shortages and rationing cannot supply a basis for constructing theories to explain the link between (1) the various demand functions or indifference curves which exist in the minds of people and (2) the more limited, take-it-or-leave-it, cut-and-dried behavioral choices which people are actually allowed to make under a system of rationing or price controls. In the same fashion, it is therefore necessary for us (1) to develop a theoretical framework which is capable of explaining whether a household member accepts or rejects a job opportunity and (2) to explain the relationship between such a theory and the traditional neoclassical theory which describes choices of optimal hours of work. Although there is not room here to go into these problems in detail, a brief outline of such an approach is formulated in the following subsection.[18]

[17] Jacob Mincer, "Labor Force Participation of Married Women," in *Aspects of Labor Economics* (Princeton: The National Bureau of Economic Research and Princeton University Press, 1962).

[18] Obi Keiichirō, "Rinkai Kakushotoku Bunpu ni Yoru Kinrō Kakei no Rōdō Kyōkyū no Bunseki" [An Analysis of Labor Supply in Employee Households Based on the Distribution of Critical Incomes], *Mita Gakkai Zasshi* (vol. 62, no. 1: January 1969), pp. 17–45. Also see Obi Keiichirō, "Analysis of the Household's Supply of Labor in Terms of a Numerical Income-Leisure Preference Field," a mimeographed paper presented to the Third Far Eastern Meeting of the Econometric Society at Tokyo in 1968.

C. The Critical Level of Primary Income and Its Distribution

The foregoing discussion makes it clear that a theory of labor supply must explain two observed behavioral patterns without any contradiction. The first is the inverse relationship between the labor force participation rate of secondary earners in a given group of households and the household's primary income at a given point in time. The second is the change in the relationship between these two variables over time. In the paragraphs below, such a theory will be outlined briefly.

Let us begin by considering the simple case in which the two-member household is composed of two adult members: the husband, who is the primary source of income, and the wife. Let us further imagine that the wife is given the choice of working a certain number of fixed hours at a given wage rate. This situation is illustrated in Figure 1. Leisure time OT on the vertical axis shows the number of hours of leisure available to the household, which daily totals forty-eight less the number of hours the husband works. In the case of this type of household, changes in the household's leisure time (or hours worked) can be expressed by the changes in the amount of the wife's leisure time since the husband's hours of work are assumed to be fixed at the firm in which he is em-

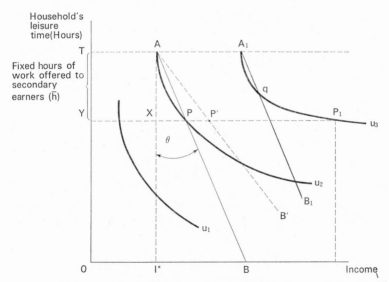

Figure 1: An Analysis of Wage Rates and Indifference Curves for Hours of Work, Leisure, and Income Preferences.

ployed. Curves u_1, u_2, and u_3 are indifference curves for different combinations of leisure and income. The amount of the wife's assigned hours of work is shown by $\bar{h}$ on the vertical axis. Therefore, in Figure 1, the time measured along the vertical axis represents the wife's leisure time. The hourly wage rate $(\bar{w})$ offered to the wife is defined by the slope of line AB (or similar parallel lines such as A_1B_1). Accordingly,

$$\bar{w} = \tan \theta = \frac{AI^*}{I^*B}.$$

The horizontal axis indicates the total amount of household income.

Let us further denote the hours of work assigned by the firm as h, which is shown by TY on the vertical axis. Now, the wife has to choose whether to accept the job opportunity, by which she can earn the amount wh, or to reject it. If we let the husband's income change, then it is easy to see that the wife will accept the job opportunity when the husband's income is in a lower range and reject when it is in a higher range. Between those two ranges there should be a level of husband's income at which the wife is indifferent between accepting and rejecting the offered job opportunity. This specific level of husband's income for this particular household is shown by I^* in Figure 1. In the case in which the actual level of husband's income (primary income) is I^*, the choice of the household between income and leisure is represented by position A in the diagram when the wife rejects the offer, and by position P on line AB when the wife accepts the offer. In the case of a household such as the one described in the diagram, the indifference curve passes through both point A and point P. This household, therefore, is indifferent between accepting and rejecting the job opportunity which is defined by a given wage rate $\bar{w}$ and assigned hours of work $\bar{h}$.

As we noted above, job opportunities present themselves largely as package deals where the number of hours of work are fixed. In Figure 1, the fixed hours of work $(\bar{h})$ are such that they intersect the wage-rate line (AB) and the leisure-income indifference curve (u_2) at point P. If the amount of income for $\bar{h}$ hours of labor exceeds the value of XP, the wife will choose to work; if it is less than the amount XP, she will stay home. Similarly, if we consider the wage rate $(\tan \theta)$ to be fixed, and consider a variation in the income of the household head, it is readily apparent that a lower income will shift a household back to an indifference curve with less utility and thereby make the offer of employment attractive; a larger income will mean that the indifference curve is such that the job offer will be refused. The amount of primary income such that the household is indifferent to the wife's accepting the job offer shall be referred to as "the critical level of primary income" *(rinkai kakushotoku)*.[19] For the household shown in the diagram (whose preference with respect to income and leisure is specified by the shape of indifference curves u_1, u_2, etc.), the actual level of primary income happens to be equal to this critical level of primary income. Now consider a household with an indifference curve different from that shown in Figure 1. For this household the indifference curve passing through point A in Figure 1 will intersect horizontal line YY' at a point p' other than point P. This means that the critical level of primary income of this household differs from that of the household shown in Figure 1.

Thus, the critical level of primary income varies among households according to the difference in the slope of their indifference curves. The critical level of income will vary according to the fluctuation in any or all of the three key variables: (1) a change in the hourly wage rate for the wife, (2) a change in the hours required for her to work, and (3) a change in the shape of the leisure-income indifference curve.

Given the above analytical framework, it would seem likely that the critical level of primary income varies from household to household. If it were the same for each household, a given job opportunity would result in a labor force participation rate for wives of either one (1.0) or zero (0). However, the empirical data clearly suggest that the wives' participation rate is between zero and one for households in the same primary income grouping. For this reason, it seems logical to conclude that the critical level of income varies even among households in the same primary-income groups.

A more detailed analysis of the probability distribution of households according to their critical levels of primary income seems to be needed. Figure 2 shows how we might calculate the wives' participation rate for any group of households in the same primary income class (j). As the area under the curve is set to equal one (1.0), the area S to the left of the vertical line drawn through the point representing actual amounts of primary income (I_j) will correspond to the group's rate of non-participation for secondary earners. The area to the right ($1-S$) will correspond to its labor force participation rate.

We can now go one step further with our example of two-member households confronted with the choice of accepting or rejecting an employment offer with a given wage rate and a set number of working hours. Given a fixed wage rate ($\bar{w}$) and a set number of hours ($\bar{h}$) for members in each income class (j), for each group of households with

---

[19] Refer to the articles listed in note 18.

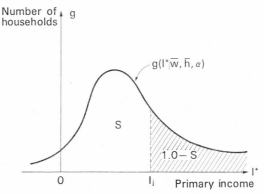

Figure 2: The Probability Distribution of Households in the Same Income Grouping by Critical Primary Income.

Note: The probability density function as indicated by the values of g shows the percentage distribution of households according to their critical levels of primary income. The distribution is affected by the values of w (the wage rate), h (the hours of work assigned by the firm), and α (the shape of the leisure-income indifference curves).

primary income I_j $(j=1, \ldots, n)$, there exists a distribution curve of critical level of primary income. If we assume that the shape of the distribution curve is common to all groups of households with primary income I_j $(j=1, \ldots, n)$, it will easily be seen from Figure 2 that the higher the primary income I_j, the lower the wives' participation rate. Thus, a curve can be drawn to show the wives' labor force participation rate for each group of households classified according to primary income (Figure 3). The curve itself expresses the first DLA effect: the inverse relationship between the primary income and the wives' labor force participation rate.

Suppose that a wife's wage rate rises as is shown by the line AB_1 in Figure 1. More wives will choose to be gainfully employed because the indifference curve passing through P_1 is located above the one shown by u_2 which passes through point A. This means that the critical level of primary income has increased along with the increase in the wife's wage rate. Hence, an increase will cause the curve in Figure 2 to shift to the right. Accordingly, wives' participation rates of households with common primary income I_j increases if their wage rate increases. In Figure 3, an increase in participation rate for each of the groups of households will result in an upward shift of the curve. This means that we can synthesize the first and second DLA effects. Working

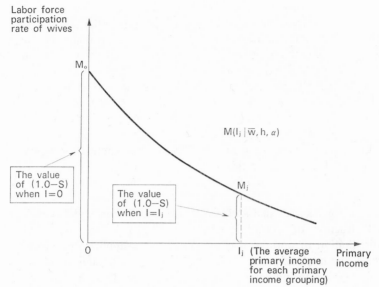

Figure 3: The Participation Rates for Wives in Households Classified by Primary Income.

back from Figure 3 to Figure 1, we can say that a change over time in the labor force participation rate of secondary earners (meaning wives in our example of two-member households) implies a change in the distribution of critical level of primary income. Given (i) the wage rate for wives ($\bar{w}$) and (ii) the hours of work required ($\bar{h}$), both of which are set by employers, a clear mathematical relationship exists between the curves in Figures 1, 2, and 3. Accordingly, we can use the data on the labor force participation rate of wives and primary income to derive numerical values for parameters defining the preference function for given wage rates and hours. The usefulness of Figure 2 (showing the household distribution of critical incomes) as an analytical tool is not limited to two-member households. Although there is insufficient space here to elaborate on this model, the basic analytical framework can be used to handle households of any size.[20]

Given this framework, a wife either accepts or rejects the entire employment package,. This means that her hours of work will either be the fixed number given in the offer of employment or zero. In

[20] Obi Keiichirō, "Rōdō Jikan to Yūgyōritsu no Kankei" [Working Hours and the Labor Force Participation Rate], *Nihon Rōdō Kyōkai Zasshi* (vol. 10, no. 9: September 1968), pp. 13–21.

other words, we are left with a discontinuity which prevents us from adopting the conventional techniques of differentiation to estimate the preference function. However, we are able to evaluate the integral of the probability function for the critical level of primary income (Figure 2) in order to derive the curve of the wives' participation rate (Figure 3). The parameters which delineate the preference functions can only be estimated with the observed wage rates and the observed number of standard hours of work. Assigning some appropriate value to the parameters, we can compute the definite integral (estimated rate of participation) which approximates the cumulative probability curve in Figure 3. For this reason, we must simulate the structural parameters in our search for approximate values by using a set of initial values.

Having derived an indifference curve for income and leisure, the construction of a traditional labor supply function gives us the distribution of optimal working hours to be supplied with given wage rates and levels of primary income. Using our estimates of the amount of variation in indifference curves (u in Figure 1) among households, in addition to our estimates of the distribution of critical level of incomes, we can also determine the distribution of the minimum wage rates at which labor will be supplied. That value will be the lowest business firms can offer and still obtain the services of secondary earners for a given number of hours from households at a set level of primary income. If in Figure 1 we arbitrarily set the income of the primary earner at A_1 and offer a workday of $\bar{h}$ hours, the minimum supply price of labor will be given by the slope A_1P_1. Because the indifference curve for income and leisure will vary, the minimum supply price for each household will differ and result in a distribution like that found in Figure 2.[21] Unfortunately, there is insufficient space here to discuss the determination of parameters for the income-leisure preference function in more detail. Putting such technical considerations aside for the time being, I wish to introduce briefly the results of our analysis of the Japanese data using the analytical framework developed here, and then discuss their significance.

4. Some Tentative Results and Their Significance

The analysis for the years 1955–1958 was based upon the special

[21] The minimum supply price of family members in entrepreneurial households can be obtained from the scheme for estimating the general supply of labor described in the article by Tsujimura, Sasaki, and Nakamura cited in note 11.

tabulations of the Family Income and Expenditure Survey for households with three adult members. For the years 1961–1964, the same data were used for households having a husband and wife and an unspecified number of children. In constructing the indifference curve for income and leisure, both Bernouille-Laplace and quadratic functions were used. Unfortunately, our data are limited in many ways, and we are able to draw only tentative conclusions about the two types of households described above. In the future it will be necessary to use a more extensive data base in order to further enlarge the universe for which we can make generalizations.

A. Ambiguities in the Function for the Aggregate Supply of Labor

The labor supply behavior of household members other than the primary earner will depend not only on the wage rate offered to secondary earners but also on the wage rate paid to the household heads, who are mainly adult males. In other words, the influence on the total supply of labor exerted by a change in the wage rate offered to each individual in society will depend upon the way in which those individuals are organized into households. Hence, we can define precisely the individual's optimal hours of supply of labor if and only if we know the way in which the wages offered to each individual will be distributed within each household. However, even when the situation has been defined in this way, it is still impossible at the present time to predict how a given change in average wage rates will affected the aggregate supply of labor. For example, if there is an across-the-board rise in all wage rates, it is difficult to know whether secondary earners will be more sensitive to the fact that the income of the primary earner has risen (thereby lowering the labor force participation rate of secondary earners) or to the fact that the wage rate for secondary earners has also risen (thereby boosting the participation rate). The shift in the aggregate supply curve of labor will depend upon the relative sensitivity of secondary earners to these two types of change.

If we think only in terms of average wages and the total supply of labor, it is impossible to construct a stable labor supply curve. Accordingly, it is also impossible to define precisely the level of unemployment that will result from a surplus of supply over demand. Accordingly, a consistent theory of labor supply will be formulated not in terms of the behavior of individuals but rather in terms of the behavior of households (or even groups of households). Such a theory requires that we clearly distinguish between the behavior of household heads and the behavior of other household members who depend on the income of the household head.

B.   Some Empirical Results of an Investigation into the Household Labor Supply Function and the Preference Function for Leisure and Income

(1) *The labor force participation of secondary earners.* The preceding sections presented an analytical framework which can be used to analyze quantitative data in order to explain the mechanism that determines how secondary earners will respond to a given employment opportunity. It is through this mechanism that the DLA effects work themselves out in terms of the principle of utility maximization as understood within the framework of the indifference curve for hours of leisure and income. The supply function in terms of *human numbers* (as distinct from hours worked) which emerges from this kind of analysis of indifference curves is characterized by the following three propositions: First, an increase in the income of the primary earner will result in a lower labor force participation rate among other household members (assuming that the offer to them of a given wage rate and fixed hours does not change). Second, a rise in the wage rate offered to secondary earners will, other things being equal, result in a higher labor force participation rate. Finally, a shortening of the workday offered in the employment package will, other things being equal, result in a higher participation rate.

(2) *Hours of labor supplied by secondary earners.* The supply function in terms of the total number of hours of labor supplied by secondary earners may be characterized in the following manner: First, if the hourly wage rate offered to secondary earners does not change, an increase in the income of the primary earner means a drop in the optimal number of hours of labor supplied (equal to the number of hours resulting in maximum utility). Second, a rise in the wage rates offered to secondary earners will, other things being equal and in the vicinity of the rates actually observed, result in an increase in the optimal number of hours of labor supplied.

(3) *The labor force participation rate for women.* The above results for sections (1) and (2) were obtained with both Bernouille-Laplace and quadratic preference functions for income and leisure. The general conclusions stated above in paragraph (1) suggest that the general rise in the participation rate of women over time can best be explained in terms of the improved conditions offered with employment for second-

ary earners. The conclusions in paragraph (2) suggest that the opportunity to work shorter hours has more than offset the effect of higher incomes for the household head in attracting secondary earners to the work force. The countervailing forces also determine the total number of hours worked by women. To the extent that the wage rate offered to women remains constant, it would seem likely that the long-term rise in the incomes of household heads has served to reduce the optimal number of hours worked by women. On the other hand, to the extent that primary income remains the same, a rise in the wage rate offered to women will result in an increase in the optimal number of hours worked by women. In explaining a drop in the number of hours worked by women, it would seem that the rise in the income of the household head has had more effect than the rise in the wage rate offered to women.

(4) *The significance of understanding the labor supply mechanism for secondary earners.* The above analysis suggests that the labor supply mechanism will introduce into the economic system a disequilibrating element which will work to limit the ability of the system to automatically restore equilibrium once an imbalance is introduced. Here two types of disequilibrium are envisaged.

Suppose that for some reason there is a drop in the wages of adult males. This drop in primary income will result in an increase in the labor force participation rate of other household members. If the demand for the labor of these other members remains fixed (or, more likely, falls), it is inevitable that the hourly wage rate will fall. Even if the demand of firms for labor as measured in hours of labor remains fixed, it is possible that the drop in primary income will result in an increase in the standard workweek (according to the first proposition in (2) above), with the end result being a drop in the demand for labor in terms of the number of secondary earners. If this process results in a drop in the income of the household head because of a drop in demand for consumer goods (owing in a circular fashion to the drop in household income), the supply of labor from the household will increase. As long as the income of the household head is falling, the secondary earner's minimum supply price of labor cannot be maintained.

In an opposite example, assume that economic growth results in a continuous rise in the income of primary earners. The demand for secondary earners will remain constant or increase, and their wage rate will also increase. The rate at which wages for secondary earners rise depends on the rate of increase in wages for primary earners. However, it is very possible that a rise in primary income will result in a change in the indifference curve showing the relative preference for leisure and income, and thereby promote the willingness of the household to supply labor despite higher levels of income.[22] However, before we can make predictions about the likelihood of either scenario actually occurring, further research will be necessary. Given the possibility that the labor supply mechanism contains this latent ability to undermine the stability of the economy and cause a downward spiral in wages and income, it would be wise to consider the need for institutional brakes should such a contingency arise.

[22] A very important factor affecting the equilibrating mechanism in the system is the function describing the preference of households for various combinations of leisure and income. The marginal utility of income will have a marked effect on how changes in wage levels will affect the aggregate supply of labor. It is possible that an increase in either primary or secondary income will be accompanied by a rise in the marginal utility of income—the importance which the household attaches to income. As a result, the amount of labor supplied by the household might well increase. The increase in the income of the household will serve to lower the labor force participation rate of other household members only if there is no change in other factors. However, in real life the change in income likely affects the marginal utility of income and thereby the decision to work. It is thus entirely possible that the latter effect more than cancels out the former so that an increase in primary income results in an increase in the labor force participation rate. If this is the case, there is through the labor supply mechanism an accelerator effect which serves to exaggerate disequilibrating tendencies. Using a semi-logarithmic function to examine the preference for leisure and income in the 1955–1958 data and a quadratic function for the years 1961–1964, we found that such behavior does in fact exist.

The Effect of Reductions in Working Hours on Productivity

Tsujimura Kōtarō

1. The Economic Significance of Shorter Working Hours

During the 1960s Japan increasingly attracted attention as an economic power. The nation's GNP and foreign exchange reserves were no doubt one source of such attention. Even after the upward revaluation of the yen in the early 1970s, the economy has remained internationally competitive. Nevertheless, the length of Japan's average workweek suggests that Japan is not as competitive as many would like to think.

Although international comparisons are complicated by various dissimilarities in the data from different countries, data rearranged for comparative purposes by the Ministry of Labour clearly indicate that hours of work in Japan are rather long by international standards, in spite of the fact that the workweek in Japan has been considerably reduced over the past decade. The average workweek of 48.1 hours in 1960 was shortened to 43.1 hours by 1970. However, the American workweek in 1970 was 37.5 hours; in West Germany it was 39.1 hours. Although a difference of several hours per week may not seem like much, the weekly difference of 5.6 hours between Japan and the United States means an annual difference of 291 hours per worker. The annual difference between Japan and West Germany is 208 hours. This means that annually the Japanese are working four to six weeks more than their counterparts overseas. A difference of more than one month per year is not insignificant.

This paper originally appeared as "Rōdō Jikan Tanshuku wa Seisan o Bōgai Suru ka," *Keizai Hyōron* (vol. 21, no. 12: November 1972), pp. 56–67. The author is Professor of Economics at Keio University.

The disparity lies not so much in the longer workweek itself as in the practice of having shorter annual paid vacations and the lower propensity of employees actually to use the full time allotted for vacation leave. Shorter paid vacations came about when the general gist of the International Labor Organization's Convention Fifty-Two, ratified by the ILO in 1936, was written into Japan's Labor Standards Law of 1947; the Convention gave minimum acceptable standards for annual vacations, and private firms have used the law as a guideline in drawing up their own policies. However, the original standards which were intended as a legal minimum were soon institutionalized in most Japanese enterprises as the accepted guidelines. In contrast to Japan's rigid adherence to the 1936 convention, most of the countries in Western Europe improved their conditions so as to satisfy the new standards laid down in Convention One Hundred Thirty-Two, which was approved by the ILO in 1970. Whereas the old convention calls for six days of annual paid vacation for employees who have worked more than one full year at the same establishment, the new convention stipulates that workers be eligible for a minimum of three weeks' vacation after six months of continuous employment. While the U.S. and the countries of Western Europe have matured considerably in their thinking and practices concerning vacation leave, Japan has remained stationary, still relying on concepts which were first introduced some thirty years ago.

In recent years considerable attention has been given to the situation, and the facts mentioned above are generally well understood. In its interim report, *Nanajū Nendai no Tsūshō Sangyō Seisaku* (Industrial and Trade Policy in the 1970s), which was issued in May 1971, the Council on Industrial Structure (Sangyō Kōzō Shingikai) emphasized the importance of shorter working hours and stated that considerable effort would be required to achieve parity with the United States. In contrast to the 5 percent reduction in working hours which occurred during the 1960s, the Committee estimated that a 12 percent reduction would be necessary in the 1970s. To achieve these goals, it called on all firms to use the five-day workweek and to considerably extend annual vacation leave.

In January 1972 the Research Group on the Labor Standards Law (Rōdō Kijun Hō Kenkyūkai) issued a report recommending the following goals: (1) thorough reorganization of working hours, (2) introduction of the two-day weekend, (3) revision of the system of annual paid vacation leave, (4) improved use of time off, (5) greater consensus between labor and management on these issues, and (6) the development of effective measures to help small and medium-sized enterprises cope with the various problems they encounter in improving working hours. The Group further recommended that the forty-eight hour week (which is provided for by the present Labor Standards Law) be reconsidered. Many of the proposals were later reflected in the policies and administrative directives of the Tanaka Cabinet which took office in July 1972.

The interest in shorter working hours which has suddenly appeared in Japan in the early 1970s is the outgrowth of two different processes. One involves the general orientation of the economy as many Japanese have come to question the policies of high economic growth. Emphasis has shifted to the more broadly conceived welfare needs of the people and their "quality of life." The second involves changes in the realities of international competition and the pressures coming to bear on Japan as a result of excessive foreign exchange holdings.

The number of hours spent working is closely linked to working conditions in general. The work environment is in turn intricately related to the standard of living. However, although the connection between life styles and hours of work seems to be quite obvious on a theoretical level, the actual interaction between the two is extremely complex. In terms of economic theory we are talking about the preference for and marginal utility of additional increments in income as opposed to leisure. It is commonly posited as basic knowledge that with a given hourly wage rate each individual will choose the most appropriate division of time into work and leisure. Accordingly, it is not simply a matter of shorter hours of work; other things being equal, nearly everyone would enjoy shorter hours. Rather, it is a complicated process of judging the trade-off between hours of work and income, and then making a choice. The recently expressed popular sentiment that hours of work are too long comes only after a decade of hard work and a remarkable rise in the overall standard of living. Had such growth never occurred, the question of long workweeks likely would never have been raised. It is in terms of the imbalance between income levels and leisure that people have come to query the length of the workweek. Although per-capita income in Japan is still below that in the U.S. or West Germany, it would still seem that working hours are, by international standards, unreasonably long in Japan.

Considering the problem of working hours from this perspective, the recent trends in Japan would seem to be part of a quite natural process which is working to restore an equilibrium between hours of work and levels of income. There is today no real problem with the idea that such a restoration should occur, and few would argue that a reduction in working hours is undesirable. One remaining task in this regard, however, is the derivation of the preference function for various combinations of working hours and income levels. In other words, given a level of income, at what rate should hours of work be reduced?

2.   International Competitiveness and Working Hours

Although we have mentioned the natural desire of people to maintain a balance between their level of income or material standard of living and the amount of leisure they enjoy, and the fact that most people would enjoy having more leisure if other things remained equal, there is a small minority which is opposed to any reduction in working hours. In particular, many managers remain opposed to cutbacks in hours of work. Although their position has not been publicized, it is not necessarily a surprise when viewed in terms of the long history of labor-management relations in Japan. Unions have in the past occasionally made an issue out of working hours, but only as a kind of appended demand; their basic demands have consistently concerned wage rates. It is thus reasonable to expect that some managers will continue to view demands for a shorter workweek as an unacceptable and trivial demand by labor unions. Moreover, when demanding shorter hours of work the union leadership has often failed to make clear the relative preferences of their members for income and leisure; indeed many leaders have used the demand for shorter working hours as a strategic measure to aid in the achievement of more important wage demands.

In the United States the movement toward a shorter workweek was initiated by the depression in the 1930s. With 14 million unemployed, the shorter workweek spread employment. A reduction in the work load from ten to nine hours a day meant an 11 percent increase in the work force. The reduction of working hours meant that the burden of unemployment was shared throughout society. Americans were thus able to move toward a shorter workweek with a different kind of choice between income and leisure. For many, the increase in unwanted leisure meant a commensurate loss of income, but some leisure and some income was no doubt better than the possible outcome of all leisure and no income. Although the choice on a societal level was between the lesser of two evils, it was nevertheless not one made freely but one which was imposed by the exigencies of the situation. The pressure for shorter working hours generated by the fear of massive unemployment is quite different from that which arises from a feeling that more free time is necessary to obtain further utility from the material level of affluence already achieved.[1]

Although the American experience is often cited, the unique situation of the world economy in the 1930s and certain peculiarities of the American case make it difficult to generalize in a way which is altogether useful for understanding Japan's problem today. It is important that a number of the assumptions built into the American experience be explicitly discussed before further considering whether or not there are lessons for Japan. The first assumption is that hourly labor productivity remains the same. This means that the hourly productivity of newly employed persons must at least equal that of those whose hours have been shortened. The second assumption is that productivity per unit of labor cost remains the same. In other words, the amount of wages paid to each individual must be tied to the amount of labor he or she supplies. The third assumption, which is related to the first, is that a reserve of unemployed persons exists. Such a reserve may consist of either formally unemployed workers or otherwise under-utilized labor. Some of the problems experienced in Japan arise because these conditions cannot be assumed for the Japanese economy.

Looking initially at the last assumption, what happens when the employable population is already gainfully employed, as in Japan? The general application of Keynesian economics in the postwar years has resulted in continuous economic expansion for all countries. Widespread economic contraction and massive unemployment on the scale of the 1930s have not characterized the postwar capitalist economies. As part of this general milieu, the Japanese economy has moved from a state of full employment to one in which a keenly felt labor shortage exists. Consequently, a reduction in working hours in Japan means a cutback in the total supply of labor. If the hourly productivity of labor is maintained, the drop in overall productivity will be proportional to the reduction in the hours of work. As a measure to counter unemployment, the reduction of working hours might be interpreted as an attempt to limit the ability of persons already employed to supply labor. Perhaps it is the commitment of the unions to full employment and the fear that a small cutback in hours of work is the first step to large-scale retrenchment which accounts for the fact that, despite the existence of full employment, labor unions have continued to take a rather ambivalent stance on shorter hours of work.

---

[1] In fact, as the U.S. economy recovered from the depression, many American workers used their additional increments in leisure to engage in side jobs, a phenomenon known as "moonlighting".

On the same point, many managers have also found it difficult to go along with the move toward shorter hours of work. They argue that shorter hours and the concomitant reduction in the supply of labor make impossible the maintenence of competitive levels of production for either the domestic or the international market. Coupled with the unions' concern for maintaining levels of employment, management's fear of losing the competitive edge has been a major deterrent to progress.

In contrast to these types of concerns, particularly the traditional emphasis of the unions on full employment and higher wages, the most important consideration for many is the connection of leisure to further improvements in the material standard of living. Here it is necessary to distinguish clearly between the demands of the union leadership and those of the individual employee. Those arguing for more leisure are not unaware of the need to be internationally competitive, but they tend to appraise the problem differently. They point to the fact that Japan is criticized for continuing to build up foreign exchange reserves partly through long hours of work while other governments seek to better their citizens' standards of living by shortening hours of work and promoting the effective use of leisure. Japan's long hours of work are often cited as one kind of social dumping. Even if per-hour productivity is the same, Japan's extra month or six weeks of work per year gives it that much more productivity in terms of the individual worker. More important, however, is the increase in productivity per unit of capital and the overall ability to enter and take advantage of world markets. One major source of this competitiveness is, as mentioned above, the shorter annual vacation leave given to Japanese employees.

When improved technology results in a superior international competitive position by raising the hourly productivity of each worker, there seems to be no problem with world opinion. However, when the Japanese derive their competitive edge by continuing to work while everyone else is taking a vacation, the international repercussions are considerable. Views frequently expressed in certain circles of contemporary Japanese society reflect the impact of this world opinion. Somehow it is no longer a virtue to be diligent and hard-working. Somehow it is wrong to improve one's competitive position in the world economy simply by working hard. Those who argue otherwise have likely forgotten the fallacy of composition: that which is universally accepted as being good for the individual is not necessarily good for society as a whole.

In *The Protestant Ethic and the Spirit of Capitalism*, Max Weber describes how Methodists in the eighteenth century were ostracized and oppressed because they were overly imbued with the desire to work hard. The same thing can be said for the movement in California to exclude Japanese migrants in the early twentieth century. The Japanese were disliked not because they were dishonest or dirty, but rather because they worked excessively and ignored the custom of resting on the Sabbath. Their behavior violated the norms of society. Profits earned at the expense of those who observe such norms or customs invite the appellation of "miser" and even outright anger when the others feel that their standard of living is threatened.

The world today is being brought together as never before by improved communications. Thus, in a very real sense an international society has been formed which, though still in its embryonic stages, has formulated generally accepted standards of behavior. Regardless of the fact that many of these standards may be defined in terms of Western cultural norms, it is important that these norms be observed as much as possible if Japan is to participate profitably in the world community. Other countries will criticize Japan if their unemployment rates increase as a result of Japanese imports which are competitive because Japan does not abide by international norms with regard to working hours, wage rates, and environmental protection. To prevent an international backlash, Japan has revalued the yen upwards. Nevertheless, the extent to which Japan can import cheaper foreign goods is limited even if all trade restrictions are lifted. This is partially because a large portion of household expenditures in Japan is taken up by the high cost of housing and services. Accordingly, the upward valuation of the yen does not easily yield the expected results in terms of the real standard of living.

Driven by the fear of restrictive trade legislation abroad against Japanese imports, Japan moved quickly to revalue the yen in the early 1970s. However, despite the cutback in export trade, domestic prices have not dropped, and much hard work has gone unrewarded. At present, foreign countries are not pointing accusing fingers directly at Japan's long working hours. Nevertheless, the message is clear: if the present situation continues much longer there will be a swelling tide of protest sooner or later. Even the diehard proponents of GNP growthmanship have come to accept the fact that Japan's hours of work are too long.

3.   Some Economic Issues Raised by the Move to Shorten Working Hours

The decision to shorten hours of work must be agreed to by all firms in the economy. In this regard it is similar to the decision to attack environmental pollution: such problems will never be settled if left to the initiative of individual firms. At present the economy is so organized as to prevent individual firms from bearing extra costs because of the tremendous competition. However, as in the case of the installation of pollution prevention equipment, a minimum amount of consensus can result in the creation of a social norm which demands the kind of conformity described above. Only when firms are convinced that others are bearing the same kinds of costs are they willing to cut back on hours of work. By requiring that all firms follow the same guidelines, such norms actually work to preserve competition. Given the principle of free competition associated with the capitalist system of production, firms which cannot compete within the normative framework laid down by society are regarded as unfit to survive. To successfully promote competition rather than hinder it, such norms must be based on a certain amount of consensus. Moreover, the rules of competition must be fairly enforced, with few loopholes and little room for wavering in the application of such principles.

With the need for a national policy on working hours clearly understood, we can now move on to consider two rather technical problems involving economic theory. One is the development of criteria for judging the relative preference of individual households for increased leisure and larger incomes. The solution clearly does not lie simply in introducing the American workweek. The per-capita income of the Japanese is still slightly less than half that of Americans and about two-thirds that of West Germans. It is thus quite reasonable that Japanese work longer hours to maintain or even improve their relatively low levels of income, although the extra month or six weeks of work done to narrow the income gap is perhaps too much. The questions are how to equalize hours of work and at what pace such equalization ought to occur. If we move too quickly there will soon be an imbalance in the opposite direction. Too much free time without the material standard of living to enjoy such time simply means lying around doing nothing. In deciding upon the optimal workweek, economic theory on indifference curves and preferences for income and leisure is instructive. It first suggests that we must take a closer look at theories which attempt to account for the labor supply behavior of households.

The second technical problem involves the rise in productivity which is necessary if working hours are to be successfully shortened. Given the labor shortage in Japan today, any cut in hours of work without a change in productivity will result in a proportional drop in output. The end result would be a drop in the level of GNP and a similar dip in the real wages of all employees. Since this is undesirable for all households concerned, the relationship of shorter working hours to productivity must be examined more closely.

The monthly average for the number of total hours worked per employee decreased 8.2 percent during the 1960s (from 207 hours in 1960 to 190 hours in 1969). The standard work load decreased 6.6 percent from 182 to 170 hours per month, while overtime dropped 20 percent from 25 to 20. Although there is considerable variation from industry to industry and the relationship between changes in productivity and hours of work is not so clear, Figure 1 indicates that past reductions in the hours of work have been accompanied by more than proportional increases in productivity. Even in the timber industry,

Increase in productivity $= \dfrac{\text{(1970 levels)}}{\text{(1960 levels)}}$	Industry	Percentage reduction in hours $= 100 - \left(\dfrac{\text{Hours of work in 1970}}{\text{Hours of work in 1960}}\right) \times 100$
3.9	Steel	9.0
2.9	Non-ferrous metals	6.7
3.7	Machinery	11.2
2.5	Pottery and earthenware	8.0
3.9	Chemicals	5.0
2.0	Rubber	10.9
2.0	Tanned leather	10.3
2.7	Pulp and paper	10.0
2.3	Textiles	7.7
1.3	Lumber	8.3

Figure 1: Reductions in Hours of Work and Productivity Improvements by Industry, 1960–1970.

Source: The relevant issues of Rōdō Shō, (Ministry of Labour), *Maigetsu Kinrō Tōkei Chōsa* [Monthly Labor Survey] and Nihon Seisansei Honbu (Japan Productivity Center), *Kikan Seisansei Tōkei* [Quarterly Statistics on Productivity].

which registered only a 30 percent improvement in productivity, the rise in productivity was more than three times the reduction of 8.3 percent in hours worked. In the machinery industry, however, the 11.2 percent reduction in hours of work was offset by a 270 percent improvement in productivity.

Although these two variables have moved in a more or less parallel fashion over time, the cause-and-effect relationship is not clear, for a great many variables are involved. Nevertheless, higher labor productivity seems to be fundamentally tied to increased capital outlays. This was particularly true for Japan during the 1960s: the capital stock of private firms increased from 8.29 trillion yen in 1960 to 28.50 trillion yen in 1969, an increase of 243 percent. During the same period the work force increased only 50 percent. The value of capital stock per worker increased about 130 percent. The tremendous increase in the amount of capital equipment per worker was certainly responsible for much of the improvement in productivity.

Our major task is the careful examination of how shorter hours of work and improved capital-labor ratios interact to produce higher labor productivity. For example, given a fixed ratio of capital to labor, how do reductions in the number of working hours affect labor productivity?

To protect the gains in productivity rendered by further investments in capital, reductions in working hours must be offset by commensurate improvements in the productivity of labor itself. If reductions occur without such improvements in labor productivity, the costs of reducing hours of work are, in the first instance, thrown onto management. The resultant rise in costs for management, however, means a decline in its ability to pay and hence a decline in the rate of wage increases. Although it seems likely that the effect of a reduction in the hours of work on productivity would be negligible, meaningful discussion requires that we isolate the effects on productivity of changes in the capital stock and changes in hours of work.

To be sure, capital stock and hours of work are not the only factors affecting productivity. Although the capital stock increases as a long-term trend, there are also short-term considerations such as the capital utilization rate, which varies with the business cycle. It has been shown in every country that physical per-hour productivity falls in periods of recession and rises in periods of economic expansion. Accordingly, even if the total amount of capital continuously expands over time, a short-term drop in the utilization rate may mean a deterioration in labor productivity.

Consideration of how both the long- and short-term trends interact requires a distinction between standard or regular hours of work and overtime. The movement in total hours of work may well be different from that in regular hours. Past experience suggests that regular hours of work are determined by long-run factors such as the accumulation of capital, whereas overtime tends to fluctuate considerably as the economy alternately speeds up and slows down in response to short-term factors. These general facts are borne out by the data in Figure 2.

The total number of hours increased between 1955 and 1960, and then declined, whereas the decline in regular hours has been steady. More-over, the downward movement in the total number of hours worked was interrupted between 1964 and 1968. Changes in regular hours reflect long-term trends, whereas movements in total hours (including overtime) reflect the presence of short-term fluctuations in the business cycle. It would seem that short-term changes in overtime cannot exert a lasting effect on the long-term trend in total hours of work, but can

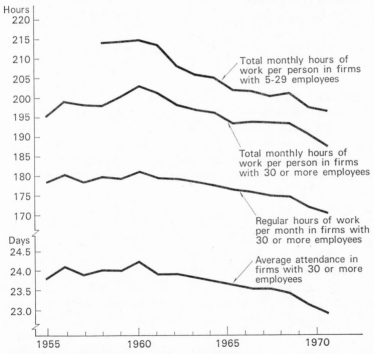

Figure 2: Average Monthly Hours Worked and Work Attendance for All Industries.

Source: Rōdō Shō (Ministry of Labor), *Maigetsu Kinrō Tōkei Chōsa* [Monthly Labor Survey].

account for temporary reverses in the long-term trend. The result may therefore be a kind of ratchet effect.

In considering the data for Japan, it is important to remember that the cutback in regular working hours began in the early 1960s, just as Japan was shifting from a labor surplus to a labor shortage. According to the statistics of the Public Employment Security Office, the ratio of demand to supply for middle school graduates rose from 1.2 in 1959 to 2.7 by 1963. The ratio for high school graduates rose from 1.1 in 1959 to 2.7 by 1962. This was the first time that firms began to feel the labor shortage.

The move toward shorter working hours in the early 1960s cannot be explained by the simple unemployment model introduced above. Given the increasingly acute labor shortage, the cutback in man-hours seems to be a paradox. Unlike today, there was no public campaign in the 1960s to shorten working hours. Rather, there occurred a kind of spontaneous agreement among labor and management that hours could be shortened. As the labor market began to tighten, the competition among firms to secure labor intensified. One aspect of this competition was the effort by many firms to provide more attractive working conditions. Consequently, wages, which had risen at an average annual rate of 6.1 percent during the pentad prior to 1960, suddenly attained an average annual rate of increase equal to 10.3 percent in the first five years of the 1960s. The change is even more remarkable if we consider the improvement in wage rates for new graduates. Wages rose 1.9 percent for male high school graduates in 1959, jumped 10.6 percent in 1960, and then 21.5 percent in 1961. For female middle school graduates, the comparable figures are 5.7, 18.6, and 21.0 percent.

In addition to improved wage rates, companies also sought to compete by offering favorable hours of work. This is a particularly important consideration in Japan since nearly all permanent employees, blue collar or white collar, are on a salary system. Given the need for a balance between leisure and the material standard of living, it is perhaps only natural that shorter hours of work would be introduced in order to make the higher pay all that more enticing to the prospective employee. The introduction of shorter working hours was aimed not only at attracting new graduates but also at keeping presently employed personnel with the firm for as long as possible. Since many firms were unable to increase the cash income of older workers at the rate they were increasing starting salaries, improvements in working hours became an important secondary measure. Accordingly, although the movement toward shorter working hours was often initiated by the labor unions, the efficacy of the unions was not a result of better organization or more *esprit de corps* among the rank and file. Rather, it was a reflection of the improved bargaining position of unions owing to changes occurring within the labor market as the labor shortage grew more acute.

A number of surveys have underlined the effectiveness of a shorter workweek in attracting labor. The data in Tables 1 and 2 show that the initial motivation to introduce the two-day weekend in the late 1960s was closely tied to the recruitment and retention of labor. Particularly with regard to the effects of introducing the new system (Table 2), it is interesting to note that over 40 percent of all enterprises, regardless of size, improved their ability to recruit employees. Moreover, 12 percent found it easier to retain their current work forces. Given the basic trade-off between income and hours of work, increases in income will invite demands for more leisure.

4. Shorter Hours of Work and the Effect on Production

In the background of labor-management negotiations to gradually lower monthly working hours during the 1960s was the increasingly acute labor shortage. The question which still remains, however, concerns the effect of shorter hours of work on production. Do they in fact act as a brake on the rate at which production expands and thereby lower the rate of economic growth itself?

To find an answer to this question we built a mathematical model for the manufacturing industries. Per-hour labor productivity becomes the dependent variable; the four independent variables are (1) capital-labor ratio, (2) rate of capital utilization, (3) standard hours of work, and (4) overtime. The statistical fit for the ten-year period 1960–1969 was such that 99 percent of the change in productivity could be explained with the above-mentioned four variables. Although the exact formula involves considerable technical manipulation, which cannot be discussed here, the coefficients for the independent variables were quite stable. Therefore, we feel rather confident about the results.

In looking at the effect of changes in the four independent variables on productivity, we used a measure of elasticity which showed the percentage change in productivityi nduced by a change of one percent in any of the independent variables. Although the elasticity varies slightly depending upon the point at which the one-percent change is recorded,

Table 1: Reasons for Introducing the Two-day Weekend

Size of the firm (number of employees)	Total number of firms with some form of two-day weekend (actual numbers in parentheses)	Reason for introducing the two-day weekend							
		To bolster attendance	To improve productivity	One way to compensate workers for improved productivity	To attract new employees	For the health of employees	Because of problems in commuting	Other reasons	Not clear
Total	100.0 (1,449)	19.6	44.2	13.7	28.8	67.9	2.3	7.9	6.7
1000+	100.0 (535)	17.2	49.2	15.3	29.2	77.2	3.6	7.9	5.2
300–999	100.0 (418)	18.2	43.5	14.8	31.3	70.6	3.1	6.9	5.0
–299	100.0 (496)	23.4	39.5	10.9	26.2	55.6	0.4	8.7	9.7

Note: In some cases several answers were supplied.   Therefore the totals do not equal the number of firms surveyed.
Source: Rōdō Shō Rōdō Kijun Kyoku (Labor Standards Bureau, Ministry of Labour), *Shūkyū Futsukasei Jittai Chōsa* [Survey on the Two-day Weekend] [Tokyo: Rōdō Daijin Kanbō Rōdō Tōkei Chōsa Bu Rōdō Shō, 1970).

Table 2: The Effects of Introducing the Two-day Weekend

Firm size (number of employees)	Total number of firms with some form of two-day weekend (actual numbers in parentheses)	Effects									
		Positive Effects							No change	Ill effects	Not clear or no answer
		Subtotal	Improvement in attendance	Improvement in productivity	Decrease in industrial accidents	More competitive in the recruitment of new employees	A decrease in attrition due to retirement or changing jobs	Other beneficial effects			
Total	100.0 (1,449)	72.7	35.2	36.1	8.6	44.6	12.5	7.2	20.2	0.5	6.6
1000+	100.0 (535)	73.6	32.7	40.2	8.2	47.5	12.0	12.0	17.6	0.7	8.0
300–999	100.0 (418)	72.3	32.5	37.1	10.5	46.4	14.1	5.0	20.6	0.2	6.9
–299	100.0 (496)	72.0	40.1	30.8	7.3	42.9	11.7	4.8	22.8	0.4	4.8

Note: In some cases several answers were supplied. Therefore the totals do not equal the number of firms surveyed.
Source: Same as for Table 1.

the following conclusion seems to be generally sound: A one-percent reduction in hours of work accounted for a two-percent increase in productivity. This refers to the net effect of such reductions isolated from the effect of changes in the other variables. A one-percent increase in the amount of capital resulted in an increase of 0.9 percent in productivity. However, a one-percent change in the rate of utilization produced a four-percent change in productivity. The short-term effect of economic fluctuations is thus very big. This effect occurs because the size of the labor force is, like the stock of capital, relatively fixed despite changes in the level of economic activity. However, this effect is perhaps greater in Japan than in other countries because of the greater emphasis on employment security and the difficulty of laying off employees during recessions. The effect is thus really in terms of productivity per person rather than in terms of the individual's labor productivity per hour.

Although the elasticity of per-hour labor productivity in terms of changes in the amount of capital per unit of labor seems small at 0.9 percent, we need only recall that the per-capita stock of capital expanded 130 percent during the 1960s to understand how important capital formation was to the expansion of labor productivity at an annual rate of 10 percent. Accordingly, despite the short-term impact of fluctuations in the rate of capital utilization on the level of productivity, the major source of rapid economic growth and the concomitant rise in labor productivity in the 1960s was capital formation. It is with this tremendous amount of capital investment in the background that the reduction of working hours served to lift productivity even further.

An increase of one percent in the number of overtime hours was associated with a drop of 0.4 percent in productivity. In other words, a one-percent increase in the volume of labor resulted in an increase of only 0.6 percent in physical output. This drop in the marginal efficiency or productivity of labor is no doubt due to the onset of fatigue; however, the concept of fatigue must be understood within the broader context of labor supply behavior. This is also true when examining changes in the regular hours of work. The drop in productivity is due not to physical fatigue alone but also to a drop in the overall desire or willingness to work when the equilibrium between leisure and the material standard of living is upset.

This fact seems to be substantiated by the number of firms which have recognized the contribution of shorter hours of work to improved attendance, higher productivity, and fewer accidents (Table 2). It is in this broader sense that the contribution of shorter working hours to productivity and the negative effects of excessive overtime can be fully appreciated.

Our analysis suggests that the common myths associated with a reduction in working hours need to be reviewed. In particular, the fear that a reduction in working hours will undercut economic growth or undermine a firm's competitiveness is quite groundless. However, one must remember that reductions in working hours contribute to improved productivity only to the extent that such reductions serve to restore a balance with the material standard of living. The relation with productivity is not a mechanical one in which successive cuts in hours of work will always result in higher productivity. Rather, the loss in productivity occurs when the material standard of living rises with rapid and sustained economic growth while the hours of work remain unchanged. It is in restoring equilibrium that shorter hours serve to push up productivity. In any case, we must carefully examine the behavior of households in terms of their preferences for different combinations of leisure and income. Only then can concrete recommendations be made.

From our analysis of the data it would seem that the recommendation of the Council on Industrial Structure for a 12-percent reduction in hours of work during the 1970s is quite reasonable in terms of the favorable effects on productivity. Indeed, one might even say that shorter hours are desirable as a means of improving productivity. In firms which have exceptionally long hours one might expect favorable results from an annual reduction of even 3 or 4 percent. At the same time, however, it would be wrong to conclude that working hours can quickly be sliced across the board simply because the coefficient of elasticity derived from a study of variables in the 1960s is 2.0. We again return to the need for a broader consensus and for further examination of the individual employee's relative preference for further increments in leisure and income.

The Economic Return to Tertiary Education and Educational Subsidies: An Empirical Study on Japan

Horiuchi Akiyoshi

1. Introduction

In recent years the role of tertiary education in Japanese society has been examined from various points of view, with considerable attention being given to the broad economic and social implications. The relationship between society and education is extremely complicated, and any attempt to simplify the relationship will result in a serious distortion of reality. However, if we limit our concern to the economic considerations involved in education, and tertiary education in particular, two major issues immediately come to mind. First is the impact on the distribution of income effected by the equality of opportunity for education. In this regard, the tertiary system in Japan appears regressive, in that the system of education serves to reinforce existing income differentials rather than narrow them. Second is the financial position of the private tertiary institutions which educate about 70 percent of all tertiary graduates in Japan. Their position has been allowed to deteriorate.

There is not room in this essay to examine fully all aspects of the economic problems associated with tertiary education. Accordingly, our analysis focuses on the individual's private returns from a tertiary education and the public and private costs. With regard to the costs, how much is the education of students subsidized with public funds, and how does each student's subsidy compare with the household income of his or her family?

This paper originally appeared as "Daigaku Kyōiku no Rieki, Hiyō Oyobi Hojokin —Nihon ni Tsuite no Jisshōteki Kentō," *Nihon Rōdō Kyōkai Zasshi* (vol. 15, no. 4: April 1973), pp. 28–39. The author is Professor of Economics at Hitotsubashi University.

2. Toward a Definition of the Costs and Returns Involved in Tertiary Education

The costs and returns involved in tertiary education are easily illustrated if we place ourselves in the shoes of the eighteen-year-old secondary-school graduate who must choose between a tertiary education and immediate employment. Assuming that each graduate desires to maximize income, the decision will be based on a comparison of the likely earnings from each possible career, one beginning immediately without the costs of a tertiary education and the other starting after graduation from a tertiary institution and involving the costs of that "extra" education. It goes without saying that such a comparison will rest upon some calculation of the present discounted values for each career. Although the value of either career obviously depends upon the number of years in the labor force, for this study retirement from the labor force is arbitrarily assumed to be at 65, and entry into the labor force is assumed to occur at 18 for secondary-school graduates and at 22 for graduates from four-year tertiary institutions. To calculate the earnings from both careers over the same period (for the years from age 22 to 65), we let V_t stand for the present discounted value of the tertiary graduate and V_s stand for that of the high-school graduate. The extra return to the tertiary graduate will be B_p (which equals $V_t - V_s$).[1]

The earnings of high school graduates from the time of graduation (age 18) until age 22, which we will represent as F, are not included in V_s. This income is treated as income foregone by tertiary graduates; it is their opportunity cost. This becomes a sizeable component of the total costs of tertiary education which are borne by the student himself. In addition to the foregone income, the student must pay a rather sizeable university entrance fee as well as tuition and other miscellaneous fees. Transportation, textbooks, other study materials, and extracurricular activities also require large outlays.[2]

If we let E_1 represent the expenses paid to the university and E_2 represent the non-institutional costs, the total cost (C_p) of tertiary

---

[1] In reality many graduate from a tertiary institution after the age of 22 owing to the time spent preparing for entrance examinations, traveling, or otherwise broadening their experience. These variations are not dealt with in this paper. We also overlook those who are unemployed or ill after graduation and those who die before the age of 65.

[2] There are some who argue that living expenses should be included as an expense. However, whether they are in school or in the work force, young people's living expenses are about the same. Therefore they are not included in our calculations.

education borne by the individual will equal $F+E_1+E_2$. Note that C_p represents only the costs to the individual student, not the total cost of education. In addition to C_p there are a variety of social costs. Strictly speaking, any resources diverted from other social uses and not reflected in estimates of F, E_1, or E_2 must be accounted for. Here we are talking about possible loss of externalities (particularly in the case of F) and direct transfers from public funds which represent a redistribution of income. Since the first category is difficult to measure, it is excluded from our analysis. Transfers, easier to measure, can be entered into our calculation when the costs of the university are not met by student payment.

From the point of view of the educational institution, the costs include operating costs (*keijōteki hiyō*) (P) and capital or investment costs (*kizoku hiyō*) (I).[3] Accordingly, the total social cost of a tertiary education (C_s) can be expressed as $C_s=P+I+F+E_2$. Here F represents the loss to society due to the student's absence from the labor force and E_2 represents the use of the individual's income for educational expenses outside the school, resources which might be used for other social ends. The difference (S) between individual cost and institutional cost may be expressed in the following manner:

$$S=C_s-C_p=P+I-E_1.$$

The difference (S) is the subsidy paid by society to those receiving a tertiary education. The value of S is obviously considerable at institutions run by the national government and local governments, but, as the following analysis will demonstrate, it is also substantial at private institutions.

3. Estimates of the Monetary Return to Tertiary Education

Estimates of the monetary return to tertiary education are derived from the average earnings profiles for college and high school graduates. The profiles are calculated from the average income for each age group. Although the earnings profile will differ according to occupational groupings even for those with the same education, it is difficult to ob-

---

[3] This terminology is a little different from that used by the Ministry of Education. In its statistics, school expenses (*gakkō keihi*) are frequently referred to as the sum of consumptive-type expenditures (*shōhiteki shishutsu*) and capital expenses (*shihonteki shishutsu*), the latter including expenditures for land and facilities. However, these definitions are not very precise. Although capital outlays are expenses, they do not necessarily correspond to the costs of educating the student.

tain sufficiently detailed information. Income estimates for the self-employed and the free-lance professional are particularly difficult to obtain. Table 1 gives the annual income for male employees in supervisory posts, administrative positions, and technical jobs in manufacturing. The figures are for fiscal 1968 (1 April 1968–31 March 1969) and are available for eight age groups and three levels of education; estimates indicate income before and after the deduction of personal income tax. Unfortunately, however, more detailed data on a greater number of industries are not available.[4]

It should be emphasized that the values in Table 1 are from cross-sectional data. The figure for any age group represents what that age group is earning in a given year (1968). The figures for the 30–34 age group do not represent the actual income to be earned in 1980 by those aged 18 or 19 in 1968. In the future, time series data will be needed to substantiate our estimates.[5] This study relies on projections of the estimated rise in real income levels which were derived from cross-sectional data taken over the five-year period prior to 1968. Table 2 gives the present discounted value for both the projections (which are used as our time series data) and the cross-sectional data available for specific years. Four different interest rates are used for discounting. The discounted value of income for high school graduates includes the four years' income foregone by college graduates (F) and is therefore equal to V_s+F. In Table 3 these values of F and V_s are shown separately. The figures in the lower half of the table are for comparison with junior college graduates; the foregone earnings are smaller and the lifetime earnings are greater, but the two totals are the same.

The pecuniary benefit of a four-year university education (B_p) is the difference between V_t and V_s. That of a two-year junior college education (B_p') is the difference between V_t' and V_s'. The pecuniary benefits of the two types of tertiary education are shown in Table 4. These are the values which must be compared with the costs of education in order to render a final judgment about the economic return to an individual from a tertiary education. Before considering the cost component, however, two comments on the tremendous effect of changes in the discount rate should be made. First, as will later become apparent, the going interest rate will be critical in determining profitability. Second, even with an

[4] The statistical problems are numerous. For example, since nearly all doctors and barristers are university graduates and earn an income considerably above that for the university graduates shown in Table 1, it is quite likely that the returns to tertiary education are underestimated. For the time being, these inconsistencies will be overlooked.

[5] On this point, see H. P. Miller, "Life-time Income and Economic Growth," *The American Economic Review* (vol. 55, no. 4: September 1965), pp. 834–843.

Table 1:   Annual Income for Age and Educational Groupings: 1968

(Unit: ¥1000)

Educational group-ing; highest institution of graduation	Status of taxes	Age grouping							
		18–19	20–24	25–29	30–34	35–39	40–49	50–59	60–
Old universities or new universities	before taxation		614.4	796.8	1,056.0	1,292.8	1,702.4	1,976.0	1,144.0
	after taxation		577.7	761.9	991.8	1,193.5	1,484.5	1,629.1	1,060.0
Old higher technical schools or new junior colleges	before taxation		558.4	760.0	940.8	1,252.8	1,512.0	1,624.0	1,006.4
	after taxation		528.4	749.1	889.1	1,162.5	1,351.1	1,406.1	952.4
Old middle schools or new high schools	before taxation	433.6	574.4	761.6	931.2	1,086.4	1,270.4	1,259.2	888.0
	after taxation	418.6	542.6	730.7	890.9	1,033.0	1,175.6	1,150.5	853.1

Note: For details on data compilation, please refer to item A in the appendix.

Source: These data are taken from the Chingin Kōzō Kihon Tōkei Chōsa (Basic Survey of Wage Structure) as reprinted in Rōdō Daijin Kanbō Tōkei Jōhō Bu (Statistics and Information Department, Minister's Secretariat, Ministry of Labour), *Dai Nijūichi Kai Rōdō Tōkei Nenpō* [Yearbook of Labour Statistics: 1968] (Tokyo: Rōdō Hōrei Kyōkai, 1969), p. 140–171.

Table 2:   Estimates of the Present Discounted Values of Lifetime Earnings by
Educational Background

(Unit: ¥1000)

		Selected interest rates			
		5%	8%	10%	12%
A. Time series data					
University graduates	Before tax	72,057.6	31,994.2	20.067.6	13,508.2
	After tax (V_t)	63,458.9	28,504.7	18,044.8	12,751.7
Junior college graduates	Before tax	50.509.8	28,282.1	18,597.1	12,948.7
	After tax (V'_t)	53,758.7	25,791.4	17,073.0	11,966.0
High school graduates	Before tax	46,690.8	25,315.0	17,956.4	13,392.8
	After tax ($F + V_s$)	44,129.9	23,793.5	16,930.6	12,662.3
B. Cross-sectional data					
University graduates	Before tax	18,015.8	10,258.4	7,460.7	5,629.2
	After tax	16,213.0	9,351.3	6,851.5	5,201.9
Junior college graduates	Before tax	17,175.2	10,235.2	7,691.0	6,001.9
	After tax	15,817.8	9,511.7	7,183.6	5,629.3
High school graduates	Before tax	16,376.7	10,355.4	8,099.9	6,576.7
	After tax	15,440.2	9,800.8	7,681.6	6,246.9

Note: For details on data compilation, please refer to the appendix, item B.

Table 3:   The Present Discounted Value of the Lifetime Earnings of Secondary
School Graduates and the Foregone Earnings of Tertiary Graduates
of Four-year and Two-year Institutions

(Unit: ¥1000)

Variable	Selected interest rates			
	5%	8%	10%	12%
F (4-yr.)	2,060.8	1,963.1	1,905.2	1,850.5
V_s	42,069.1	21,830.4	15,025.4	10.811.8
$F + V_s$	44,129.9	23,793.5	16,930.6	12,662.3
F (2-yr.)	846.8	834.9	827.3	820.0
V_s	43,283.1	22,958.6	16,103.3	11,842.3
$F + V_s$	44,129.9	23,793.5	16,930.6	12,662.3

Table 4:   The Pecuniary Benefit of a Tertiary Education ($B_p = V_t - V_s$)

(Unit: ¥1000)

	Selected interest rates			
	5%	8%	10%	12%
For graduates of four-year institutions (universities)	21,389.8	6,674.3	3,019.4	1,939.9
For graduates of two-year institutions (junior colleges)	10,475.6	2,832.8	969.7	123.7

interest rate of 5 percent, the differential return to junior-college graduates is less than half that to four-year graduates; an interest rate of 12 percent causes it to fall to less than one-fifteenth.[6]

4.   The Private and Social Costs of Tertiary Education

The cost components can be deduced from the two concepts introduced above in the second section. The first involves the private cost borne by the individual recipient or his family. The second focuses on the full social cost borne by the institution in educating one person. The latter concept subsumes the first; accordingly, social costs will include private costs.

Private costs can be estimated from the data on the educational costs to students in 1968 which are provided by a survey conducted by the Ministry of Education. The data are broken down for national, public,[7] and private institutions in Table 5. These are cross-sectional data for 1968; no doubt there is some variation from year to year, although this should not greatly affect our conclusions. The average annual cost is slightly higher for students in four-year programs. Of major significance is the fact that foregone earnings account for a very sizeable percentage of total private costs: roughly 90 percent in the case of national institutions and about three-fourths of the total cost at private institutions.

---

[6] It should be noted that approximately 80 percent of two-year junior college students are female as opposed to approximately 20 percent of those at four-year tertiary institutions.

[7] The term "public" refers to institutions run by prefectural and local governments, which are distinct from those operated with funds from the national government. The following figures (again, for 1968) give some idea of the size of the various institutions:

Type of institution	Number of institutions	Number of full-time teaching staff	Number of students
Four-year institutions			
National	81	42,020	357,772
Public	34	5,602	50,880
Private	305	42,060	1,325,430
Two-year institutions			
National	31	654	13,143
Public	48	1,617	17,973
Private	434	13,286	322,666

Table 5: Cross-sectional Data on the Average Annual Private Costs of Education for Students in Different Types of Institutions

(Unit: ￥1000)

Type of cost	Type of institution					
	National (*kokuritsu*)		Public (*kōritsu*)		Private (*shiritsu*)	
	Four-year	Two-year	Four-year	Two-year	Four-year	Two-year
Institutional fees (E_1)	13.8	12.0	21.3	29.2	107.9	113.2
Additional personal costs (E_2)	45.3	42.0	46.1	36.8	47.7	42.6
Foregone earnings (F) a. for the first two years b. for the third and fourth years	418.6 or 542.6	418.6	418.6 or 542.6	418.6	418.6 or 542.6	418.6
Total private cost (C_p)	477.7 or 601.7	472.6	486.0 or 610.0	484.6	574.2 or 698.2	574.4
F/C_p (using the average foregone earnings for four-year institutions)	89.0%	90.2%	87.7%	86.4%	75.5%	72.9%

Note: In calculating the figures for E_2, students in medicine, dentistry, and pharmacy are excluded. For more details on the calculations refer to the statistical appendix.

Source: Mombu Shō Daigaku Gakujutsu Kyoku Gakusei Ka (Student Affairs Division, Bureau of Higher Education, Ministry of Education), *Shōwa Yonjūsan Nendo Gakusei Seikatsu Chōsa Hōkoku* [Report on the Survey of Student Life: 1968], an unpublished mimeographed document.

Accordingly, although there is considerable variation in institutional fees (E_1) and, therefore, in the cost borne directly by the student or his or her family ($E_1 + E_2$), the greatest proportion of private cost is foregone earnings. In other words, the private cost of a tertiary education does not depend much upon the type of institution attended; if we accept the commonly heard complaint that education at a private university is expensive, we must then also say that the same is true for education at the national and public universities. The alleged advantage of national and public institutions in terms of the actual private cost borne is thus a myth which exists because people fail to consider foregone earnings and the way in which they, as the largest part of private costs, tend to diminish the significance of whatever inequalities might exist in terms of other private costs such as fees.

Turning to consider the full social cost of tertiary education, we use the same values for foregone earnings (F) and private costs outside the institution (E_2). The remaining portion of social costs is equivalent to the costs incurred by educational institutions. As explained above, we can break this portion into two components: running or recurrent costs (P) and imputed capital investment (I).

In the case of operating costs (P), the Ministry of Education's data for consumptive educational expenses are close enough to allow their use as a proxy for P. The problem is with the data on investment or capital costs (I), which ought to include the implicit rents paid on land, buildings, and other durable equipment. Until 1965 the data gathered by the Ministry gave only the present value of buildings and equipment held by the schools. We used these figures to calculate the per-student value and then took 8 percent of that value as the imputed cost of fixed capital (I). The estimates for each variable are given in Table 6. One should note that information on the value of library holdings is not available; the annual expenditure on library materials is, however, included in the statistics as a capital expenditure and is included here in the value of P.[8]

Table 6 shows that there are noticeable differences among the several types of institutions in terms of the values of P and I. The average

Table 6:   Average Annual Per-capita Social Cost Components for 1968

(Unit: ¥1000)

Type of cost	Type of institution					
	National		Public		Private	
	Four-year	Two-year	Four-year	Two-year	Four-year	Two-year
Recurring costs (P)	382.8	99.4	313.0	208.4	146.8	94.8
Investment costs (I)	100.3	7.7	73.7	49.9	27.5	32.1
Institutional costs (P+I)	483.1	107.1	386.7	258.3	174.3	126.9
Non-institutional costs (F+E₂)	463.9 or 587.9	460.6	464.7 or 588.7	455.4	466.3 or 590.3	461.2
Total social costs (C_s)	947.0 or 1,071.0	567.7	851.4 or 975.4	713.7	640.6 or 764.6	588.1

Source: Mombu Shō Daijin Kanbō Tōkei Ka (Research and Statistics Division, Minister's Secretariat, Ministry of Education), *Gakkō Kihon Chōsa Hokoku Sho* [Basic Statistical Survey on Schools] (Tokyo: Ministry of Education, 1975), pp. 24–40: and Chūō Kyōiku Shingikai (Central Council on Education), *Kongo ni Okeru Gakkō Kyōiku no Sōgōteki na Kakujū Seibi no Tame no Kihonteki Shisaku ni Tsuite* [Basic Guidelines for the Reform of Education], Basic Materials No III-12 (Tokyo: Ministry of Education, 1971), p. 465.

[8] Chūō Kyoiku Shingikai (The Central Council on Education), *Kongo ni Okeru Gakkō Kyōiku no Sōgōteki na Kakujū Seibi no Tame no Kihonteki Shinsaku ni Tsuite* [Basic Guidelines for the Reform of Education], Basic Materials No. III-12, (Tokyo: Ministry of Education, 1971), p. 465. Also see the statistical appendix.

cost per student at the national universities is about 33 percent above that at the public universities and 200 percent above that at the private universities.

One might argue accordingly that the private universities are much more efficient in educating their students. However, such an interpretation does not go well with our common understanding of the situation. Rather, it is more likely that the extremely small budget of a private institution is offset by a variety of non-monetary impositions or costs borne by the student. In other words, the quality of education is inferior. Students must cram into lecture halls like sardines to hear their lectures. The facilities are poor, often in want of repair, and the classrooms are frequently dirty and without heating or air conditioning. Consequently, the students have to withstand various kinds of mental stress, physical discomfort, and considerable inconvenience. It is only when the students willingly put up with these shortcomings that their private university education is on a par with that received from the national universities.[9]

A comparison of social costs (C_s) in Table 6 with private costs (C_p) in Table 5 shows that students bear only 50.4 and 56.2 percent, respectively, of the total costs for four- and two-year national institutions. For public institutions the figures are 57.1 and 62.5 percent; for private institutions, 89.6 and 91.5 percent. If the low level of expenditures (P and I) at the private schools is partially offset by the willingness of students to bear a variety of non-monetary costs, then the percentage of total costs borne by the students is even higher.

As expected, the social cost (C_s) is greater than the private cost (C_p) for all institutions. As hypothesized above in the second section,

Table 7: Per Capita Subsidies in 1968 by Type of Institution

(Unit: ￥1000)

Type of cost	National		Public		Private	
	Four-year	Two-year	Four-year	Two-year	Four-year	Two-year
Social cost (C_s)	947.0 or 1,071.0	567.7	851.4 or 975.4	713.7	640.6 or 764.6	588.1
Private cost (C_p)	477.7 or 601.7	472.6	486.0 or 610.0	484.6	574.2 or 698.2	574.4
Subsidy $(S = C_s - C_p)$	469.3	95.1	365.4	229.1	66.9	13.7

[9] This does not mean that facilities at the national universities are adequate. Much improvement is needed there as well. But here we are only discussing relative differences between the two.

students receive a subsidy in kind. From society's point of view the subsidy is a social service. The cost of this social service in 1968 is shown in Table 7. Although the actual absolute cost borne by the student does not vary much, the disparity in subsidies to students at the various types of institutions is considerable. Accordingly, the real disadvantage for students at private institutions lies in the size of the subsidy paid to the university on their behalf by other parties in society at large.

5.   Subsidies for Tertiary Education

The preceding sections considered briefly the returns and costs involved in tertiary education. Taken as a whole, the discussion suggests a number of interesting propositions. The rate of return to a tertiary education can be calculated by comparing the present discounted value of the profit margin (B_p) and the present discounted value of the cost (C_p). The rate of return is equivalent to the interest or discount rate at which B_p and C_p are equal.

A comparison of the figures in Tables 3 and 8-A yields an immediate answer. If we exclude two-year private institutions, it is obvious that the rate of return is somewhere between 10 and 12 percent, and in no instance is the return over 12 percent. This is the return to the private investment of the students and is different from that to the total social cost.[10]

Strictly speaking, in defining the private rate of return to a tertiary education, one ought to consider the social subsidy as being a net transfer to the tertiary graduate. When this is done the rate of return will rise to over 12 percent. Finally, Table 9 shows the ratio of the discounted value of subsidies to those for private returns. The results could have been predicted.

In order to estimate the social rate of return to tertiary education, the present discounted values of the social costs given in Table 8-B are compared with those for the social returns as measured with the before-tax

[10] It is instructive to compare these returns with those calculated for the United States. Over the past ten years a number of researchers have done work in this area; G. S. Becker's work would be most typical. Although he has calculated returns for a variety of situations, the rates of return for white males living in urban areas was 14.5 percent (1939) and 13.0 percent (1954). It should be pointed out that a number of other variables are also involved in accounting for the different rates of return to secondary and tertiary education. In addition to education there is natural ability and on-the-job training. Becker was confronted by the problem of trying to exclude the influence of these other variables, and we can offer no solution to this dilemma. See Gary S. Becker, *Human Capital: A Theoretical and Empirical Analysis* (New York: National Bureau of Economic Research, 1964), pp. 69–113.

Table 8: Present Discounted Values for the Private and Social Costs of Education and Subsidies by Type of Institution, 1968

A. Private costs (C_p)   (Unit: ￥1000)

Type of institution		Selected discount rates			
		5%	8%	10%	12%
National	Four-year	2,280.7	2,174.2	2,110.9	2,051.1
	Two-year	952.3	939.0	930.5	922.1
Public	Four-year	2,311.4	2,203.8	2,139.8	2,079.3
	Two-year	975.7	962.1	953.4	945.1
Private	Four-year	2,644.7	2,526.7	2,456.3	2,389.7
	Two-year	1,151.9	1,136.5	1,126.6	1,117.1

B. Social costs (C_s)   (Unit: ￥1000)

Type of institution		Selected discount rates			
		5%	8%	10%	12%
National	Four-year	4,028.1	3,853.2	3,747.7	3,648.0
	Two-year	1,137.9	1,122.1	1,111.9	1,102.2
Public	Four-year	3,672.2	3,511.3	3,414.3	3,322.8
	Two-year	1,423.0	1,403.2	1,390.7	1,378.6
Private	Four-year	2,887.4	2,757.2	2,679.3	2,605.7
	Two-year	1,177.7	1,161.3	1,150.9	1,140.8

C. Subsidies ($S = C_s - C_p$)   (Unit: ￥1000)

Type of institution		Selected discount rates			
		5%	8%	10%	12%
National	Four-year	1,747.3	1,678.7	1,636.4	1,596.5
	Two-year	185.7	183.2	181.6	180.0
Public	Four-year	1,360.5	1,307.1	1,274.1	1,243.0
	Two-year	447.3	441.2	437.4	433.7
Private	Four-year	249.1	239.3	233.3	227.6
	Two-year	26.7	26.4	26.2	25.9

income figures in Table 2. The index of social benefit ought to include private returns plus any other returns to society at large. Unfortunately, we cannot measure the various externalities, but we can measure the effect of tertiary education on before-tax income. In calculating private benefits, the individual's tax is excluded. In the case of social returns, however, we can consider the effect on before-tax income minus any other levies. The discount rate which brings social cost (C_s) into alignment with the social return to society will be between 9 and 10 percent for all types of tertiary institutions.

The amount of subsidy which tertiary students receive in the form of educational services cannot be ignored. The present discounted values for these subsidies are shown in Table 8-C: with a discount rate of 8 percent their value totals nearly 1.7 million yen (about U.S.$5,000–

Table 9:   The Ratio (S/B_p) of the Discounted Value of Subsidies to Private Benefits for Various Types of Four-year Institutions at Various Discount Rates

(Unit: percentage)

Type of institution	Selected discount rates			
	5%	8%	10%	12%
National universities	8.1	25.2	54.2	82.3
Public universities	6.4	19.6	42.2	64.1
Private universities	1.2	3.6	7.7	15.6

$6,000) for students at national universities, 1.3 million yen (about U.S. $4,000–$5,000) for students at local public universities, and 240,000 yen (about U.S. $800) for students at private universities.* To gain a better perspective on these subsidies, the following comparison is perhaps useful. As a result of receiving the subsidy while a student, the college graduate will earn a higher income and therefore pay a progressively higher income tax. In other words, we can compare the present discounted value of the subsidy with the present discounted value of the taxes he will pay after graduation. Using the data in Table 2 and assuming that the tax schedule remains the same, the present discounted value of national income tax and the local government tax is calculated, and the difference in the total amount of income taxes paid by university and high school graduates is deduced. That difference is given in Table 10. A comparison of Tables 8-C and 10 shows that discount rates of over 10 percent result in the present discounted value of the subsidy's being greater than that of the extra taxes to be paid by graduates of national and public universities.

In short, national and local public universities provide for a net transfer of income to their graduates. Moreover, if only the difference in the amount of taxes paid back to defray educational expenses were considered, the redistributive effects of education over the individual's lifetime would clearly be greater. Finally, even if the present discounted value of the subsidy was lower than that of the graduate's future tax burden, it could still be claimed that the organization of tertiary education worked to offset the effects of progressive taxation. This possibility

* *Editor's note:* These U.S. dollar figures, and those which follow in this article, are based on an exchange rate of $1.00=¥300, the prevailing rate at the time the article was originally published. As this book goes to press, the dollar, having dropped to a record low of $1.00=¥180, has stabilized at roughly $1.00= ¥220. At this rate of exchange, the dollar figures would be much higher than those here. For instance: given ¥1.7 million=$7,700; ¥1.3 million=$6,000; ¥240,000 =$1,100.

Table 10: The Present Discounted Value of the Differential Tax Paid by Graduates of Tertiary Institutions for Various Discount Rates

(Unit: ¥1000)

	Selected discount rates			
	5%	8%	10%	12%
I. Present discounted value of tax to be paid by				
a. graduates of four-year tertiary institutions (I)	8,598.7	3,489.5	2,022.8	756.5
b. graduates of two-year tertiary institutions (II)	5,751.1	2,490.7	1,524.1	982.7
c. graduates of secondary schools (III)	2,560.9	1,521.5	1,025.8	730.5
II. The additional tax burden for				
a. graduates of four-year institutions (III)−(I)	6,037.8	1,968.0	997.0	26.0
b. graduates of two-year institutions (III)−(II)	3,190.2	969.2	498.3	252.2

brings us to the last issue: Who receives these subsidies? How are they distributed throughout the society?

6. The Distribution of Subsidies for Tertiary Education

A comparison of the pattern of income distribution among the households of tertiary students with the distribution of income in society at large will give us some idea of the distribution of subsidies for tertiary education. [The Ministry of Education's survey on student finances contains income estimates for the families of tertiary students. Data from this source are arranged in Table 11. Among students at the national universities, for example, only 5.6 percent come from households with an annual income of less than 400,000 yen (about U.S. $1,300–$1,400).

The Family Income and Expenditure Survey gives us the distribution for all households. For our purposes we wish to focus only on households which are likely to have members in the 18-to-22 age bracket. The survey gives a breakdown of the distribution according to the age of the household head. The distribution among households in which the household head is aged between 40 and 59 is shown in Table 11.

The relationships in Table 11 are presented graphically in Figure 1. Regardless of the type of university, the percentage of students from households with annual incomes over 1 million yen (about U.S. $3,300–

Table 11: The 1968 Percentage Distribution by Income Class of the Households of Tertiary Students and All Households in Which the Age of the Household Head is Between 40 and 59

Annual income (¥10,000)	Percentage of households of students at various types of institutions (percent)						All Japanese households in which the age of the household head is between 40 and 59 (percent)	Annual income of all Japanese households in which the age of the household head is between 40 and 59 (percent)	Subsidies from national and public institutions (¥1,000,000)	Subsidies from private institutions (¥1,000,000)	Total amount of subsidies received (¥1,000,000) (percent)
	Four-year			Two-year							
	National	Public	Private	National	Public	Private					
Less than 40	5.6	2.3	0.9	4.6	1.4	1.0	9.3	2.8	7,398	803	8,201 (4.1)
40–50	6.5	4.0	1.2	2.0	2.8	0.8	6.9	3.2	8,563	832	9,393 (4.3)
50–60	5.8	4.0	2.0	5.8	4.6	1.3	7.6	4.2	7,838	1,326	9,164 (4.6)
60–70	6.9	5.9	2.5	6.9	5.8	2.7	9.1	6.0	9,523	1,695	11,218 (5.6)
70–80	7.3	6.8	3.6	6.9	4.6	2.8	9.9	7.5	10,150	2,336	12,486 (6.2)
80–90	8.4	8.3	5.1	8.9	7.1	4.6	9.7	8.3	11,683	3,282	14,963 (7.4)
90–100	7.1	7.6	4.8	7.9	8.2	4.3	8.5	8.2	10,032	2,961	12,993 (6.5)
100–120	15.4	17.4	13.9	21.6	15.7	13.2	12.0	13.3	21,875	8,668	30,543 (15.2)
120–140	13.0	14.5	15.7	13.8	19.9	16.0	8.9	11.6	18,552	9,477	28,029 (13.9)
140–200	13.9	16.6	22.6	16.7	21.8	25.4	12.0	19.9	20,023	13,847	33,870 (16.8)
Over 200	10.1	12.6	27.7	4.9	8.1	27.9	6.0	15.1	14,302	16,197	30,499 (15.1)
Total	100.0	100.0	100.0	100.0	100.0	100.0	100.0	100.0	139,939	61,422	201,361 (100.0)

Note: Night students, who account for 11 percent of all university students, are not included in these figures.

Source: Mombu Shō Daigaku Gakujutsu Kyoku Gakusei Ka (Student Affairs Division, Bureau of Higher Education, Ministry of Education), *Shōwa Yonjūsannen Nendo Gakusei Seikatsu Chōsa Hōkoku* [Report on the 1968 Survey of Student Life] (Mimeographed report). Sōrifu Tōkei Kyoku (Bureau of Statistics, Prime Minister's Office), *Shōwa Yonjūsan Nendo Kakei Chōsa Nenpō* [The 1968 Annual Report on the Family and Income Expenditure Survey] (Tokyo: Ōkura Shō Insatsu Kyoku, 1969), pp. 62–63.

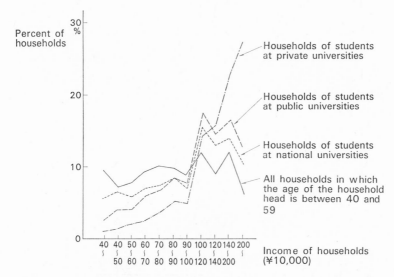

Figure 1: The 1968 Percentage Distribution by Income Class of the Households of Tertiary Students and All Japanese Households in Which
the Age of the Household Head is Between 40 and 59.

$3,400) is above the percentage of households with such incomes in the
population at large. In other words, young people from households
with annual incomes of less than 1 million yen are underrepresented, and
increasingly so as household income falls. Since the young people from
richer households are receiving a disproportionately large share of the
subsidies for tertiary education, the system of tertiary education in
Japan redistributes income regressively.

This fact is shown even more dramatically in Table 12, where the
total subsidy per income class is calculated by multiplying the number
of students at each institution by the average amount of subsidy
received (see Table 7).

Households with annual income below 1 million yen account for
about 61 percent of all households, but they receive only 39 percent of
the subsidies. At the other end of the income scale, about one-third of
the richest households receive over 50 percent of the subsidy.

Table 13 shows the amount of subsidy received on a per-household
basis for each of the income classes. Again the regressive nature of these
subsidies is demonstrated. There is a very high correlation between the
subsidy received and household income. The public institutions tend to
be slightly less regressive, but nonetheless they clearly fit the overall
pattern.

Table 12: The Distribution of Subsidies for Tertiary Education by Income Class: 1968

(Unit: ¥1 million)

Annual income (¥10,000)	Type of institution						Total
	Four-year			Two-year			
	National	Public	Private	National	Public	Private	
0–40	6,876	435	767	34	53	36	8,201
40–50	7,810	615	803	39	99	29	9,395
50–60	7,013	643	1,280	39	143	46	9,164
60–70	8,343	944	1,610	44	192	85	11,218
70–80	8,817	1,094	2,245	62	177	91	12,486
80–90	10,062	1,305	3,135	77	239	147	14,963
90–100	8,504	1,196	2,822	57	275	139	12,993
100–120	18,517	2,696	8,265	110	552	403	30,543
120–140	15,588	2,252	9,000	68	644	477	28,029
140–200	16,690	2,558	13,093	72	703	754	33,870
200–	12,080	1,912	15,385	36	274	812	30,499
Total	120,300	15,650	58,403	638	3,351	3,019	201,361

Table 13: The Amount of Per-household Subsidy by Income Class: 1968

(Unit: Yen per household)

Annual income (¥10,000)	All national and public tertiary institutions	All private tertiary institutions	Total
0–40	7,232	785	8,016
40–50	11,282	1,096	12,378
50–60	9,376	1,586	10,962
60–70	9,513	1,694	11,207
70–80	9,320	2,071	11,391
80–90	10,949	3,074	14,023
90–100	10,729	3,167	13,896
100–120	16,459	6,567	23,026
120–140	18,950	9,680	28,630
140–200	15,169	10,490	25,659
200–	21,670	24,541	46,211

7. Conclusions

The foregoing discussion has uncovered two important facts. First, the subsidy to tertiary education is considerable. This is particularly true in the case of national and public institutions. Second, these subsidies are distributed regressively in favor of the wealthy. The conclusions are as one would expect; the specifics of the data are really not too important.

The research leaves unanswered a variety of theoretical and moral issues involved in the distribution of the subsidies: Is the present state of affairs desirable in terms of criteria such as equality, equity, or efficiency? Or, if revision of the present system is in order, what direction should such revision take?

Although there is no room here to do more than broach these questions, it should be mentioned that the system of education seems to change more slowly than other subsystems within the economy, many of which have experienced the impact of extremely rapid technological change in recent years. For this reason it is likely that the cost of education as an industry will rise in the future. Nevertheless, as W. J. Baumol suggests, the education industry is an important component of modern industrial society and cannot be ignored any longer.[11] If the situation is left as it is, the position of the education industry will deteriorate. This will in turn mean higher costs, some of which will be defrayed by the student and some by increased subsidies. There are many reasons to expect also that the distribution of subsidies for tertiary education will become even more regressive. In terms of the openness of the social system as a whole and the dynamics of economic efficiency, this regressiveness would have numerous undesirable consequences. It is hoped that some of these can be avoided by an early study of these problems. This paper is offered as one small step in that direction.

Statistical Appendix

A. Table 1

The figures are taken from the Chingin Kōzō Kihon Tōkei Chōsa (Basic Survey of Wage Structure) as presented in *Rōdō Tōkei Nenpō* [The Yearbook of Labor Statistics] (Tokyo: Ōkura Shō Insatsu Kyoku, 1969). The average monthly salary is given for different groups based upon age and level of education. To obtain the before-tax annual income used in Table 1, we multiplied the average monthly earnings by 16 in order to take account of the bonus (here assumed to be equal to four months' income). The amount of national income tax was calculated according to the 1968 schedule made available for tax returns. To estimate the appropriate deductions for dependents, we made several

---

[11] W. J. Baumol, "Macroeconomics of Unbalanced Growth: The Anatomy of Urban Crisis," *The American Economic Review* (vol. 57, no. 3: June 1967), pp. 415–426.

assumptions about family size and the age of the household head:

Age of the household head	Spouse and other dependents (number of persons)
18–24	0
25–29	1
30–34	2
35–39	3
40–49	3
50–59	2
over 60	2

Although the local government taxes vary from one location to another, here we assumed that these were 50 percent of the national income tax. The amounts of the two taxes were added together and subtracted from before-tax income to obtain after-tax income.

B.   Table 2

Using data from the Ministry of Labour's *Rōdō Tōkei Nenpō*, comparable breakdowns for groups based on age and the level of education exist only for the years beginning with 1964. Using data from 1964 through 1968, the rate of increase in real wages was calculated. These rates are given in the table below. An annual 5 percent rise in consumer prices was assumed. Using these rates of increase in real income, the lifetime earnings in Table 2 were calculated. It is assumed that the income tax schedule will remain the same for each age grouping.

	(Unit: percentage rate of annual increase)							
Level of education	Age group							
	18–19	20–24	25–29	30–34	35–39	40–49	50–59	60–
Old university and new university		5.6	6.1	5.8	4.0	4.0	5.7	7.2
Old higher technical schools and new junior colleges		6.4	6.4	3.3	4.7	4.5	5.9	5.8
Old middle school and new high school	7.4	9.7	7.0	5.9	5.4	4.4	5.4	3.0

C.   Table 5

The figures on institutional costs (E_1) represent all payments on behalf of the student to the educational institution. These include entrance fees, examination fees, and tuition.

Other expenses or additional costs (E₂) represent all other expenses except living costs. These include commutation and extra-curricular activities. They are averages for all students except those in medicine, dentistry, and pharmacy. The latter types of students are excluded because they rarely enter supervisory, administrative, or technical positions in manufacturing industries.

D. Table 6

As mentioned in the text, operating expenses *(keijōteki hiyō)* include (i) consumptive expenditures *(shōhiteki shishutsu)*, such as salaries for teaching and general staff, professorial research funds and repair work, and (ii) funds used for library acquisitions. Using figures from *Kongo ni Okeru Gakkō Kyōiku no Sōgōteki na Kakujū Seibi no Tame no Kihonteki Seisaku ni Tsuite* [Basic Guidelines for the Reform of Education], the total value of all buildings and equipment in 1965 is estimated at ¥438 billion (U.S.$1.4–1.5 billion). The annual rate of increase in the value of these assets over the previous ten years was 18.4 percent. Using that rate and the 1965 figures, the capital stock for 1968 was estimated at ¥727 billion. To obtain a breakdown for the different types of institutions, the total floor area of buildings was used as an index. The national universities, for example, accounted for 44.5 percent of all floor space at all tertiary institutions. Accordingly, its assets were estimated as 44.5 percent of ¥727 billion or ¥323 billion. The annual outlay was taken as being 8 percent of the value of the assets. The student enrollments used for calculating per-student P and I were were as follows:

Type of institution	Student enrollment
National universities	257,870
National junior colleges	9,020
Public universities	43,880
Public junior colleges	15,630
Private universities	787,120
Private junior colleges	205,120

The Future of the Fixed-age Retirement System

Kaneko Yoshio

1. Introduction

One of several on-going research groups within the Japan Institute of Labour, the Labor Economics Research Subgroup has spent two years (April 1971–March 1973) examining the fixed-age retirement system common to many large firms in Japan. This article is an initial report on the group's findings.

During the past two years public interest in problems associated with the fixed-age retirement system has grown rapidly. Since the announcement of Labour Minister Tamura Hajime that the Ministry would actively work to promote an extension of the retirement age, which has normally been 55 in most large firms, a number of valuable reports, many from the Ministry itself, have appeared in rapid succession. They include the interim report of the Employment Policy Research Committee (Koyō Seisaku Chōsa Kenkyūkai) in August 1972, the report of the Second Subgroup of the Conference on Future Living Styles for Employee Households (Rōdōsha Seikatsu Bijon Kondankai, Daini Bunkakai) in December 1972, and a report entitled *Teinen Enchō to Chingin Seido ni Tsuite* [Extended Retirement Ages and the Wage System] issued by the Research Group on Wages (Chingin Kenkyūkai) also in December 1972. Without exception these reports have called for an extension of the fixed retirement age from 55 to 60. In this recommendation two lines of reasoning appear. One stresses the desirability of improving the welfare of older persons in the work force. The

This article was originally published as "Teinensei no Shōrai," *Nihon Rōdō Kyōkai Zasshi* (vol. 15, no. 5: May 1973), pp. 2–10. The author is Director of the Japan Wage Research Center.

other argues for a more rational allocation of manpower and thereby a higher level of economic activity for the nation.

While these viewpoints have been set forth by governmental agencies or so-called "third parties", a similar stance can be found among management groups and organized labor. Although in the past Nikkeiren (The Japan Federation of Employers' Association) has been reluctant to move ahead in this area, some sign of change can be seen in a recent report entitled *Teinen Encho Mondai ni Kansuru Kenkai* [Views on Extended Retirement Ages and Accompanying Problems] which appeared in March 1973. In the report Nikkeiren argues that "even from the viewpoint of improving the welfare of older employees and solving the future labor shortage, it will be necessary for us to go beyond the partial solutions and *ad hoc* arrangements of individual firms. For the future a commonly accepted approach is necessary."

The labor movement has long favored an extension of the retirement age, arguing for the abolition of the fixed-age retirement system altogether or at least for a minimum retirement age of 65. Judging from the white papers issued by labor unions before the recent spring wage offensive, they too would agree that the move to change the fixed retirement age from 55 to 60 is a step in the right direction.[1]

It would thus seem that a considerable consensus exists in the call for an extension of the fixed retirement age to 60, and, as the conference on Future Living Styles for Employee Households suggests, it is very likely that a common retirement age of 60 will become the norm in the next five years.

However, the real problems are not in merely extending the age of retirement, but rather in actually obtaining a more rational allocation of labor and in really improving the welfare of the older employee. The extension of the retirement age is nothing more than a first step. Although it is an important first step, it is possible that the wrong approach and merely good intentions will yield a result quite contrary to our initial expectations. For example, some argue that entry into a second career is possible at 55 but extremely difficult, if not impossible, at 60. The five years are crucial. Excessive haste may well result in our overlooking such important facts.

In other words, even if one assumes that the present system of compulsory retirement at the age of 55 is no longer desirable, it is wise

[1] Two white papers are particularly important, one from the Sōhyō-based Shuntō Kyōtō Iinkai (Spring Offensive Joint Struggle Committee) and one from Dōmei. Each publishes its own annual white paper entitled *Chingin Hakusho* [White Paper on Wages] several months before the spring wage offensive begins. In addition to these, white papers are published by the Japan Council of the International Metalworkers' Federation and by Nikkeiren.

to be fully aware of the multifarious aspects of social change. An awareness of all the ramifications of change is of the utmost importance. The
remaining sections of this paper will focus on some aspects of the discussion on the retirement age in light of my own research in this area.

2. Career Employment and the Retirement System

It is common knowledge that the Japanese approach to retirement is
unique among industrialized societies. In Europe and North America
there certainly are examples where employees retire upon reaching a
certain age, either voluntarily or in compliance with company regula-
tions. However, in these instances the retirement age is 65 or above.
Moreover, the social significance of retirement abroad differs considerably from that in Japan. In these other societies the decision to
retire is seen as an indication that one has reached the end of his productive years in the labor force. The decision means that one is retiring
from *the labor force* itself. There is thus a certain rationale to the
decision to retire.

In the case of Japan, however, retirement at the early age of 55
indicates retirement from *a particular firm*, not retirement from the
labor force. In Japan, employees who still possess the ability and the desire to continue working in a productive fashion are summarily dismissed or compelled to retire. This approach to personnel management
has been institutionalized over the years, and is now viewed legally as
a kind of voluntary retirement which is part of a long-term agreement
whereby the firm guarantees employment to the individual until that
age; such retirement is in fact compulsory from the position of the
individual employee. The fact that the system of compulsory retirement
at 55 has received much criticism within Japan in recent years needs
no substantiation. The responses of the retired to surveys focusing
upon their living conditions and their sentiments are well publicized.
The criticism is indeed a quite natural outcome of rising life expec-
tancies and other changes occurring within Japanese society.

The uniqueness of the Japanese system is also intricately tied to a
number of other characteristically Japanese institutions. The system of
career employment sometimes referred to as lifetime employment and
the seniority-merit wage system come readily to mind. On the interrelationship of these various institutions, Nikkeiren argues that

> the system of a fixed retirement age cannot be understood apart

from the practice of lifetime employment and the seniority-merit wage system. The guarantee of firms to employ individuals until a certain age and the willingness of individuals to retire at that age has in the past allowed for necessary adjustments in the firm's personnel levels.[2]

One might enlarge upon this opinion by citing the views of Ohbori Teruji:

> For the employee, employment has meant a guarantee of career employment. This has in turn implied a moral commitment to work for the duration of one's career with a given firm. For the employer, the decision to employ an individual has meant that once the decision to employ is made there is a moral obligation to throw one's lot in with that of the worker for better or for worse unless there is some overriding consideration imposed upon the firm from the outside by forces beyond the control of the firm.
>
> In this system it is natural for employees to think in terms of maintaining the continuity of the firm by preparing for the next generation to gradually take over the running of the firm. Thus, in the very assumption of employment there is an understanding that retirement will occur at a certain age. This is the system of retirement.[3]

He goes on to point out that

> the postwar courts have handed down a number of judgments which argue that the practice of lifetime employment, an approach to personnel management which was first introduced by management purely out of a moral sense of duty, has become generally accepted as a social practice requiring that there be more than adequate reason before an employee is fired or otherwise dismissed. Given this broad interpretation of the right of the employee to be continuously employed by the same employer, compulsory retirement at the age of 55 has become the only recognized exception to the accepted obligation of the employer to continuously employ a regular employee.[4]

[2] Nikkeiren, Chūkōnen Mondai Shoiinkai (The Subcommittee on the Problems of Middle-aged and Older Workers), *Teinen Enchō Mondai ni Kansuru Kenkai* [Views on the Problems of Extending the Age of Retirement] (Tokyo: Nikkeiren, March 1973), p. 3.

[3] Ohbori Teruji, *Teinen Seido* [The Retirement System] (Tokyo: Rōdō Hōrei Kyōkai, 1968), pp. 11–12.

[4] Ohbori, *Teinen Seido*, p. 50.

With regard to this relationship between the fixed-age retirement system and the practice of career employment, two general characteristics should be mentioned. First, the system of career employment is closely linked with paternalistic management and the family system. Once the firm is seen as a united, family-like group, the transition to being an organization with a built-in system of retirement is easy. When the head of a family has served his full time as head of the family, the eldest son will have been nurtured to maturity and the senior figure will be able to hand over his position as household head to his son and look forward to a comfortable life in retirement. In the same fashion, the older worker in the firm hands over his position to a younger employee. In return, the enterprise awards the older worker with a lump sum payment on retirement to show its gratitude for his many years of hard work. In other words, the retirement system has emerged as a way of handing down the top positions from one generation to the next. The original rationale for this system can be found in the proposals for a typically Japanese system of remuneration based upon scientific principles and the concept of a lifetime earnings profile (the so-called "livelihood wage").[5]

However, the conditions for maintaining this kind of system which assures career employment, indeed lifetime employment, are no longer present. We are now in a period when the nuclear family has become the standard and the older paternalistic family system is breaking down. The retirement age of 55 more or less matched the life expectancy of the average worker in the Taishō period, whereas life expectancy is now over 70 for men. An equivalent system today would call for a retirement age of perhaps 65.

---

[5] See, for example, Godō Takuo's *Shokkō Kyūyo Hyōjun Seitei no Yō* [The Essentials of Standardized Wage Systems for Workers], which was published in 1922. He gives the following description:

> From birth until the age of fifty-five there is a close relationship between income and life-cycle needs, between one's salary and his age. For example, there was the average man working at the munitions factory who, at age thirty-nine, would find his eldest son graduating from primary school and entering an apprenticeship at the same munitions factory. At age forty-three his oldest son would finish his apprenticeship, and his fourth child (second son) would graduate from primary school and follow his older brother into an apprenticeship at the munitions factory. At forty-seven his second son would have finished the appreticeship, and at fifty-two his eldest son would marry to produce a granddaughter the following year. Finally, at fifty-five the employee would be greeted with a grandson upon retirement. In this way the life cycle was conceived."

This quote is from Magota Ryōhei, *Nenkō Chingin no Ayumi to Shōrai* [The History and Future of Japan's Seniority Wage System] (Tokyo: Sangyō Rōdō Chōsa Jo, 1970), p. 272.

In addition to this historical background, a full understanding requires an awareness of the relationship between the fixed-age retirement system and the system of retirement allowances. The Japanese approach seems to be unique. Despite the differing theories as to the true nature of the allowances in the prewar period, one cannot understand the prewar system without being aware of the very sizeable lump sums paid out by the largest firms, sums which are unimaginable by today's standards.[6] Given the status system which existed before the war, qualification for the career employment system was limited to a small number of white-collar employees for whom it was possible to guarantee "a comfortable life in retirement." For the system to work as an established institution, a very handsome lump sum payment upon retirement was essential. In contrast to the prewar period, today all employees in large companies now participate in the system. It is thus impossible to guarantee all "a comfortable life" upon retirement. The postwar period is thus different from the prewar period in a number of respects, and the relationship between career employment practices and the system of retirement pay has weakened considerably.

This fact is linked to a second characteristic which appears for the first time in the postwar period: the system of career employment which has generally tied the hands of employers in laying off employees. Since employees have had to carry unproductive persons on their payrolls, compulsory retirement at a fixed age has become the only means whereby they can make the necessary adjustments. Statistics suggest that the system of fixed-aged retirement began to spread during the early part of the Shōwa period and again after the Second World War. Both periods were times when depressed business conditions forced severe retrenchments in personnel levels. These were also periods when retirement pay became less generous and fixed-age retirement became more firmly entrenched.

Given the tendency to associate closely the fixed-age retirement system with the postwar system of career employment, many feel that career employment itself is responsible for the retirement age being set at 55. Management has firmly based its position upon this kind of thinking, and there are not a few labor leaders who would take a

---

[6] In Kawada Hachirō's *Kaishain Kyūyo Shirabe* [An Investigation of Salaries of Company Employees] (Tokyo: Tokyo Keizai Sha, 1925), the lump sum payment made upon retirement by the largest firms was equal to between 120 and 150 months' regular pay for employees who had worked thirty years for the same firm. Among the firms surveyed there were even some which paid up to 250 months' salary as a retirement allowance. The average amount paid today by large firms (with over 1,000 employees) to employees with thirty years' service is equal only to about thirty months' salary. In smaller firms, the amount is less.

similar view. Nevertheless, there is a big error in such a conclusion. To be sure, the retirement age of 55 and the practice of career employment were closely linked together in the prewar period. However, the situation today is quite different; in several respects the early retirement age denies the continued existence of "lifetime employment", and it certainly makes a joke out of the word "lifetime". Indeed, the rationale of those who first institutionalized career employment depends on firms paying a retirement allowance which would cover the needs of retiring employees for the rest of their lives. This could be done by raising the retirement age to 65.

The literature on the retirement system compounds the problem by lending credence to the belief that management is constrained in adjusting personnel levels solely by the practice of career employment. While it is reasonable to acknowledge the differences in the way employment is viewed by Japanese and Western Europeans, one must not exaggerate the importance of these differences. To do so only hinders our understanding of the problems facing Japan. In Europe and America there are many examples of hiring and firing according to criteria such as job performance or job commitment; but taken overall the number of people so treated is quite small. Most employees are able to work at the same job until they retire. Systematic or "forced" retirement before the age of 65 is rare, and the practice of seniority rights protects the jobs of those who have held them for long periods of time. Indeed, in some ways overseas practices do more to guarantee lifetime or career employment than do employment practices in Japan. Moreover, despite the lip service given to the practice of career employment in Japan, personnel retrenchments do occur, and in the vast majority of the cases it is the worker with seniority who is asked to leave even before the compulsory retirement age. Finally, both in Japan and abroad there are a number of court decisions on cases involving dismissals. Everywhere the right of the employer to dismiss employees is limited, and employers have reacted by criticizing the courts for interpreting too broadly restrictions concerning the firm's responsibility in providing employment. This fact does not so much reflect the spread of career employment as it does general changes occurring in social norms.

For this reason it is easy to understand why even today management continues to feel a moral obligation to maintain employment levels. It is a commonly recognized value throughout industrialized societies. We are even quite prepared to accept lower levels of productivity as a trade-off for greater employment security. Nevertheless, we must also realize that the normative commitment to career employment has been one of the ideological underpinnings of the Japanese system of labor-management relations. It has contributed in no small way to the growth of the large firm sector: a balance sheet of the pluses and minuses of career employment would clearly show tremendous over-all advantages for the large Japanese firms.

It should be clear that the fixed age of 55 (or even 60) for retirement does not have to be part of a trade-off for the guarantee of career employment. Not only does the fixed retirement age of 55 tend to undermine the system of career employment; given the situation today, the benefits generally associated with the guarantee of career employment no longer cover the costs of early retirement for the work-er. Moreover, the guarantee in Japan is not as extensive as most people believe, and considerable guarantees do in fact exist overseas without the system of early retirement. If the concern with career employment continues to be an obstacle to the extension of the retirement age or even its abolition, then it is high time we set about the task of ridding ourselves of such misconceptions. The first step in this direction is the realization that the right to dismiss employees is limited not by the continued presence of some system of career employment, but rather by the overwhelming sense of public concern which is embodied in the social norms of the times. To this end it might well be useful to consider a "Dismissals Restriction Act".[7]

3. The Fixed-age Retirement System and the Seniority-Merit Wage System

Given the fact that the fixed-age retirement system spread most rapidly and was institutionalized primarily in the early years of the Shōwa period and in the years immediately after the war, the institutionaliza-tion of the seniority-merit wage system would seem to have no direct bearing on the problem. The latter system was really institutionalized after 1955, although a scheme with certain similarities can be found for white-collar employees in the prewar period and then again right after the war in the age-based livelihood wage systems, such as that in the electric power industry, often demanded by the labor unions.

[7] It has been suggested that one good way to abolish retirement systems of a compulsory nature, particularly those which require retirement before the age of 60, is to publicize the fact that such systems are in contravention of public morals and therefore antisocial in nature. See Shimada Nobuyoshi, "Teinensei Gōrikaron no Hōteki Hihan" [A Legal Criticism of the Discussion on Rationalizing the Retirement System], *Kikan Rōdō Hō* (vol. 22, no. 4: December 1972), pp. 59–72.

It is important to remember, however, that the major objective of management in introducing the fixed-age retirement system in both periods was personnel retrenchment.

Regardless of these historical facts, the seniority-merit wage system is often cited today as a major obstacle to the extension of the retirement age beyond 55.[8] It is clearly felt by many that the seniority-merit wage system insures that older workers will receive a salary which is disproportionately large compared with their skills and the content of their jobs. Extension of the retirement age, it is argued, would serve only to widen the gap between income and output, thereby pushing personnel costs to unbearable levels. Consequently, many firms have adopted "reemployment" schemes whereby individuals are officially retired with the right to continue working for the same firm, often in the same job, but without the guaranteed wage increases they enjoyed before retirement. Statistics on these new arrangements show that 59 percent of the reemployed continue to do the same work, but 76 percent experience a drop in status and 52 percent experience a drop in salary. If we include those who do not suffer wage cuts but also do not receive the customary wage increase given annually to all employees, it is clear that the large majority of rehired retirees experience a drop in real income.[9]

Management's argument for early retirement owing to the gap between the older employee's wages and his productivity is quite narrow-minded and wholly in the interests of management. If at the other end of the age continuum young employees give much more in terms of productivity than they receive in wages, the pyramidal age composition of the labor force (the fact that younger employees clearly outnumber those in the older age brackets) guarantees that management has received more labor than it has paid for. The gap between productivity and wages among younger workers has more than offset any over-

---

[8] For example, one survey of employers taken by Nikkeiren suggests that a major factor preventing a rise in the fixed age for retirement was the existence of the seniority-merit wage system. In response to a question asking for the major difficulties in making such a change, the following factors were cited most frequently:

The presence of the seniority-merit wage system	75.3%
The presence of a seniority-merit promotion scheme	55.6%
The growth of retirement allowances	55.4%
The low productivity of older workers	37.9%

See Nikkeiren, *Teinensei ni Kansuru Ankēto Chōsa Kekka* [Results of a Survey on Retirement Systems] (Tokyo: Nikkeiren, November 1972), p. 3.

[9] Rōdō Daijin Kanbō Tōkei Jōhō Bu (Statistics and Information Department, Minister's Secretariat, Ministry of Labour), *Shōwa 45 Nen Koyō Kanri Chōsa* [The 1970 Survey of Personnel Practices] (Tokyo: Rōdō Daijin Kanbō Tōkei Jōhō Bu, 1971), p. 18.

payment to older employees. The higher wages paid to the older worker are in part a return for the relatively low wages paid to him when he was younger. Accordingly, it is difficult to substantiate the frequently heard argument among management that the older worker is overpaid. If management wishes to rationalize wage rates for older workers on the grounds of productivity, the only fair thing to do is to rationalize wage rates for everyone and pay younger workers higher rates in keeping with their higher productivity. However, the switchover is not quite so easy. One cannot simply pay the younger worker in accordance with his productivity and then reduce wage payments to the older worker. The older worker has already put in his thirty years with the firm under the old seniority-merit criteria and must still be compensated for all those years of hard work with low pay and nothing more than the expectation of something better to come in the future. For this reason the transition to a system in which pay is commensurate with the work load will require a considerable amount of time. In the process of changing over to such a rationalized system of wage payments, the income of the older worker, an income which was earned some time in the past, should not be sacrificed in order to raise the wages being paid to the younger employee. In order to make the shift and thereby lower the income of the older worker in relative terms, it will be necessary for firms to establish some kind of special fund for compensating older employees— or, as a more serious attempt to come to grips with the whole problem of the retiree in society, to have the government take the lead in guaranteeing that the older worker will be covered in terms of housing and the costs of sending his children on for a higher education.

For these reasons, the policies suggested in the chapter entitled "Wages" in the above-mentioned report of the Research Group on Wages can be criticized for inviting a number of misunderstandings. The report looks forward to a shift away from the seniority-merit wage system towards a system based upon productivity and specific skills, and argues that certain difficulties inherent in the fixed-age retirement system can be remedied by introducing such a system. The report goes on to conclude that "it is doubtful whether it is necessary to be continuously raising the worker's wages until the age of 55 simply because the number of the years with the firm is increasing. In any case, there is certainly no reason why the seniority-merit principle needs to be implemented for all employees beyond the age of 55."[10]

[10] For additional comments on the report itself, see Rōdō Kijun Kyoku (Bureau of Labor Standards), Ministry of Labour, *Shūkyū Futsukasei, Yoka, Teinensei* [The Two-day Weekend, Leisure and the Fixed-age Retirement System] Tokyo: Nihon Rōdō Kyōkai, February 1973), p. 117 onwards.

I personally support the move toward a wage system stressing the productivity and skills of the employee. However, in making the transition to such a system, it is important to consider fully how a new wage system will tie in with life-cycle needs and the concept of a livelihood wage, concepts which were at the core of the older seniority-merit wage system. Until the nation's various social security and social welfare programs can guarantee the most important life-cycle needs of the average household (and the examples of Europe and the United States suggest that it will be impossible to meet all needs), I feel it is necessary for us to retain certain parts of the seniority-merit wage system. In other words, although business is clearly moving toward the adoption of productivity-based wage differentials, it is important that we don't go overboard and do away completely with the seniority component until an appropriate replacement is found. A balance between life-cycle needs and productivity requirements should be maintained.

The real problem lies in how the seniority component, or that part of the wage package tied to life-cycle needs, is retained. The report of the Research Group on Wages states that this component need not be paid until the age of 55 and indeed argues that it should be cut off at a younger age. The real intention of the report was that the standard of living now guaranteed at age 55 ought to be provided at a much earlier age. The report does not specify what that earlier age should be, nor does it define the appropriate standard of living. The action sought by the Research Group on Wages is nearly the same as that demanded by many labor unions, which also suggest that a higher standard ought to be guaranteed at an earlier age. For this reason it is a little difficult to understand why labor's Joint Spring Offensive Struggle Committee should criticize the Group for ignoring the problem of the wage level to be guaranteed for the older worker.[11]

Looking next at the age payment system itself, one should be aware that a productivity component is already added to most seniority wage systems. In theory the productivity component is calculated according to the worker's actual output or productivity, and the payment of this component ought to change as the worker's job responsibilities change. According to the report of the Research Group on Wages, which wrongly accepts the case presented by management, the productivity component must be strengthened as the retirement age is extended

[11] Shuntō Kyōtō Iinkai (The Spring Offensive Joint Struggle Committee), Chingin Semmon Iinkai (The Specialist Committee on Wages), "Chingin Kenkyūkai, Teinen Enchō to Chingin Seido ni Tsuite" [On the Research Group on Wages, Extension of the Fixed Age for Retirement, and the Wage System], *Sōhyō Chōsa Geppō* (no. 79: April 1973), p. 19.

because the wage system is intricately connected with personnel policies. However, changes in the level of wages resulting from personnel transfers within the firm are not tied so closely to the fixed age for retirement. Personnel administration involves much more. Changes in status, promotions, and personnel transfers within the firm are also a very fundamental part of personnel practices and as such are directly related to the level of wages.

When a system of personnel management based upon productivity is replaced by one which emphasizes the seniority principle, extension of the retirement age is accompanied by the accumulation of redundant personnel in upper positions and the lowering of morale due to the decrease in opportunities for promotion among younger employees. Moreover, when seniority is stressed as the basic guiding principle in personnel practices related to the promotion and allocation of employees, the wage system will also come to reward seniority despite official documents acclaiming the importance of job-related criteria or occupational skills. Consequently, the disadvantages of a seniority wage system are soon added to those of seniority personnel practices related to the promotion and allocation of employees: in addition to the undesirable effects on personal motivation and productivity, the costs of expensive seniority payments must be borne.

Accordingly, personnel structures (*e.g.* promotion and assignment criteria) based upon seniority principles are also considered major obstacles to extending the retirement age. Indeed, it is argued that such personnel practices are much more important than the seniority wage system in this regard, and thus that it is necessary to retain the present system of fixed-age retirement in order to offset the disadvantages arising from the seniority-based system of personnel management.

However, the argument that the fixed-age retirement system is necessary because the seniority principle is embedded in Japan's personnel practices resembles the argument for retaining the present retirement system because wages are tied to the employee's age. Both involve the same type of *non sequitur*. If the seniority wage system and seniority personnel management practices are no longer suited to the needs of today, they should be abandoned. If an extension of the retirement age is somehow incompatible with the seniority wage system or the seniority principle of personnel management, then an effort ought to be made to revise these practices. One can even argue that the very existence of the fixed-age retirement system itself works to conceal the shortcomings of the seniority wage system and the seniority approach to personnel management, and thereby to preserve these two institutions. It is therefore important that we take advantage of the opportunity being presented by the demands for the extension or even the abolition of the fixed age for retirement to completely rationalize these two institutions.

4. Lump Sum Retirement Allowances and Pension Schemes

Another problem presented by extensions in the retirement age involves the retirement allowance. The present formula for calculating the retirement allowance emphasizes the number of years worked at a given enterprise. Additional years worked before retirement will mean larger retirement allowances and, therefore, management resistance. On the other hand, some suggest that a significant increase in the retirement age would allow for retirement in the true sense since the retiree would be able to receive a social security pension immediately upon retirement. Accordingly, it is argued that the lump sum normally paid by the firm should be converted into a pension to supplement that received from the government. The report of the Research Group on Wages states that the retirement allowance ideally serves not only to provide daily sustenance for the retiree's remaining years but also to provide him with enough funds to purchase a home and bear the costs of higher education for his children. For this reason, the report argues, the present system of making lump sum payments ought to be continued for the time being. However, the choice between lump sum payments and pension schemes involves several other considerations.

With regard to the various social security pension schemes, it should be pointed out that the bill presently before the Diet calls for some form of indexation tied to the cost of living. Wage agreements in private industry will also likely provide some form of indexation. These developments will require similar mechanism for any private pension scheme which firms might establish. Without indexation, employees would certainly choose to receive the customary lump sum upon retirement. However, various considerations prevent the firm from guaranteeing indexed pension payments.

Returning to the first point, it is interesting to note that the Research Group on Wages argues for a review of the practice which has retirement allowances increasing geometrically for each additional year worked by the most senior employees. At least there is no need, the Group's report says, to accelerate increases after the age of 55. This point also invites misunderstanding. The real concern is that the maintenance of geometric increases becomes a barrier to the free flow of labor between firms. The intention of the Research Group on Wages was not to argue for lower retirement allowances. The stance taken on this point is essentially the same as that taken on changing the seniority wage curve so that the peak will occur at an earlier age. We will return to the problem of labor mobility in the next section; here we need only underline the Group's view that "to protect the employee's opportunities for changing jobs it is important for employers to implement a system in which persons working a certain minimum period with the firm can leave the firm of their own volition and still receive the full retirement allowance without undue prejudice."[12]

5. Early Retirement

Japan has set for itself the goal of changing the fixed retirement age from 55 to 60. Those involved are now groping for the various conditions under which this goal can be achieved. However, in terms of improving the welfare of the older worker while also better utilizing his labor for the economy (concerns which initially prompted us to deal with the problem), a mere shift in the fixed retirement age from 55 to 60 may be quite shortsighted.

Such revision serves only to stabilize the life of the employee for an additional five years and thereby simply postpones the problem of retirement until the age of 60. Moreover, the difficulty of finding new employment is much greater at 60 than at 55. From this perspective, it would seem more reasonable to speed the age of retirement so that the individual could successfully make the transition to a second career.

A major unknown, however, is hidden in the psychological and cultural strain accompanying compulsory retirement. One survey of retirees in the United States suggests that, regardless of occupation, job status, social status, or relative economic well-being, retirees show the symptoms of psychological strain, feelings of failure, worthlessness, anxiety, and a certain irritability.[13] One researcher who has interviewed Japanese retirees aged between 55 and 60 suggests that their psychological state is not too different from that of retirees aged between

[12] Persons leaving the firm before the accepted retirement age of 55 are at a marked disadvantage if they leave at their own convenience. If they leave at the suggestion of the firm, however, they are more likely to receive full retirement benefits. There is thus a compulsion to remain with the firm until the normal retirement age (which has been 55 in most firms) or until some other appropriate age designated by the firm.

[13] Paul W. Boynton, *Six Ways to Retire*, third edition (New York: Harper and Row, 1952).

65 and 70 in the United States.[14] There is also Parkinson's suggestion that people lose interest in their work three years before retirement.[15] In other words, concern with retirement may well influence the productivity of the worker even before he retires. One might conclude from these studies that no further thought should be given to early retirement. Carrying this line of reasoning even further, one might argue that, from the perspective of maintaining human dignity, the various programs of reemployment currently being introduced by many private enterprises are also doomed to failure.

A compulsory retirement age of 60 is no doubt better than one of 55, but the shift from one to the other is only an intermediate step and will not by itself solve the fundamental problems. With the fixed retirement age at 60, neither private enterprises nor the government will be able to provide the retiree with a satisfying life style comparable to that enjoyed by salaried employees in the large firms before the war. Moreover, the later retirement age will worsen the retiree's prospects of finding suitable reemployment. Consequently, it is imperative that we think through carefully the meaning of retirement and the full implications of the system of compulsory or fixed-age retirement found in Japan.

During the 1950s a similar discussion occurred in the United States. A most important aspect of that debate was the attention given to the concept of retirement. Here one might consider the definition given by E. H. Moore, who argues that retirement in the true sense represents the individual's decision midway through life to give up his past work in order to enjoy a freer and more leisurely life style. This implies that a large share of his income must derive from sources other than wages, salary, or profits directly tied to his labor input.[16]

This concept of retirement coincides with the traditional concept of a "comfortable life in retirement" envisioned by the large firms in the prewar period. However, Moore suggests that the institutionalization of earlier retirement will result in a more enjoyable or fulfilling retirement. He thus gives positive encouragement to early retirement.

Another important focus of the discussion in the United States concerns the system of compulsory or fixed-age retirement. In general, the labor movement has been against compulsory mechanisms that

[14] Douglas Sparks, in an oral report to the study team on the retirement system set up by the Labor Economics Research Subgroup at the Japan Institute of Labour (Tokyo: Chūtaikin Building, 1972).

[15] For example, see G. Hamilton Crook and Martin Heinstein, *The Older Worker in Industry* (Berkeley: The Institute of Industrial Relations Institute, University of California, 1958).

[16] Elon H. Moore, *The Nature of Retirement* (New York: Macmillan, 1959).

"force" early retirement. Although the younger worker has supported the concept of a compulsory retirement age, the union leadership formally has come out in opposition to such systems and actually has been more concerned with the establishment of adequate pension schemes despite the increased economic burden on the workers.

Both the leadership and the younger members are concerned with job protection and the expansion of the younger worker's opportunities for promotion. In considering this example from the United States, however, we must not overlook the extent to which the general institutionalization of the seniority system operates to fully protect the older worker's right to his job. In other words, the system of fixed-age retirement is seen as an integral part of a highly sophisticated arrangement which also guarantees employment, and the two are supported together as a set. In Japan it is the system of career employment which is closely linked with the system of fixed-age retirement. Accordingly, the approach to voluntary retirement at an early age adopted in the United States can be seen as one way of minimizing the problems which arise in providing both guaranteed employment and fixed-age retirement.[17]

It is often said that the American worker considers it quite natural for his job and income to change as his abilities change. Moreover, unlike his Japanese counterpart, he is able to accept a job with less status without a loss of face. Nevertheless, despite this positive attitude, it is clear that a sudden drop in income is a serious problem.[18] Accordingly, some economic guarantee must accompany early retirement. In 1964 the United Auto Workers took a big step forward in concluding agreements calling for an early retirement pension scheme. By 1972 the system had evolved to a point where all employees with thirty years' work experience could retire. This was the so-called "thirty-and-out" pension scheme. Those who retired at the age of 56 received a monthly income of $500.00 until age 62. From 62 until 65 the worker was guaranteed a monthly income of $450.00, excluding his social security pension. From age 65 the worker received, in addition to his social security benefits, a private pension of $171.00.[19] This type of early

[17] For example, see Melvin K. Bers, *Union Policy and the Older Worker* (Berkeley: Industrial Relations Research Institute, University of California, 1957), or The [California] Governor's Council, *Employment and Retirement of the Older Worker* (Berkeley: Industrial Relations Research Institute, University of California, 1959).

[18] Richard Barfield and James Morgan, *Early Retirement* (Ann Arbor: University of Michigan, Institute for Social Research, 1969).

[19] For a detailed explanation of the United Auto Workers' Scheme, see Barfield and Morgan, *Early Retirement*. The following table indicates the monthly amounts paid at various ages for different retirement ages, as outlined in the union's 1971 agreement and which become effective on October 1, 1972:

retirement scheme has in recent years spread to other industries; by 1968 more than 49 percent of all workers receiving pensions had retired early.

The report of the Research Group on Wages is concerned with limiting the extent to which such institutions as career employment and the seniority wage system discourage early retirement. However, if early retirement is to be promoted, it is important that early retirees be given conditions of retirement which are not too different from those afforded employees working straight through until the fixed age for retirement. It is also important that attention be given to the need for education, occupational training, and various kinds of facilities. This fact was also emphasized by the various reports coming out of groups associated with the Ministry of Labour. However, acceptance of the findings, which suggest that the problem of insufficient income is the major constraint preventing employees from retiring early, implies the need for a radically new approach similar to that taken in the United States. For example, an increase in the lump sum retirement allowance for early retirees or the payment of a monthly pension may be necessary.

Many are quick to argue that such a system would invite the most able employees to retire early, leaving the firm with the non-productive employees. This view merely underlines the lack of confidence on the part of those responsible for personnel management. Indeed, if we accept the fact that the inter-firm mobility characteristic of the United States is

Age at which retirement occurs	Current age of pension recipient		
	Until 62	62–65 not including 80% of social security benefits to which the individual is entitled	Over 65 not including the full social security benefits to which the the individual is entitled
62		450	225
61	500	450	216
60	500	450	207
59	500	450	198
58	500	450	189
57	500	450	180
56	500	450	171
55	460	414	162
48	180	162	99

Taken from United Auto Workers, ed., *UAW—Jidōsha Sangyō Kōshō ni Kansuru Hōkokusho: 1970–1973 Nen Shin Kyōyaku no Gaiyō* [The UAW's Report on Collective Bargaining in the Auto Industry: A Summary of the 1970–1973 Agreement] (Tokyo: International Metalworkers' Federation—Japan Council, 1971).

becoming the backbone of personnel management practices which stress productivity, such fears are unwarranted. The very proposition that the ablest employees would leave the enterprise suggests that the firm should develop programs for raising the productivity of employees who are presently working below their full potential. Moreover, higher turnover rates should motivate younger workers to work all the harder since the chances for early promotion would be enhanced. On this point, it is important to remember that we are concerned with the overall utilization of labor for the national economy as a whole, not for the individual firm. A good example of how this has worked in Japan can be found in the civil service, which does not have a fixed-age system of compulsory retirement but does provide for the full payment of pensions at age 55 and partial payment before that age. One result is that many talented persons do leave the civil service early and take jobs in private enterprises.[20] It is clear that the bureaucracy has maintained a very high level of efficiency, and part of the secret to that success no doubt lies in this system of early retirement. Here we have a system already in operation not too unlike that established by the United Auto Workers in the United States.

In considering extension of the retirement age, it is important to look beyond the problem of employment guarantees. It is also necessary to consider carefully the concept of a second career and the consequences of a sudden change in life style. From this perspective the concept of early retirement assumes a new importance: it implies a new way of looking at the problem of retirement and its relationship to the whole process of aging. Since our way of thinking about these problems is ultimately closely tied to more general attitudes found in society at large, it may be difficult for us to change our notions about the retirement system overnight. Nevertheless, the very difficulties embodied in such change mean that systematic institutional changes are indeed necessary.

Moreover, whether a pension system is introduced or lump sum retirement payments are used, it is certain that the problem of rising personnel costs will be aggravated. Indeed, management opposes an extension of the retirement age because personnel costs will rise. It is here, perhaps, that a shift in thinking is most needed. The recent revaluation of the yen was in part tied to the problem of very low labor costs. Moreover, the increase in costs associated with the introduction

---

[20] So many high-level bureaucrats switch at around age 55 to responsible positions in private industries (often the companies they regulated as government officials) that a term has been coined to describe the practice: *amakudari*—literally, descending from heaven.

of the two-day weekend, the shortening of working hours, and the extension of the retirement age are part of the necessary cost involved in realizing a socially accepted standard of living and work for all employees. Accordingly, these broader considerations must be given priority over narrower concern with the post-revaluation policies for dealing with inflation. The costs associated with early retirement schemes and other revisions in the retirement system will be great, and they must be considered in the same package with wages. On this point there is much to learn from the United Auto Workers experience.

6. The Future of Fixed-age Retirement: A Proposal for a "Flex-age" System

An early retirement system is by definition one which encourages the employee to retire voluntarily before he reaches an age at which retirement is compulsory or before the age at which he can receive some form of social security or a public pension. In recent years such systems seem to be designed to keep people active in the work force even beyond the customary retirement age, which in most European countries is the age at which persons qualify for their public pensions.[21] In other words, by increasing the benefits paid by private and public pension schemes, individuals are encouraged to continue working, a result which might seem contrary to the whole notion of early retirement. However, at least with regard to the system of public pensions, it is desirable to view early retirement as the gateway to a second job or career which can be continued after the commonly accepted retirement age. A system of early retirement also may include the payment of limited amounts before one qualifies for the full amount of the public pension.

Given the emphasis on full employment and full utilization of a nation's manpower resources, the concern with promoting employment beyond the common age for retirement is most prevalent where labor shortages exist. Moreover, a growing amount of research in recent years has suggested that retirees feel alienated from society once they are not working or otherwise contributing to the social good. It thus behooves us to consider as a general social problem the need to supply senior citizens with meaningful jobs.

From this perspective, then, the whole idea of an appropriate retire-

[21] Organisation for Economic Co-operation and Development, *Flexibility of Retirement Age* (Paris: OECD, 1970).

ment age may be changed. The productivity of the individual employee obviously depends upon both the content of his job and his own capabilities. Accordingly, there is no single retirement age which is appropriate for everyone, and, ironically, the fixed-age retirement system clearly underlines this fact.

Those dealing with this problem in Japan have tended to overemphasize the importance of extending the fixed age for retirement from 55 to 60. Even if we accept that this is an inevitable, perhaps even necessary, step in revising the system, it somehow seems that a more fundamental review of the problem from a long-term perspective is required. Grave consequences are built into any discussion of the retirement problem which assumes that the institutions of career employment and seniority wages are a given. Such an approach inevitably prevents us from considering the real options which, other things being equal, will give the individual employee the optimal system. It will rather result in a mere shift in the fixed age for retirement from 55 to 60 without any significant change in the compulsory or coercive aspects of the system. In other words, our efforts will serve only to rigidify the present system. Rather than solving the problem of the older employee, we only postpone it for five years, after which time the inevitable transition becomes even more excruciating.

Recognizing the need for a flexible approach integrating the two concepts of early and delayed retirement, I would like to propose serious consideration of a "flex-age" retirement system. Such a system is not suggested as a panacea for the older employee; nor would it involve only minor costs. However, from the viewpoint both of better serving the individual employee and of improving the system of labor-management relations, I feel a new approach to retirement is required.

Employment and Unemployment: 1970 to 1975

Nishikawa Shunsaku and Shimada Haruo

1.   Macroeconomic Changes and Employment

This paper examines the levels of employment and unemployment in Japan between 1970 and 1975. We will first discuss the more conspicuous changes which have occurred in the demand for and supply of labor, and then consider the trend toward shorter working hours during this period.

The decade following 1960 was characterized by a high economic growth rate. Measured in terms of gross national product at fixed prices, the Japanese economy grew at an annual rate of 10.7 percent. Since the number employed increased only 1.4 percent annually, GNP per employed person grew at an annual rate of about 9.3 percent. During the same period, wholesale prices rose 1.3 percent annually, and consumer prices at a rate of 5.9 percent. The relative stability in wholesale prices reflected the sustained expansion of mining and manufacturing (13.2 percent annually) and the rapid increase in labor productivity (10.5 percent annually). The rise in consumer prices, on the other hand, was generated by wage hikes and rising transportation costs which were not offset by the meager increases in productivity in the sectors producing consumer goods and services.

The overall performance of the Japanese economy between 1960 and 1970 was fairly good. Since that time, however, the economy has ex-

An earlier version of this paper was read at the Seminar held by the Japan-German Cultural Exchange Association in Tokyo on October 8, 1975. The paper itself was originally published under the same title in *Keio Business Review* (no. 13: 1974), pp. 43–58. The authors are Professors of Economics at Keio University.

perienced a number of setbacks, beginning with the "Nixon shock" in 1971. Nixon's surprise freeing of the dollar-gold exchange rate was followed immediately by a crisis in the international monetary system, and Japan's economy was rocked by world-wide inflation and sharp rises in import prices for foodstuffs and raw materials. However, it was the oil crisis in late 1973 which really started the Japanese economy off on a course of erratic change. The recession in 1972 and the somewhat abnormal boom in 1973 were followed by a slump in 1974. The impact of these shocks from abroad was amplified by the very belated response of the government in developing policies to immunize Japan from the spread of inflation overseas.

Table 1 gives a breakdown of gross national expenditure (GNE) and shows the implicit deflator for selected years beginning with 1955. It also gives the annual rate of change in these figures for the four years since 1970. The right-hand half of the table suggests that the fluctuations in the rate of capital formation in both the public and private sectors have been more pronounced in recent years. After a long period of stability, wholesale prices began to increase appreciably late in 1973, and in the first half of 1974 they increased at an annual rate of more than 35 percent. Consumer prices increased 20 to 25 percent during the same period. Accordingly, real wages began to drop, decreasing at an annual rate of 4.1 percent in March 1974. Carried out under such circumstances, the spring wage offensive resulted in large wage hikes of up to 33 percent. Well in advance of the spring wage offensive, the government requested that both labor and management show restraint in readjusting wage rates. After the huge wage increases in the spring of 1974, the government strengthened its efforts to promote price stability. Its austerity measures included cutbacks in government spending and a tight money policy. As a result, the pace of inflation eventually slowed. The rate of increase in wholesale prices fell below 20 percent by the fourth quarter of 1974, while that in consumer prices returned to about 20 percent by the beginning of 1975 and dropped to 15 percent fairly early in the year.

These dramatic changes were accompanied by a substantial decline in the demand for labor. Many firms took steps to save on labor costs. Overtime was reduced and partial or temporary shutdowns occurred. In the latter half of 1974, unemployment increased sharply. According to the Labor Force Survey, unemployed persons in fiscal 1974 numbered 790,000, the highest level in fifteen years. The number of employed persons declined to 51.85 million, the first absolute decline in the work force since the Labor Force Survey was initiated in 1948. By March 1975 the unemployed had increased to 1.12 million, up by 230,000 or 25

Table 1:   Changes in Selected Components of Japan's GNE

(in 1970 yen)

	In trillion yen					Annual rate of change (%)				
	1955	1960	1965	1970	1973	1970	1971	1972	1973	1974
1. Personal consumption	10.50	15.28	23.45	36.26	45.97	7.8	7.3	9.2	8.1	1.4
2. Current government purchases	2.83	3.23	4.55	5.80	7.1	5.3	7.2	7.8	7.0	4.3
3. Gross domestic capital formation										
a. Government	0.93	1.67	3.50	5.81	8.53	10.6	25.4	12.1	7.3	7.4
b. Private	1.80	4.48	8.10	18.96	25.30	14.3	4.3	8.7	17.0	10.6
4. Inventory increase	0.61	0.62	0.78	3.03	3.09	74.0	-43.5	-3.1	85.9	6.9
5. Current balance of payments	0.23	0.13	0.50	0.78	0.77	-18.1	149.3	0.1	-60.6	139.7
6. Gross national expenditure	16.90	25.41	40.88	70.63	90.85	10.9	7.3	8.7	10.2	-1.2
7. GNE deflator	51.0	61.0	78.2	100.1	122.2	6.8	4.4	4.8	11.5	20.7

Data: Economic Planning Agency, *Kokumin Shotoku Tōkei Nenpō* [Annual Report of National Income] (Tokyo: Ōkura Shō Insatsu Kyoku, 1976).

percent compared with March 1974. The unemployment rate for March 1975 was 2.2 percent, more than double the 1 percent level to which the Japanese had been accustomed since the early 1960s.

Even so, the statistics on unemployment did not accurately reflect the true situation. There were, for example, a substantial number of female workers (approximately 500,000 as of March 1975) who had dropped out of the labor force without reporting the fact to the Public Employment Security Office. The real number of such workers in disguised unemployment probably approached one million. This rapid increase in unemployment was one result of the government's anti-inflation policies.

The present government and the ruling Liberal Democratic Party evaluate the success of their anti-inflation policies in terms of the annual rate of increase in consumer prices. The policy is based on the theory that the rate of the annual spring wage hike is tied to the rate of increase in consumer prices as measured immediately before the negotiations begin. The return of the consumer price index to a level below 15 percent by the end of March 1975 created a political atmosphere in which the average wage hike arising out of the 1975 spring wage offensive was held to a "meager" 13 percent. Previous experience suggested that labor-management agreements contained implicit escalator clauses. However, the negotiations in the spring of 1975 suggested that wage hikes were also related to other factors such as the supply of and demand for labor—in particular, on the demand side, the profitability of firms. Since the spring wage hikes in 1975 were slightly lower than the rate of consumer price inflation over the previous year, many feared that real wages would decline.

Nevertheless, the major concern of many people has been the possibility that the economy will stabilize at a level characterized by undesirably low economic activity or under-utilization. The real fear is that continued austerity on the part of the government will result in decreased demand in the private sector and increased unemployment. Added to this is the inevitability that the officially regulated prices for postal services, tobacco, water, and basic materials such as iron and steel will be allowed to rise. This would add to the generally steep price hikes occurring in the fall of 1974 for rice, transportation, electric power, and so forth. These increases serve only to aggravate the impact of the spring wage increase upon the rate of inflation.

In this fashion, then, increased unemployment and further contractions in the size of the work force are sources of considerable anxiety. Although from a long-term perspective of five or more years there may be less cause for pessimism, the state of affairs since 1973 has resulted in a certain uneasiness about the immediate future. One might also question the use of 1973 as the comparative standard, since it was quite abnormal in many respects. Nevertheless, the year 1973 has come to symbolize the high point in Japanese economic growth. Accordingly, the psychological impact of minus growth the following year was greater than it otherwise would have been.

2. Female Labor and the Peripheral Labor Force

Nakamura Takafusa has carefully analyzed recent changes in the structure of the labor market which have occurred during the past decade.[1] He attaches particular importance to the "peripheralization" of the female labor force. The research of Douglas and Arisawa shows that the labor force participation of women (whether married or unmarried) tends to vary (1) negatively with the income of the head of their household (either husband or father) and (2) positively with their own wage rate.[2] Rapid economic growth resulted in larger income for the breadwinner, and thus lowered the participation rate for women. At the same time, higher female wage rates tended to encourage participation. The net result, however, has been a consistent decline in the labor force participation rate for women from 69.2 percent in 1960 to 65.7 in 1965, 65.4 in 1970, and 64.4 by 1972, according to the Labor Force Survey. The downward shift was especially notice-able between 1960 and 1965. Since 1965, the rate of decline has slowed.

The decline is due primarily to decreases in the agricultural popula-tion, as the wives of farmers are usually members of the labor force. According to the Labor Force Survey, the number of workers classified as self-employed or unpaid family workers dropped steadily during the period of high economic growth. Female self-employed workers, most from farm households, found new employment in non-agricultural sectors of the economy. This "new" female labor force is highly mobile. "Peripheral" thus refers to those able to enter and leave the labor market rather easily, a group which is very sensitive to changes in wage rates and other working conditions.

[1] Nakamura Takafusa, "Gendai no Rōdōryoku no Kōzō to Mondai" [Some Problems on the Structure of the Labor Force], *Tōyō Keizai*, Special Issue No. 31 (January 1975), pp. 95–103.

[2] Paul H. Douglas, *The Theory of Wages* (New York: Macmillan, 1934); Arisawa Hiromi, "Chingin Kōzō to Keizai Kōzō—Teichingin no Igi to Haikei" [Wage Differentials and the Structure of the Economy: Some Background Factors and the Meaning of Low Wages], in *Chingin Kihon Chōsa* [A Study of Wages], ed. by Nakayama Ichirō (Tokyo: Tōyō Keizai Shimpō Sha, 1955), pp. 40–57.

The Employment Status Survey (Shūgyō Kōzō Kihon Chōsa) is conducted by the Bureau of Statistics on the first day of July every year. It provides important data on the employment status of the population during the year preceding the date of the survey. Using data from this survey, Nakamura classified female workers into two major categories: (1) a core labor force consisting of persons who list work as their principal activity and (2) a peripheral labor force consisting of (a) persons regarding their jobs as a secondary activity, (b) those currently without jobs who are actively searching for work, and (c) those currently without jobs who are willing to accept work under certain conditions but are not actively searching for work. Those in the last group (2c) are usually excluded from the labor force, while those in group (2b) are counted as unemployed persons. The exclusion of the last group from the index of unemployment is not unrelated to the insensitivity of the index in Japan to the business cycle. Accordingly, Nakamura includes all three of the peripheral groups in his estimates of the labor force. His compilations are given in Table 2.

Nakamura's analysis shows that the relative size of the peripheral labor force declined until the late 1960s because of the relative decline in the first component (2a). Since 1965, however, the relative importance of all three components has increased. The figures for 1974 suggest that female workers are the first group to be discharged. Using Nakamura's vocabulary, female workers have served as a "cushion" in the process of employment adjustment. In the latter half of 1974, when

Table 2:   The Female Population, Its Labor Force Participation Ratio, and Designation of a Core and Peripheral Labor Force

Year	Female population aged 15 and over (1000 persons)	Labor force participation ratio (percentage)	Core labor force (percentage)	Peripheral labor force		
				Working secondarily (percentage)	Unemployed (percentage)	Jobless and not searching for a job (percentage)
1956	31,397	49.6	32.2	17.3	6.0	7.2
1959	33,357	46.3	32.8	13.5	5.4	6.4
1962	34,823	45.9	34.8	11.3	4.4	7.0
1965	37,553	44.2	34.0	10.0	4.4	7.2
1968	39,519	47.5	33.4	14.1	6.2	10.2
1971	40.970	46.5	32.2	14.3	6.0	11.3
1974	42,836	44.0	30.7	13.2	6.4	11.7

Note: The divisors for the percentages come from the first column.
Source: Sōrifu Tōkei Kyoku (Bureau of Statistics, the Prime Minister's Office), *Shūgyō Kōzō Kihon Chōsa* [Employment Status Survey] (Tokyo: Ōkura Shō Insatsu Kyoku, published every three years).

employment dropped still further, the relative weight of the latter two components of the peripheral labor force (2b and 2c) grew as female core workers were shifted into the peripheral labor force. It is not clear into which subcategory many of these "transfers" fit: whether they are willing to work at the going wage rate if a job were available (2b), are searching for a better job (2b or 2c), or are waiting for improvements in wages and working conditions (2c).

While many of the "transfers" are unemployed, it may be possible to regard their unemployment as not a really serious social problem since many female workers participate in the labor market simply to earn additional pocket money for school tuition and fees, electric household appliances, or clothing and other personal accessories. However, in addition to the factors identified by Douglas and Arisawa, the female labor force participation rate tends to rise with the educational level of women and decrease with a rise in the number of children per household. These members of the peripheral labor force were enjoying an optimal situation prior to 1974 in terms of their income-leisure prefence, and a sizeable increase in their unemployment would certainly not have been desirable.

3. Changes in the Composition of the Female Labor Force

Table 3 summarizes another aspect of the structure of employment. The table shows changes in the role of regularly employed women in blue- and white-collar occupations in manufacturing industries as reported in the Monthly Labor Survey. Here the term "white-collar" or "non-production workers" includes technical, administrative, and office workers. As a percentage of all employees, the number of white-collar workers has steadily increased throughout the period under investigation: it has risen about ten percentage points within two decades. During the same period, the number of "regular" employees in manufacturing firms with more than thirty employees has grown from 3.07 million in 1955 to 7.91 million by 1974, with 38.6 percent of the increase being accounted for by white-collar types.

The relatively rapid increase in the number of white-collar employees is a general trend observable throughout the industrial sector. As automation proceeds, the relative importance of maintenance and other support staff increases, and production lay-out, the regulation of material inventories, and the administration of personnel become more important. Consequently, the demand for white-collar employees

Table 3:   Changes in the Proportion of Production and Non-production and
Female Employees in Manufacturing

(Unit: %)

Year	Percentage of all employees in non-production occupations	Percentage of female employees in different occupations		
		Employees in production	Non-production employees	Average for all occupational groupings
1955*	22.0	36.4	22.5	33.3
1960	22.8	35.7	25.6	33.4
1965	26.9	35.9	26.2	33.3
1970	28.4	36.6	27.2	34.0
1971	29.2	36.0	26.3	33.2
1972	29.8	35.2	25.3	32.3
1973	31.1	35.5	25.0	32.2
1974	32.3	33.2	24.4	30.8

* At the end of 1955.
Source: Rōdō Shō (Ministry of Labour), *Maitsuki Kinrō Tōkei* [Monthly Labor
Survey].

increases more rapidly than the demand for line production workers.[3]
These changes result in a loss of flexibility in terms of the firm's ability
to adjust to changes in the amount of output and in the overall level of
plant utilization. Indeed, while the number of production workers has
consistently fallen since 1970 (except in 1973, an abnormal year), the
number of non-production workers has steadily increased, jumping 7.8
percent in 1973. While this results in more stable employment situations,
it also means that it has become more difficult for the firm to reduce production costs when wages are persistently rising.

From the viewpoint of allocating the labor force among various sectors, especially among manufacturing and non-manufacturing industries, the relative increase of non-production workers within manufacturing industries no doubt will result in several problems. First, this trend
will retard the development of enterprises specializing in important
services such as repair, security, and maintenance, since the demand
for such services is self-contained within the manufacturing sector.
Second, this trend will deter the improvement in labor productivity
of the service sector as a whole since much of the demand left for the
service sector *per se* is for personal services which are supplied by
very small businesses with low productivity and often run by self-
employed entrepreneurs. Third, this trend will detract from efforts to

[3] G. E. Delehanty, *Non-Production Workers in U.S. Manufacturing* (Amsterdam:
North Holland, 1968).

expand or create more knowledge-intensive industries, which is an important goal of current industrial policy, since the attempt by manufacturing industries to supply their own needs will diminish the opportunities for those specializing in knowledge-intensive services.

The second and third columns of Table 3 show the percentage of production workers and non-production workers, respectively, who are women. In the case of production workers, the proportion of women workers did not change much until about 1970, but then it began to decline rather rapidly. This change partially reflects the decline of the textile and apparel industries which traditionally depended heavily on female labor. The number of female production workers decreased from 830,000 in 1970 to 734,000 in 1974 in the "female-using industries" which, in addition to textiles and garments, include the food and tobacco manufacturing industries. This reduction of nearly 100,000 persons accounts for nearly a third of the total drop in the number of female production workers in manufacturing. Another 100,000 female production workers were dropped by the electric machinery and precision instrument industries, which are also heavily dependent on female labor.

In the case of non-production workers, the ratio of female workers increased rather substantially (5 percent) until 1970, but then declined by more than 3 percent over the following five years. Non-production female workers are engaged primarily in office or clerical work. The decline in their numbers is partially due to the "cushion effect" and partially due to declining birth rates and the increase in levels of education.

Regardless of the occupational type, the proportion of female regular employees in manufacturing has decreased in recent years. While the core labor force has come increasingly to consist of males, female workers have been employed in increasing numbers as part of the peripheral labor force. They are available to supplement the labor supply in the economic upswing and to "cushion" the core labor forces in the downswing.

4.   Employment and Hours of Work

Working hours have declined since 1970. Table 4 gives the monthly averages for actual hours worked (including overtime), the regular hours of work, and the number of days worked. Winston's regression analysis of international cross-sectional data for 1953 through 1960 suggests that the elasticity of the workweek (number of hours) with respect to wages in manufacturing ranges between minus 0.10 and minus

Table 4:   Reduction in Working Hours

	Average working hours per month	Regular working hours per month	Working days per month
1955	194.8	178.3	23.8
1960	202.7	180.8	24.2
1965	192.2	176.4	23.6
1970	187.7	169.9	22.9
1971	185.7	169.9	22.9
1972	184.7	169.3	22.8
1973	183.1	166.8	22.4

Source: Nihon Seisansei Honbu (Japan Productivity Center), *Katsuyō Rōdō Tōkei* [Handbook of Labor Statistics] (Tokyo: Nihon Seisansei Honbu, 1975), p. 126.

0.15.[4] The report of the Economic Advisory Council Subcommittee on the Labor Force uses international cross-sectional data for 1960 and 1969 to estimate an elasticity of minus 0.17 for working hours with respect to per-capita national income. However, a regression analysis of inter-industry cross-sectional data for Japan gives an elasticity of slightly less than 0.2. Needless to say, we have to be very careful in using these estimates from cross-sectional data in time series analysis. Nonetheless, the observed changes in hours of work presented in Table 4 roughly coincide with what one would expect from the analysis of cross-sectional data. It is thus "economic growth" which has resulted in the reduction of working hours.

The shorter hours of work have been realized through an increase in annual paid holidays and the spread of the five-day workweek. However, this trend has continued at a steady pace even since 1970, when the pace of income growth began to slow down (see Table 5).

Table 5:   Annual Number of Holidays

(days)

	Weekly holidays	Other holidays during the year	Total
1966	53.2	11.8	65.0
1968	54.1	14.4	68.5
1970	55.5	14.6	70.1
1972	61.1	15.6	75.7
1974	71.6	16.6	78.2

Source: Rōdō Shō (Ministry of Labour), *Chingin Rōdō Jikan Seido Sōgō Chōsa Hōkoku* [Survey on Payment Schemes and Working Hours].

[4] G. C. Winston, "An International Comparison of Income and Hours of Work," *Review of Economics and Statistics* (vol. 48, no. 1: February 1966), pp. 28–39.

Flex-time has been introduced in only a small number of firms on an experimental basis; whether it will prevail is yet to be seen. Although many large firms have a five-day week on an every-other-week basis and some even have a two-day weekend every week, such practices are not so common in most small and medium-sized firms (see Table 6).

The spread of part-time work also shortens the workweek. The introduction of part-time arrangements certainly works to promote the mobilization of female labor, as mentioned above. Statistical data presently available do not show precisely the number of part-time female workers. We can, however, be fairly sure that part-time work has expanded more rapidly for females than for males (see Table 7).

The irreversible trend toward a shorter workweek probably will continue in the future, even with low economic growth. It is unlikely that a complete five-day workweek will appear in banks, schools, or government offices in the very near future. Such changes will require legislation and certain social and psychological changes. Nevertheless, the workweek will continue to contract as part-time work and other arrangements become more common.

However, a shortened workweek does not necessarily mean more leisure time or improved welfare. For example, it is common practice for some workers to use their paid holidays when they are ill. Some of the increase in leisure hours is offset by longer commuting hours. Commuting in crowded trains also requires more energy and means that more time is needed simply for rest.

An econometric study by Tsujimura Kōtarō and his associates shows that the shorter workweek increases labor productivity.[5] One explanation is that the morale of workers is enhanced as investments in labor-saving machinery and equipment are introduced to maintain labor productivity. Table 8 shows the increase in labor productivity which accompanies a one-percent reduction in hours of work in three sectors of the economy. The table also gives estimates of the increases in investment and employment necessary to maintain planned output levels when scheduled working hours are reduced by 1 percent. The elasticity of investment to hours of work (the marginal amount of investment required for such a reduction change to occur without a drop in production) is of course greatest in heavy industry. The same sector also

---

[5] Tsujimura Kōtarō, "Rōdō Jikan to Seisansei" [Working Hours and Productivity], a mimeographed paper by the Ministry of Labour (July 1972); and Sakuramoto Hikaru, "Rōdō Jikan Tanshuku to Rōdō Seisansei" [Reducing Working Hours and Productivity], *Mita Shōgaku Kenkyū* (vol. 17, no. 6: April 1975), pp. 65–82. Also see Tsujimura's contribution to this volume.

Table 6: Introduction of the Two-day Weekend

Firm size (persons) and years	Total	Six-day workweek	Five-and-a-half-day system	Five-day workweek						
				Total	Every week	Three times per month	Every other week	Two times per month	Once per month	Other
All firms										
1971	100.0	89.1	3.3	9.5	0.1	1.3	2.2	1.3	2.4	1.1
1973	100.0	65.6	3.8	30.0	1.5	0.6	6.9	5.7	15.3	0.7
1974	100.0	53.9	3.2	42.8	2.4	1.3	9.3	12.1	17.7	0.0
1,000 or more										
1971	100.0	55.2	6.7	37.8	5.2	1.4	10.4	7.4	13.3	0.3
1973	100.0	25.6	3.8	70.4	11.8	5.2	18.4	14.5	20.5	0.2
1974	100.0	15.9	2.7	81.4	20.6	8.4	16.7	18.4	17.3	—
100–999										
1971	100.0	81.1	5.7	12.4	0.9	0.4	3.3	2.5	5.3	0.7
1973	100.0	54.4	4.1	41.3	3.1	1.6	8.5	8.7	19.4	0.2
1974	100.0	38.2	3.6	58.2	4.7	2.8	12.0	18.7	20.0	—
30–99										
1971	100.0	93.1	2.3	3.3	0.1	0.2	1.5	0.6	0.9	1.2
1973	100.0	71.2	3.6	24.2	0.5	0.1	5.9	4.3	13.0	1.0
1974	100.0	61.6	3.1	35.3	0.9	0.5	7.9	9.2	16.8	—

Source: Same as for Table 5.

Table 7:   Number and Percentage of Female Employees by Weekly Hours Worked

Unit: 10,000 persons (%)

	1–14 hours	15–34 hours	35 hours and over	Total
1970	18 (1.7)	112 (10.3)	935 (86.1)	1,086
1971	19 (1.7)	124 (11.2)	943 (85.0)	1,109
1972	21 (1.9)	125 (11.2)	944 (84.8)	1,113
1973	23 (2.0)	146 (12.5)	978 (83.5)	1,171
1973	23 (2.0)	147 (12.5)	984 (83.5)	1,179
1974	24 (2.1)	160 (13.8)	954 (83.0)	1,163

Source: Sōrifu Tōkei Kyoku (Bureau of Statistics, Office of the Prime Minister), *Rōdōryoku Chōsa Nenpō* [Annual Report of the Labor Force Survey].
Note: The figures for 1973 and 1974 include Okinawa Prefecture.

Table 8:   Effect of a One-percent Reduction in the Standard Workweek

(%)

	Light industry	Heavy industry	Service industry
Increase in labor productivity accompanying a reduction of straight working hours	0.84	0.56	0.74
Increase in investment necessary to maintain planned levels of production	0.86	1.05	0.84
Increase in personnel necessary to maintain planned levels of production	0.17	0.45	0.26

Source: Sakuramoto Hikaru and Tsujimura Kōtarō, "Rōdō Jikan to Seisansei" [Working Hours and Productivity], a mimeographed paper by the Ministry of Labour (July 1972); and Sakuramoto Hikaru, "Rōdō Jikan Tanshuku to Rōdō Seisansei" [Reducing Working Hours and Productivity], *Mita Shōgaku Kenkyū* (vol. 17, no. 6: April 1975), pp. 65–82.

has the highest elasticity for employment levels. Light industry is the lowest in these respects. In other words, the effect of shorter working hours on labor productivity is greatest in light industries and least in the heavy industries. These results are not surprising in view of the different labor intensities in the two sectors.

We may learn from these results that the effect of the shorter work-week on employment is quite limited. Shorter working hours will result in higher productivity so that the same level of production can be maintained without much increase in employment. On the other hand, for the planned level of output to be achieved, all industries will have to increase their investments in capital equipment by over 0.8 percent for each reduction in working hours by 1 percent.

5. The New Employment Insurance Law

A very important revision in the legal framework has set the tone for the behavior of the labor market in the near future: the replacement of the Unemployment Insurance Law with the Employment Insurance Law in April 1975. Although the full impact of this legislation is yet to be seen, a number of significant innovations have been introduced to remedy the deficiencies associated with the old law, which had become increasingly anachronistic given the process of sustained economic growth and accompanying structural change in the labor market.

One problem concerned the increased number of older persons receiving unemployment benefits since 1960. Attention has been focused on the particular difficulties facing the older worker who seeks to find employment after working in the same firm until compulsory retirement. The new law exempts the older workers from paying premiums while also increasing their benefits.[6] Another major revision concerns the allocation of the burden for the employment insurance premium, with 5 permil of one's salary borne by the individual himself and 8 permil by the employer. Finally, an amount equivalent to 3 permil of the payroll may be used for the following three kinds of activities: (1) employment promotion, (2) manpower development and training, and (3) improvement of welfare programs. Of these activities, manpower development and welfare programs are long-term propositions, and their impact will depend largely on the way in which the government uses the funds. In contrast, activities for improving employment, including a new system to eliminate redundancy, were first implemented in January 1975.[7]

[6] Nishikawa Shunsaku, "Rōdō Shijo no Henka to Koyō Hoken" [Structural Change in the Labor Market and the Employment Insurance Act], in Nishikawa Shunsaku, *Keizai Bunseki to Keizai Seisaku* (Economic Analysis and Economic Policy) (Tokyo: Nihon Keizai Shimbun Sha, 1975), pp. 147–166.

[7] Known as the *koyō chōsei kyūfukin seido*, or system of Employment Adjustment Subsidies (henceforth denoted EAS for convenience), the system formally became active on 1 April 1975, as part of the new Employment Insurance Law. However, because of the critical employment situation, benefits were paid to the eligible employers beginning January 1 with funds available for this purpose under the old Unemployment Insurance Law. Under this system, the eligible employer who needs assistance is entitled to receive benefits up to the amount necessary to cover a certain portion of his total labor costs for 75 days. In other words, the employer can receive a certain subsidy for each employee for a maximum of 75 days in order to avoid laying off workers. As of the end of July, very few employers had exhausted their allotment. Indeed, most of them have used only a minor portion of their

Under the new legislation, an employer can receive benefits from the Employment Insurance Account of the government up to one-half (in the case of the large firms) or two-thirds (in the case of small or medium-sized firms) of its payments to laid-off employees in cases when the government judges that employers are obliged to reduce employment levels for an extended period because of national or regional

---

maximum allotment, the average period of use being nine days. The EAS will cover half the wages paid to employees who would otherwise be unemployed in large firms and up to two-thirds in the case of small or medium-sized firms (those with fewer than 300 employees). It is common in Japan for the "laid-off" worker to be still employed by the firm. The only difference between the laid-off worker and other employees is the fact that he does not come to the workshop and his take-home pay is somewhat lower than usual, perhaps 10 to 15 percent below his normal pay in the case of most large firms.

Eligibility for EAS is determined by how hard the industry to which the recipient employer belongs is hit by the recession. This list of designated industries has been expanded and elaborated several times since the initial list issued on 1 January 1975, which included a mixture of 39 designated manufacturing industries. By October 1975, 143 industries had been designated, covering approximately 120,000 establishments and 2.7 million workers.

The subsidies are financed by employment insurance funds which have been accumulated through payroll levies on both the worker and the employer. Under the old Unemployment Insurance Law the burden had been half-and-half, 6.5 and 6.5 permil each. Thus, the new law has shifted more of the burden to the employer. Moreover, three-thirteenths of the revenue from premiums are to be used for explicitly defined activites. In 1975, for example, the 3 permil borne by the employers for these activities probably amounts to roughly ¥100 billion. The initial budget planned by the Ministry of Labour for the EAS had called for ¥14 billion. However, that amount was exhausted in several months, and supplementary funds totaling about ¥20 billion were later made available.

The EAS do not by any means replace conventional unemployment insurance benefits. The major part of the funds accumulated under the new Employment Insurance Law, the remaining 10 out of 13 permil of the payroll, is to be used for such payments. The maximum period beneficiaries can receive insurance benefits varies with age. It may also depend upon other special conditions, such as the extent of depression in the particular industry in which the person becomes unemployed.

It can also be adjusted to geographical differentials in unemployment and consequently to the likelihood of finding employment. The maximum period of payment for persons aged under 30 will normally be 90 days, whereas persons aged over 55 usually qualify for 300 days. Under this system, the employer can receive benefits from the Employment Insurance Account of the government up to half of the wage costs in the case of large firms and two-thirds for smaller firms. Nevertheless, in place of the conventional unemployment /employment ratio, the ratio of unemployment insurance beneficiaries to the total registered or active openings/active applicants ratio were used as more convenient indicators for policy decisions. But what is important now is to prepare systematic records of unemployment rates classified by sex and age classes and analyze changes in the structure of these rates. Information of this kind is available for every fifth year from the Population Census and for each of the last five years from the Labor Force Survey. But the data have not been analyzed in depth, perhaps because of the "high economic growth" and "high-level employment" in the past. More thorough analysis of this data is needed.

economic conditions. For the period January through April 1975, 34,581 establishments actually received these benefits to cover 15.2 million man-days. The total bill was ¥5.5 billion. This system has reinforced the "temporary lay-off" system common among firms. Since the temporarily laid-off workers under this system are not counted as unemployed persons in the Japanese Labor Force Survey, this system results in a kind of disguised unemployment. In practice, the benefits are paid by the Ministry of Labour to a certain limited number of employers in depressed industries who have had to shut down their operations for more than a week. Even with selective payment, the Employment Insurance Account could not possibly continue to meet the high outlays required if a recession continued for a prolonged period. This would be true for either the lay-off benefits scheme or the unemployment insurance benefits. For this reason, the payment of employment reduction benefits to a company must be temporary in nature at any given point in time. Although payment of benefits has continued beyond March 1975, some upper limit is no doubt necessary. Perhaps a better approach would focus on steering aggregate demand so as to increase employment opportunities, thereby absorbing the unemployed.

The system of subsidies for employment adjustment has certainly made the term "employment reduction" a household word while also propping up the Japanese system of temporary lay-offs. Accordingly, the role of the new legislation should not be overlooked when we speculate about future behavior in the labor market.

Since the cushion of the female peripheral labor force has been fairly well used during the recent recession to implement reductions in personnel levels, the remaining labor force is now comprised largely of the "core labor force"—"core" for both the firm and the household. Therefore, should the recession suddenly worsen for some reason, some workers would have to be discharged, and the household economies of many people would be seriously threatened. If the temporary lay-off system actually worked to minimize unemployment under such circumstances, the new system would vindicate itself. However, since the capacity of the system is limited, and in principle should be limited, we ought not to become dependent upon it. Most essential is the prevention of an overall recession. As noted earlier, the payment of unemployment benefits is now more restricted under the new law in terms of the rate of payment and the period of payment. There is thus greater pressure on the individual to find new employment. Special care will be required in handling unemployment under the new law.

Of course, under the new law the payment of benefits will be extended when unemployment rises over 4 percent as measured with the present system used by the Labor Force Survey. Because the denominator used in calculating the unemployment rate is the labor force as a whole (including not only employees but also the self-employed, unpaid family workers, and the unemployed actively seeking work through the Public Employment Security Office), the relatively numerous self-employed and unpaid family workers (who still account for nearly 30 percent of the total labor force) will not become unemployed even if job opportunities decline; thus the Labor Force Survey figures give a superficially low rate of unemployment.

A recomputation of the unemployment rate which excludes the self-employed and unpaid family workers from the denominator gives us a 1.96 percent unemployment rate at present instead of the 1.4 percent obtained in official statistics. For this reason Mizuno argues that we ought to differentiate between the two indices.[8] I would suggest that the revised index might be more meaningful not only for the criteria for measuring levels of unemployment under the Employment Insurance Law, but also as a general concept in all policy discussions regarding the labor market and full employment. It certainly seems to be a more accurate reflection of reality than the conventional "unemployment rate." Still another option is to use the active openings/active applications ratio—a measure often used as a proxy for excess demand by those working with Phillips curves. The conventional unemployment rate is often not used in such analyses on the ground that it varies only slightly within a very narrow range, usually not more than one percentage point. Under close scrutiny, however, it does in fact demonstrate greater sensitivity to economic fluctuations than is generally known.[9] Nevertheless, other types of indices which vary more, such as (a) the index advocated by Mizuno, (b) the ratio of unemployment insurance beneficiaries to those covered, or (c) the ratio of active openings to active applicants, are more convenient indicators for a wide variety of policy decisions. Especially important now is the preparation of systematic records on unemployment by sex and age. Only then can changes in the structure of these rates be carefully analyzed. Information of this kind is available from the Population Census and, for the past five years, from the *Labor Force Survey*. But these data have not been elaborately analyzed, perhaps because the high economic growth rate and "low

[8] Mizuno Asao, *Chingin Kōzō Hendō Ron* [The Changing Wage Structure] (Tokyo: Shin Hyōron Sha, 1973).

[9] Umemura Mataji, *Rōdōryoku no Kōzō to Koyō Mondai* [The Structure of the Labor Force and Employment Problems] (Tokyo: Iwanami Shoten, 1971).

level of unemployment" convinced experts that this was not a problem area. Recently, however, Sano Yōko found that the level of unemployment in Japan is high not only for aged males and females but also for young persons.[10] These structural aspects of the labor market deserve our careful attention.

---

[10] Sano Yōko, "Kon'nichi ni Okeru Shitsugyō no Tokuchō" [Some Characteristics of Recent Unemployment], *Keizai Hyōron* (vol. 24, no. 4: April 1975), pp. 30–43.

PART II
Wage Determination

Postwar Changes in the Japanese Wage System

Ono Tsuneo

1. Perspectives and Approaches

This paper examines changes in the wage system in postwar Japan. It attempts to show how changes in the wage system are related to broader transformations occurring in a wide range of social institutions. Particular attention is given to changes occurring in business organization and labor-management relations, a chronological approach is used.

Since the paper divides a more-or-less continuous history into five- and ten-year periods, perhaps it is wise to begin with a few brief comments about these divisions. In dealing with history, past events are interpreted in terms of contemporary or immediate concerns. The past is thus rewritten as though it possessed some coherent or central themes which make it comprehensible to those existing at a later point in time. It is in the process of making such interpretations that ordinary materials become historical documents in the true sense. Accordingly, a historical interpretation goes beyond the mere identification of conflicting interests, values, and ideologies, and seeks to establish in a consistent fashion a sense of the inevitable which exists in each historical period. In dealing with a topic like the wage system, consideration of these larger historical developments is necessary as they create a certain milieu at a given point in time.

This article originally appeared as "Sengō Nihon Chingin Seido Hensen Shiryō" in *Rōsei Jihō*, a special issue entitled "Henkakuki no Chingin Mondai" [Issues Concerning the Wage System in a Period of Change] (1975), pp. 253–277. The author is a research officer at the Japan Institute of Labour.

In an article surveying the postwar wage system for an earlier com-
memorative issue of this journal,[1] I dealt with both the changes in the
ideational meanings associated with particular wage systems and the
division of history into different periods. This article uses the same
basic analytical framework, which, I feel, will remain a valid approach
for some time into the future. Nevertheless, it is not possible to apply
such a scheme in a mechanical fashion. The formulation of more dynamic and workable hypotheses about how and why the wage system
changes requires a rethinking of the ways in which the organizational
structures of management have interacted with the consciousness and
ideological identification of employees. It is only by doing so that we can
fully understand how a synthesis emerges from the historical confronta-
tion of labor and management.

In dealing with the period since the war (1945–1975), there is an abundance of historical materials. Indeed, one is overwhelmed by the task of
sorting through what might seem to be an excessive amount of material.
Nevertheless, these documents are the source of common themes which
tie together the major economic and social variables and relate them to
changes in managerial structures and the consciousness of the employee. One way to organize this vast literature and isolate some of the
major variables is to compare different time periods. Although the
varied nature of the data does not allow quantification and a statistical
time series analysis, we can nevertheless sketch in the overall picture
and identify a number of interesting relationships. However, the key
to this approach lies in the designation of the time periods, and it is
to that problem that we next turn our attention.

2. The True Meaning of the Wage System and Its Role in the Postwar Historical Period

A. The Managerial Functions of the Wage System

The "wage system" is simply a systematic approach to managing
labor or personnel costs. By looking at both the composition of the
wage package *(chingin taikei)* and the major criteria used to evaluate
the monetary value of a given labor input *(chingin keitai)*, one is able
to analyze a given wage system in terms of its functions. At the same
time, it is important to realize that the composition of the wage package
and the major criteria will in turn be the institutional expression of the

---

[1] "Sengō 'Chingin Seido' no Hensen" [Changes in the Postwar Wage System].
Rōsei Jihō (no. 2000: August 29, 1969), pp. 15–28.

power relationship between labor and management, and therefore to one degree or another reflect the basic concepts, values (goals), and policies of these two parties. In other words, the wage system serves as a mirror for personnel practices and labor-management relations. Accordingly, one cannot adequately conceive of the wage system apart from the general or socially accepted wage standard, the various kinds of wage differentials, and the mechanism set up by labor and management for determining wages. These types of variables are closely related and cannot be dissociated from the larger social and economic realities of particular historical periods.

In talking about a "wage system" we are talking about a systematized and formal set of rules which lay out the criteria and procedures for the exchange of wages for labor. From the point of view of trying to realize organizational objectives, the wage system serves simultaneously (1) to give the enterprise a kind of automatic mechanism or system which allows it to adapt to a changing environment and (2) to provide the employee with a value system which will provide the appropriate motivation by giving him a sense of being integrated into the organization.

Regardless of how rationally the system of personnel management is organized, there is ultimately no guarantee that the employee will identify fully with the goals and aims of management. Rather, in order for a system of differentiated statuses and roles, which are known as jobs or occupations, to function properly, the practical content of the wage system must be so designed as to motivate the employee to work together with others and accept the norm of teamwork while also helping him to achieve his own individual goals. The wage system functions to integrate the goals of the individual and the goals of the organization within the overall managerial system.

In practice there is a time lag following the introduction of a new system of personnel management before corresponding changes occur either in the nature of the entire organization or in the mentality of the employee. Indeed, regardless of the time sequence, there will always be leads and lags.

When the social and economic environment changes, as it does in the face of the rapid technological innovation which characterizes the transition to an "information-oriented society", management must be quick to introduce the necessary organizational changes. This obviously implies a rationalization of the system of personnel management, for it is this system which integrates individuals who occupy various roles and statuses and causes the overall organization to function. However, although management may be quick to sense changes in external business conditions and then to respond immediately with the necessary organizational adjustments, there is a time lag before the attitudes of individuals toward new roles change and a sense of balance is restored to the matrix of conflicting interests. There is, so to speak, a kind of cultural lag, and it is this lag which often produces considerable tension within the business enterprise. It is also for this reason that changes in personnel management and the wage system usually do not occur as quickly as changes in the overall organization of the firm. In the wage system, changes on the phenomenological and the ideational levels occur at different speeds, with one always taking the lead and the other following. For this reason, there is always a mix of the old and the new which makes it difficult to neatly divide a history into wholly integrated periods of time.

In considering the wage system, we are not concerned simply with the mechanics of how wage levels are set or how wages are distributed among members of a given work force. We are concerned with all forms of remuneration including semiannual bonuses, retirement benefits, and fringe benefits. In other words, we are concerned with the life-cycle earnings of the individual while he or she is employed at a given firm. This in turn means that we are dealing with the whole system of personnel management, including both the way individuals are promoted within the firm and the scheme for evaluating an individual's contribution to the firm and his own acquired capabilities. We are also concerned with the extent to which the average employee participates in the making of such decisions. In other words, we are interested in changes occurring both on the surface in formal wage agreements and informally beneath the surface. In the latter case we are referring to values and attitudes, as well as to the indirect secondary payments which in the broadest sense support the more narrowly conceived or formal wage system and account for a kind of wage drift. In understanding the wage system which has evolved in the Japanese context, it is important that one be aware of the time lag: older notions of fair or adequate compensation can still be found in these secondary payment systems. Keeping this in mind helps to explain why the Japanese wage system is referred to as a "seniority-merit wage system", why the wage system cannot be considered apart from the firm's employment policies and overall system of personnel management, and why so much attention is given to the composition, function, and administration of the basic pay package.

In evaluating any wage system, the views of labor and management naturally differ. From the perspective of the employer, the appropriateness of a particular wage system must lie in its ability to improve organizational effectiveness. The wage system will thus vary according to the supply and demand for various types of labor. For the labor union, however, there is a basic concern that the wage system guarantee a "socially accepted standard of living" and cover all necessary living costs. Given the enterprise union and the fact that wages in the Japanese context are settled within the framework of the enterprise union and individualized negotiations at the enterprise level, the wage system which emerges from the labor-management relationship fosters (1) a sense of fairness or equity, (2) motivation to perform tasks relevant to the goals of both the firm and the individual, and (3) the stability necessary for the firm to continue functioning. However, the ways in which the divergent interests of labor and management are brought together by the wage system of a given firm will depend, among other things, upon the industry, the size of the firm, the geographic location of the firm, the composition of the work force, the history of the firm, and the consciousness of the employees. Consequently, there are an infinite number of variations. Some systems emphasize the uniqueness of the firm and the employee's commitment to the firm; others stress the importance of job content and demonstrated individual achievement; still others are concerned with the inherent abilities of the individual. Many combine various criteria. Regardless of the specifics, there is an overall concern with stability in labor-management relations. From this point of view the wage system can be evaluated in terms of its ability (1) to motivate the worker to achieve individual and firm goals and (2) to integrate the employee into the organizational network of the enterprise. The organizational effectiveness of the wage system lies in its ability to foster changes in the attitudes of both labor and management as shifts occur in the relative power of each group to produce new arrangements in the wage system so that both parties can live with the new compromise. In other words, as the labor-management relationship evolves, the wage system must be able to make the necessary adjustments. Such adjustments are in part nothing more than social experiments on a small scale; changes in the wage system reflect the wisdom of trial and error and the creative powers of the individuals responsible for the design and execution of such systems. Those playing a role in this dynamic process include top management, union representatives, administrators and lower-level managers in personnel departments, shop stewards, supervisors on the "line", and various types of employee representatives organized in formal, semiformal, and informal committees at all levels of the organization.

B.   The Stages of Postwar History

What are the major features which identify or distinguish one period in history from another? In dividing history into chronological periods or stages, two general approaches are commonly used. One is the deductive approach. It seeks to find some order among the larger social and economic trends affecting the whole of society, and within that framework it seeks to identify specific kinds of changes in one subsystem or another. The second approach is inductive. It begins by looking at changes in a particular subsystem and then attempts to relate them to changes occurring in the system as a whole.

This paper uses the former approach. Looking first at changes occurring in postwar society and the economy, the paper examines (1) the ways in which labor and management have responded in terms of their demands on the wage system and (2) how these new demands have been woven into existing systems to eventually form the system which now exists.

In the case of Japan, a number of distinct periods can be identified, although each period may not necessarily wholly contain the major developments associated with it. For this paper, the thirty-year period since the end of the war is divided into six five-year segments. The first five years (1945–1950) clearly were a time of great turbulence and social upheaval, a period in which both labor and management looked for some new, but stable, arrangement.

The second five years (1950–1955) were a time of recovery and rebuilding. The third period (1955–1960) was characterized by the accumulation of capital and other preparations for the drive ahead which would make Japan a highly industrialized country. The fourth period (1960–1965) witnessed the actual take-off to high growth, and it was followed by five years of very rapid growth (1965–1970). During the last five-year period (1970–1975) the pollution problem and other types of contradiction or distortion resulting from excessive growth came to receive an increasing amount of attention. The character of each period was shaped on the domestic side by the various phases of the business cycle, which was itself considerably influenced by developments occurring in the world economy.

When we use these six periods as a framework, major changes in the postwar economy and in Japanese society can be identified and then related to the corresponding changes in the wage system. Although some periods fully contain several important changes which happened more or less simultaneously, some changes occurred over a much longer stretch of time, often bridging two or even three of the five-year periods. Furthermore, in some periods changes in the larger society and the national economy are closely linked with changes in the wage system, while other changes involve a time lag with related changes in the wage system not occurring until the next period. Given these problems, one must fully recognize the difficulty of asserting too directly the relationship between specific variables. The task is further complicated if we consider how the so-called secondary changes in personnel management and the wage system itself feed back into the system. Finally, one must be careful not to overlook the fact that many of the relationships become clear only for particular types of firms. Depending on the variables, the initial change works itself out in ways which differ considerably from one firm to another.

If we consider the wage system as one important means used by the enterprise to maintain and adapt its organization to larger changes in its social environment, it is important to evaluate the wage system as it functions to define both (1) the firm's relationship to other firms and (2) relationships within the firm. The first function concerns the ability of the firm as an organizational entity to compete in both the goods market and the labor market. In the latter case the wage system serves to bridge the gap between the worker's consciousness as an employee and his consciousness as a union member. In some cases the wage system is a compromise solution which embodies the needs of both labor and management, whereas at other times it tends to be simply the creative work of someone in the personnel department. In an effort to obtain an overview of developments occurring in the postwar period, an integrated view draws upon (1) a large body of existing literature dealing with the wage system, (2) government statistics and various white papers on the economy and labor policy in general, and (3) the policy statements of labor and management.

3. Indices of "Change" in the Wage System

A. The Sources of Change and Their Quantification

Changes in the wage system often are reflected in a number of social indicators such as the general level of wages and various wage differentials. Within the firm, such changes can be seen in personnel practices and the composition of the wage package which determines how a given pool of funds (labor costs) is allocated among employees. The wage system can also be interpreted as a product of the interplay between labor and management. Accordingly, the wage system existing at any given time will reflect the state of the labor-management relationship at that time. With the economic policies of the government in the background, the wage system adjusts itself to accommodate management's efforts to rationalize production on the one hand and the ideo-logical and economic dictates of the union movement on the other.

Shifts in the economy and the wage system, and to a lesser extent in union and management policies, can be observed by looking at statistics on the labor economy. Once these kinds of "factual" transformation have been carefully observed, the "true histories" can be filled in by closely examining the public pronouncements of the various parties involved in hammering out the wage system. Finally, to this must be added one's own observations arising from long years of personal ex-perience and involvement in these processes.

(1) *Yearly reports in the economic white papers.* Before considering the contents of the annual white paper on the economy, a brief descrip-tion of the publication may be useful. The report on the economy has been published annually since July 1947. The first white paper was entitled "A Report on the Actual State of the Economy" and was published on July 4, 1947, by the Office for Economic Stabilization (Keizai Antei Honbu) which had been organized immediately after the war. The titles for the following two years were "An Analysis of Economic Realities" and "A Report on the State of the Economy". By 1950 a format had been derived which has been used until the present. Responsibility for the publication was later given to the Eco-nomic Planning Agency when it was established in July 1955. Since 1950 each white paper has had a short subtitle succinctly indicating the state of the economy during the year covered. Since 1953 the name of the government official responsible for the white paper has appeared, and since 1956 the white paper has included a short pronouncement by the Minister of the Economic Planning Agency. In referring to the white paper of a particular year, we are referring to the year of publication. Accordingly, the white paper for a given year summarizes the state of the economy during the *preceding* fiscal year.

During the ten years following Japan's defeat in the Pacific War, the economy experienced a brief period of hyperinflation followed by a more extended push toward rehabilitation. After the signing of the Peace Treaty in San Francisco and the outbreak of the Korean War, efforts were made to achieve economic independence, and international trade revived in the latter half of the decade. It was thus generally accepted that the Japanese economy had returned to normal business conditions by the mid-1950s. Between 1955 and 1965 Japan experienced its first and second technological revolutions. At the same time the Income-Doubling Plan was introduced and the industrial structure considerably trans-formed. With entry into the period of extremely rapid growth, the economy began to experience a labor shortage. In the years following

1965 serious efforts were made to "internationalize" the economy; restrictions on both trade and foreign investment were relaxed and Japan rapidly expanded its presence abroad. As Japan reached the stage of "full development", the nation became increasingly concerned with the promotion of social welfare. In the early 1970s, various factors restricted economic activity, and the major concern of the government shifted to the problems of inflation and stagflation.

Given that the Japanese economy depends greatly upon overseas resources, it was only natural that the government continue to place great importance on maintaining export levels; however, efforts along these lines were constrained by the need to maintain an "appropriate" balance with the flow of imports. To a large extent, postwar business cycles have been closely connected with efforts to maintain or improve Japan's balance of payments within the framework of the world economy. Moreover, despite the institutionalization of a pattern in which the rate of annual wage increases were accelerated over time due to the growing bargaining power of the unions, nearly parallel increases in domestic productivity and in inflation abroad (which occurred at roughly the same rate as in Japan) allowed the Japanese economy to continue expanding until the early 1970s. However, the so-called Nixon shocks in 1971 foreshadowed a number of changes which were to restrict Japanese growth considerably by the mid-1970s. With the anti-pollution movement as the spearhead, a variety of domestic constraints coincided with the worldwide shortage of resources and global stagflation to seriously hinder the functioning of the Japanese economy.

Reflecting these trends over the past thirty years, the standard of living has risen remarkably and the Engel coefficient has fallen dramatically. Per-capita income reached prewar levels by 1952, and indices of real wages were 40 percent above prewar levels by 1960, 2.5 times those levels by 1970, and 3.2 times by 1973. The Engel coefficient, which was 53.3 percent in 1951 (indicating that the cost of food alone accounted for over half of all living expenses for the average household), fell to 39.4 percent in 1964 and to 33.3 percent by 1974. The unemployment rate dropped from 2.55 in 1955 to 1.89 in 1965 and to 1.18 by 1970. Reflecting these changes, the wage differential between large firms with over five hundred employees and smaller firms with between thirty and ninty-nine employees narrowed from 41.2 percent in 1955 to 29.0 percent in 1965.

(2) *The views of Nikkeiren on wages and personnel practices.*   In order to examine the views of management on wage systems and personnel practices, it is necessary to examine all pronouncements, policy statements, proposals, and research reports of Nikkeiren. In particular it is

useful to review the annual pamphlet on the spring wage offensive. In addition to these materials, one should consider the various summaries of Nikkeiren's activities which are published approximately every five years. These include *Jūnen no Ayumi* [Ten Years of Progress], *Nikkeiren no Ayumi* [The Progress of Nikkeiren] (covering the period between April 1958 and April 1963), *Nijūnen no Ayumi* [Twenty Years of Progress], and *Nikkeiren no Ayumi* [The Progress of Nikkeiren] (covering the period from April 1968 through March 1973). The second and fourth of these volumes give highlights from the preceding five-year periods of Nikkeiren's existence.

Surveying these materials, we can see that the period of hyperinflation was characterized by management as a period in which traditional managerial prerogatives had been lost. Following the shift in the policy of the postwar occupation authorities, however, the foundation of Nikkeiren in 1948 signaled the beginning of a new era in which management sought to reestablish its authority. During the first half of the 1950s, management sought to build up its own ranks while also restoring order among the work force. It was also a period during which efforts were made to place the overall operations of the firm on an even keel. Once the economy had begun to grow in the late 1950s, management stepped up its efforts to stabilize the organizational relationships within the firm and to invest in new plants and new technologies. These changes resulted in a considerable amount of organizational change within the enterprise, and provided the base for a new form of cooperation between labor and management. The late 1960s were characterized by further structural change in industry as management began to respond to changes in the international climate and the emergence of restraining factors at home (including the labor shortage and accelerated hikes in wage rates).

Reflecting this larger transformation, the structure of the seniority-merit approach to personnel management also changed. In the years following the end of the war, personnel management was in a confused state, but as time passed the seniority-merit principle was for the first time applied to large numbers of employees. Nevertheless, it was in the late 1950s that personnel practices were adjusted so as to "institutionalize" those practices. However, events in the early 1960s soon forced those practices to be revised as a new emphasis was placed on the individual's productivity. This in turn gave way to a concern with positive steps to foster or "develop" manpower within the enterprise. In the face of spiraling wage costs, the concern with productivity and individual ability can also be seen in Nikkeiren's stand in the "guiding light" debate and in its insistence that wage hikes be kept within the limits of productivity increases. Finally, in the 1970s there has been a growing willingness on the part of management to consider various schemes for increasing worker participation in management in order to "break out" of the difficulties in which firms increasingly found themselves.

Throughout the postwar period, management has consistently sought to reappraise the wage system's ability to guarantee an adequate supply of workers with the right qualifications. This concern can be seen in the commonly cited slogan "*seikatsukyū kara nōryokukyū e*" (from wages based on life-cycle needs toward wages tied to ability), which suggested that management desired a shift from a wage system geared to workers' needs to one which underlined efficiency as the major criteria for awarding wages. Throughout the period under consideration, the importance of the individual's job category, specific responsibilities, and actual skills or abilities became more important in determining the employee's wage rate. In 1953 the Central Labor Relations Commission began its survey of wage conditions, and the Association of Employers in the Kantō Region (Kantō Keieisha Kyōkai) soon followed suit by initiating its own Survey of Retirement Allowances. In 1953 the Survey of Model Wage Schedules, the Survey of Bonuses and Other Intermittent Payments, and the Survey of Annual Wage Increments were started. Finally, in 1958 the Commission organized the first Survey of Personnel Management Practices, a survey which has been conducted every five years since.[2] The results of these surveys show considerable change over time. The surveys are particularly useful for showing trends in different aspects of the wage system, including the composition of the paycheck, the form of payment, the criteria for wage increases, the use of bonuses, the payment of retirement benefits and annuities, and the use of various profit-sharing schemes. Particularly valuable are the data which show interrelationships between the above variables and their interconnection with the wage system and changes in other aspects of managerial organization and personnel management, including hours of work, the provision of various kinds of welfare or fringe benefits, and the introduction of training programs within the firm. These unique surveys allow us to view changes in the wage system within the larger setting of personnel management in general.

(3) *The union white papers.* Generally speaking, the wage demands

[2] The first survey in 1958 was entitled "Rōmu Kanri Tōkei Sōran" [A General Survey of Statistics on Personnel Management]. The second survey in 1963 was entitled "Wagakuni Rōmu Kanri no Gensei" [The State of Personnel Management in Japan]. The third survey in 1968 had the same title. The fourth survey (1974), however, introduced new classifications, thereby complicating comparisons over time.

of the unions, as well as their overall posture on the wage system, must be viewed as responses to management initiatives. Although the unions appear to have taken a rather aggressive stand on these matters, the truth is that unions most frequently respond in a passive or defensive manner to the lead taken by management. The aggressive posture is particularly evident in the spring wage demands and their ideological base, areas in which the influence of the national labor organizations is especially strong. At the enterprise level, however, the enterprise union has consistently shown a more flexible attitude and has been rather responsive to the initiatives of management. Unlike the situation in many Western European countries, which allows for considerable flexibility in adjusting the wage package to the needs of the individual firm and its occupational structure once a basic agreement has been reached (a situation often cited as the source of wage drift), it is common for each firm to have its own institutionalized wage structure which is agreed upon with the enterprise union. For this reason there is a built-in rigidity within the Japanese wage system unless the union is willing to take a flexible stand toward management at that level.

Immediately after the war, there were serious shortages in everyday essentials such as food and housing. Accordingly, the demand for a common minimum wage which would guarantee the income necessary to support a family was accepted by everyone in the union movement. The basic logic behind this demand was illustrated by the wage system in the postwar electric power industry, the so-called Densangata system which was established after a rather lengthy struggle between labor and management. Under this wage system, the basic component of the employee's wage packet was his livelihood wage, the amount necessary to defray the "reproduction costs" of the worker and his family—to maintain their standard of living throughout the worker's life cycle. This came to form the core of the wage system, but added to this was a small amount which would be tied to the individual's vocational skills or his occupational status within the firm. This latter component, small though it might have been, was based on the philosophy of equal pay for equal work. During the early 1950s, however, the unions found themselves increasingly hard pressed to justify the continued existence of these guarantees which covered the worker's reproduction costs. Unions came to rely heavily on data showing desirable levels of calorie or protein intake, Engel coefficient, and the accepted size of the "market basket". Confronted with these demands for what was in essence a minimum standard of living, management was not able to suggest an alternative principle for determining wages which would sound reasonable or convincing to all involved. Nevertheless, management continued to argue against this approach, and even today is commonly said simply to have an "allergy" to the theory of reproduction costs and minimum household expenditures. However, by the mid-1950s the unions had succeeded in selling their philosophy to their members and even to the public at large; the Densangata wage package had come to define the basic components of the Japanese wage system.

In this fashion, then, slogans calling for "prewar parity" served as a rallying point for labor until the economy had recovered. However, once those levels had been achieved and the "minimum standard of living" attained, arguments based on the need to cover reproduction costs gradually lost their relevance and consequently became ineffective in fully protecting the worker's interests vis-à-vis management. By the mid-1950s, revisions in the Densangata system were appearing in many industries. The federation of unions in the automobile industry, Zen-jidōsha Rōren, set off on its own, seeking a system allowing for some kind of skill differential to help adjust for differences in productivity (meaning both quality and quantity). The arrangement worked out in the auto industry was known as the *Zenji-hōshiki* wage system. In the chemical industry, Gōka Rōren took the lead in calling for a formula in which a certain amount (known as alpha) was added to a fixed amount common to all workers at a given stage in their life cycle. The alpha component was to be tied to job content and/or the skill level of the individual worker. Sometimes a second variable (known as beta) was added; this component was tied to some mixture of the individual's level of education, age, and length of employment with the same firm. Unions in other industries soon followed the pattern of the chemical industry, and before long the seniority-merit wage system (at least as it is generally conceived) had matured. In the negotiations for these various revisions, we can see the unions' efforts to force a compromise from managements bent upon introducing an occupational wage system in which wage differentials would be based primarily upon job content. Put on the defensive, unions came to argue for equal pay for equal labor (which meant not equal work in terms of job content, but rather equal labor in terms of the qualifications of the employee) and for a commonly accepted minimum wage in each industry (which was de-signed to guarantee a minimum standard of living and an ability to cover reproduction costs).

With improvements in productivity far outstripping the rise in re-production costs, management was able to accumulate considerable profit which could be reinvested in the firm. Labor was quick to appraise the situation and began to demand that the employees receive their rightful share of the profits. Thus, in part the basis for union demands shifted. At about this time (the late 1950s) the Japan Productivity Center began its movement to promote a fair distribution of the profits accruing from increased productivity. It argued that such profits ought to be divided among (1) stockholders and management, (2) labor, and (3) consumers. With these developments occurring in the background, two significant changes can be seen in the wage demands of the unions. First, the growing acceptance given to the concept of wage rates based upon productivity required both labor and management to reexamine the seniority-merit wage system. Moreover, the high economic growth rates experienced in the early 1960s and the remarkable improvement in the standard of living for all Japanese completely undermined the ability of unions to support their wage demands solely with arguments for minimum standards of living. Second, the unions were also made aware of the fact that labor productivity in Japanese factories had come to be on a par with that found in the various industrialized countries of Western Europe. Consequently slogans calling for "wage parity with Europe" or "wages appropriate for a modern industrialized nation" underlined this new consciousness.

These two changes had a big impact on the wage system in Japanese enterprises. This impact can be seen in three ways. First was the trend toward a greater equalization of wages across industries. Second was the attention given to occupational wage differentials and individualized wage packages. Third was the "average base-up formula" which has become an integral part of the annual spring wage negotiations. These trends are particularly noticeable among the unions affiliated with Dōmei and the Japan Council of the International Metalworkers' Federation.

In the late 1960s the economic growth rate reached its zenith; the labor shortage and consequent rise in wage rates offered to graduates entering the labor force did much to create an atmosphere in which unions could push for substantial wage increases and flaunt their demands for "last year's rise plus alpha" (the meaning of "alpha" here being different from that used in the chemical industry formula cited above). The focus of these new demands was clearly not on the maintenance of some minimum level, but on the achievement of a stable standard of living which could be maintained in the future and on the accumulation of capital assets such as housing and other consumer durables. The concern of unions and their membership no longer focused on immediate needs, but rather shifted to include the life-cycle needs which would arise during the remaining years of the employee's life. However, the inclusion of these kinds of demands required the establishment of a long-term wage plan for the firm, a step which would be possible only with the concerted cooperation of labor and management. One result of this cooperation was a growing concern with cross-industry and cross-firm differentials. As a result, inter-industry differentials tended to narrow despite the fact that inter-industry differences in productivity remained the same or perhaps even widened. This phenomenon in turn produced a certain amount of consumer price inflation which, when coupled with the overall acceleration in the rate of wage hikes and the rising costs associated with pollution and the world-wide shortage of resources, contributed to the phenomenon of stagflation and the fantastic rate of inflation which began to plague the Japanese economy in the mid-1970s. This period is also characterized by spreading demands for improved industrial safety, an extension in the fixed age for retirement, and shorter hours of work. In addition to these "private" demands, there is a growing voice among the populace at large for improved social welfare, some vision of life-cycle income needs, and a guarantee that the real standard of living will be maintained. Nevertheless, it is also clear that these broader demands have not seriously altered the basic demands and posture of the enterprise unions, which continue to work on the assumption that career employment and the seniority-wage system ought to be maintained.

B.   Changes in the Postwar Wage System

The wage system of an individual enterprise at any given point in time will naturally be the product of forces at work in the national economy and society as a whole. Although each firm and industry is subject to its own unique set of variables, we can nevertheless identify a number of characteristics which are common to the wage systems in most firms at any given point in time. These characteristics reflect the general forces which set the macro-economic tone and create what is known as a social milieu. Here a few such characteristics will be mentioned briefly for each of the time periods delineated above.

The annual Labor White Paper, the Survey of Remuneration and Its Components, and the Survey of Wage Systems are prepared by the Ministry of Labour and serve as indispensable sources of objective material for tracing changes in the wage system. The first Labor White Paper was published in April 1949 and was entitled *An Analysis of the Postwar Labor Economy.* In October of the same year, the second White Paper, *New Directions in the Labor Economy*, focused on trends in the first six months of the year. With the third White Paper in 1950, *Analysis of the Labor Economy for 1949*, the format for the subsequent Labor White Papers was established. The first report on the Survey of

Remuneration and Its Components, which was carried out in March 1948, was made available for internal distribution in March 1949. This survey has been continued until the present, with the title being changed to "Chingin seido Chōsa" [Survey of the Wage System] in 1963 and then to "Chingin Rōdō Jikan Sōgō Chōsa" [Comprehensive Survey of Wages and Working Hours] in 1966. With each revision the various categories used for different parts of the survey were changed in order to keep up with the actual changes occurring in the wage system itself. This is particularly true in terms of the criteria used to determine the distribution of wages among employees *(chingin taikei)* which is undertaken at a given level of labor costs determined by other criteria (the *chingin keitai*). These materials give a general idea of how the wage system has changed in postwar Japan.

During the occupation immediately after the war, the policies of the Supreme Commander for the Allied Powers (SCAP) greatly influenced developments in the public sector. Consequently, the public sector took the lead in designing new wage systems. As acute inflation began to recede, management in both the private and the public sectors began to simplify and reorder the great number of allowances which had sprung up in order to offset the inroads of inflation. During the early 1950s the basic component of pay, known as *kihonkyū*, was institutionalized, and its basic importance increased. As indicated in Table I in the Statistical Appendix to this paper, the percentage of the average monthly salary arising out of this basic component rose from 69.2 percent in 1949 to 78.2 percent by 1955 and 83.6 percent by 1965. At the same time, the content of, or criteria determining, the basic component changed as management sought to rationalize the wage system. The shift was from reproduction costs to individual productivity in terms of the firm's goals. This move to rationalize the wage system did not occur without considerable tension: the strikes which accompanied these changes in the electric power, mining, automobile, and steel industries are well known. Moreover, these shifts resulted in a widening of wage differentials between men and women and among different occupational groupings.

In the late 1950s and early 1960s the movement to "modernize" wage administration continued unabated. Much of the stimulus along these lines during this period came from attempts to introduce personnel management techniques from America. This movement was characterized by the introduction of schemes which made job content the most important criterion in calculating *kihonkyū*, and many predicted that the older seniority-merit principle would soon lose much of its weight. However, there were also those who questioned whether the occupationally centered wage systems of America would be appropriate for a country like Japan which had developed its own traditions and customs with regard to wages. The Labor White Paper for 1960 concluded that the conditions for establishing an occupational wage system were not right. Attempts to design productivity wage systems which (a) maintained the seniority-merit criteria desired by the older employees, (b) promoted traditional values toward work, and (c) stressed criteria related to actual accomplishments on the job resulted in systems which retained much of the older seniority-merit wage system and created considerable problems. Despite the common usage of the term "basic pay" *(kihonkyū)*, the willingness of firms to experiment has resulted in a word which means different things at different firms. Accordingly, in surveys on wage systems, three different types of basic pay are commonly identified. One *(kihonkyū I)* refers to systems in which the basic component is calculated according to criteria such as age, educational career, and experience (years with the same company). Another *(kihonkyū II)* is associated with systems tying the basic component to job content or responsibilities, specific job skills actually possessed by the individual, or more broadly conceived occupational clusters. The third *(kihonkyū III)* is an amalgamation of the first two types. As the salaries offered to new graduates rose in the mid-1960s, the differential narrowed between "regular" employees who had spent their whole career with the same firm and the "mid-career" employees who had worked at several firms. One result was a move to standardize wage schedules for these different groups of employees. This meant that there was a growing need for wage comparisons, and an effort was made to clarify how basic pay was calculated at different firms.

Toward the end of the 1960s, management stepped up its attack on the seniority-merit wage system. The rapid pace of technological change was making older skills obsolete and the full utilization of older employees more difficult. Rising labor costs due to the worsening labor shortage and the improved bargaining position of the unions forced management to consider new ways to save on labor, to improve the quality of its labor, to relocate workers in jobs where they could be better utilized (often requiring considerable geographic mobility on the part of the employee), and to employ "peripheral labor" such as students or housewives on a part-time basis. Reflecting these overall changes in the labor economy, the importance of job-related pay systems increased. *Kihonkyū* had come to be based upon a number of considerations by the early 1970s: on the average, 33.3 percent of basic salary was calculated according to job-related criteria, 17.2 percent according to seniority-merit criteria, and 33.9 percent by criteria which combined both aspects. Of the firms using principally one set or another of criteria, 44 percent indicated that they used job-related criteria. One result of this shift in criteria was the narrowing of differentials based upon age and/or length of employment with a given firm. Consequently, the importance of the seniority-merit principle tended to fade. On this point, however, one must be careful not to confuse percentage differentials with absolute differentials. For example, whereas in 1960 the "model wage rates" for college graduates aged 50 were 4.0 times those for their counterparts aged 25, the difference had narrowed to 2.5 times by 1974. However, the absolute difference between their salaries increased from ¥21,300 per month in 1960 to ¥112,000 per month in 1974. The distinction between these two types of comparisons is important when we consider the ideological base upon which wage demands or wage policies are based. Ultimately, we are talking about differences in concepts like equality, equity, and the notion of fair shares.

4. The Future of the Seniority-Merit Principle in Japanese Wage Systems

A given wage system is best evaluated in terms of its ability to promote organizational effectiveness. As the major tool used to implement a certain approach to personnel administration, the wage system serves both to motivate employees and to integrate or coordinate their roles within the business organization, which must be able to adapt itself to a changing economic and social environment. In terms of motivation and integration, the wage system must function (1) to promote a sense of fairness or parity, (2) to provide a stimulus or impetus to action, and (3) to guarantee a certain amount of stability or certainty in the life of each employee.

In more concrete terms, the function of promoting a sense of fairness or parity requires that a wage system insure that employees receive an income roughly on a par with that received by others doing similar work and sharing common characteristics elsewhere in society. At the same time, it also means that reasonable differentials will be maintained among the various employees within the firm, differentials which are justifiable in the eyes of the employee. The first aspect will require that better data be collected so that more accurate comparisons can be made throughout the society; the latter can be achieved by drawing up a system of personnel evaluation in which the unions actively participate. The stimulus or impetus to work can be provided by a wage system which seeks to scientifically and democratically assess the supply of and demand for specific types of labor, paying people different rates according to their output, the work environment, and the difficulty of the job. Certainty and a sense of security are provided by a wage system which considers the life-cycle needs of the employee in terms of both income (a flow concept) and asset holdings (a stock concept).

The subjective meaning of a particular wage system, as well as its effectiveness in achieving the firm's goals, will vary from firm to firm depending upon the occupational composition of the work force and the extent to which employees identify with the firm. Personality and status considerations become important because conflicting interests define cleavages not only between labor and management, but also among the employees themselves. Consequently, it is likely that each firm will continue to shop around for a wage system which can be tailored to suit its own particular needs. Moreover, other things being equal, each firm will seek to choose a wage system which allows it to maximize the employee's real income over his entire career with the firm. Finally, the overall importance and composition of the basic component of the wage package *(kihonkyū)* will likely change with the growing need for greater organizational effectiveness, but will continue to guarantee a fixed minimum to cover the employee's reproduction costs. For these reasons, we must conclude that wage systems will continue to change in the future as labor and management at each firm seek to design a wage system which will make their own firm more competitive and yet maintain the lead in setting a social standard for meeting life-cycle needs.

Appendix: Basic Data on the Wage System

I. Percentage Composition of the Wage Package for Firms with Thirty or More Employees, 1949–1972

A. 1949–1955 (*Kyūyo Kōsei Chōsa Hōkoku*)

Date of survey	Total	Basic pay (*kihonkyū*)	Incentive pay			Household support pay			Overtime pay	Other pay
			Total	Attendance pay	Skill allowance	Total	Family	Pay for geographic differentials		
November 1949	100.0	69.2	13.7	1.4	12.3	17.1	9.8	5.1	9.2	1.2
October 1950	100.0	66.8	17.3	—	—	15.9	—	—	11.7	1.2
October 1951	100.0	70.2	17.8	—	—	12.0	—	—	11.9	1.8
August 1952	100.0	73.3	15.9	—	—	10.8	6.3	—	12.2	1.5
September 1953	100.0	74.2	16.4	1.5	14.9	9.4	5.9	1.9	13.0	1.5
September 1954	100.0	75.9	14.9	1.2	13.7	9.2	5.8	1.9	11.5	1.6
September 1955	100.0	78.2	13.6	1.2	12.4	8.2	5.4	1.4	12.5	1.4

B. 1956–1958 (*Chingin Seido Chōsa*)

Date of survey	Total	Basic pay (*kihonkyū*)	Incentive pay			Household support pay				Overtime pay	Other pay
			Total	Attendance pay	Skill allowance	Total	Family pay	Commutation	Pay for geographic differentials		
September 1956	100.0	78.8	13.3	1.2	12.1	7.9	4.9	—	1.2	14.2	1.3
September 1957	100.0	79.8	12.9	1.1	11.8	7.3	4.4	—	1.2	14.2	1.2
September 1958	100.0	81.3	11.9	1.1	10.8	6.8	3.9	—	1.2	12.6	1.4

C. 1959–1962 (*Chingin Seido Chōsa*)

Date of survey	Total	Subtotal for main items (*kikonkyū*)	Basic pay (*kikonkyū*)	Incentive pay			Household support pay	Overtime pay	Other pay
				Total	Attendance pay	Skill allowance			
September 1959	100.0	86.5	81.1	12.3	1.1	11.2	6.6	12.5	1.0
September 1960	100.0	86.2	82.5	11.4	1.2	10.2	6.1	13.0	0.8
September 1961	100.0	86.2	83.5	11.0	1.3	9.7	5.5	12.8	1.0
September 1962	100.0	88.0	84.8	9.8	1.4	8.4	5.4	11.1	0.9

D. 1963–1965 (*Chingin Seido Chōsa*)

Date of survey	Total	Subtotal	Basic pay (*kihonkyū*)				Pay for results	Occupational allowance	Household allowance	Incentive allowance	Various other allowances	Overtime pay	Other pay
			Total	Type I	Type II	Type III							
August 1963	100.0	87.5	82.0	8.0	8.7	65.7	7.5	2.9	5.5	1.5	0.6	11.8	0.7
September 1964	100.0	87.9	82.3	8.8	7.2	66.3	7.1	3.1	5.7	1.4	0.4	11.5	0.6
September 1964	100.0	89.1	83.6	9.4	9.0	65.2	6.1	3.1	5.8	1.2	0.2	10.3	0.6

E.   1966–1969 (*Chingin Rōdō Jikan Seido Sōgō Chōsa*)

Wage component	Year			
	1966	1967	1968	1969
Total wage package	100.0	100.0	100.0	100.0
A. Regular wage package	88.5=100.0	88.0=100.0	87.9=100.0	87.4=100.0
1. Basic pay	82.8	83.0	82.6	82.1
a. Pay based on age, length of employment, experience, educational background	3.3	7.9	16.6	16.2
b. Productivity-based pay	8.9	10.8	13.1	12.8
1) Pay for specific job content	2.6	3.0	3.5	3.7
2) Pay for specific occupational skills	5.0	5.6	7.4	6.9
3) Pay for job content	1.3	2.2	2.2	2.2
c. Pay based on mixed criteria	70.6	64.3	52.9	53.1
1) Method I	40.5	49.5	44.1	44.9
a) Type (1)		19.3	17.4	16.8
b) Type (2)		5.2	4.8	6.2
c) Type (3)		25.0	21.9	21.9
2) Method II	30.1	14.8	8.8	8.2
2. Pay for results	5.9	5.7	5.6	6.5
3. Occupational allowance	3.5	3.4	3.4	3.4
4. Household allowance	6.0	6.0	6.5	6.3
5. Incentive (attendance) allowance	1.4	1.5	1.5	1.2
6. Other allowances	0.1	0.4	0.4	0.5
B. Additional pay (including overtime)	11.5	12.0	12.1	12.6
Total wages	¥35,140	¥39,203	¥43,983	¥50,473

F. 1971–1972 (*Chingin Rōdō Jikan Seido Sōgō Chōsa*)

Wage component	Year					
	1971	1972	1973	1974	1975	1976
Total wage package	100.0	100.0	100.0	100.0	100.0	100.0
A. Regular wage package	89.8=100.0	89.4=100.0	89.1=100.0	90.9=100.0	91.8=100.0	90.9=100.0
1. Basic pay	83.5=100.0	84.8=100.0	84.4	84.6	84.0	84.3
a. Pay for work	27.2	30.6				
b. Pay for individual characteristics	15.4	17.4				
c. Pay of mixed criteria	40.9	36.8				
2. Pay for results	5.0	3.3	3.3	2.7	2.6	2.1
3. Occupational allowance	3.8	3.8	4.1	3.8	3.9	3.9
4. Incentive (attendance) pay	1.2	1.1	1.0	1.0	1.0	0.9
5. Household maintenance allowance	6.0	6.3	6.6	7.1	7.9	8.2
6. Other allowances	0.5	0.6	0.6	0.8	0.7	0.6
B. Additional pay	10.2	10.6	10.8	9.1	8.2	9.1
Total wages	¥69,004	¥78,435	¥94,325	¥120,405	¥130,508	¥138,368

G. 1971–1976 (*Chingin Rōdō Jikan Seido Sōgō Chōsa*): Percentage of Firms with a Particular Type of Wage System

Type of wage system	Year of survey					
	1971	1972	1973	1974	1975	1976
A. Systems based on work criteria	31.4	37.8	43.8	47.9	39.8	42.6
1. Single criterion systems	20.2	26.5	32.6	36.9	30.4	32.5
2. Multiple criteria systems	11.2	11.3	11.2	10.9	9.4	10.1
B. Systems based on personal characteristics	10.1	11.4	10.8	11.3	11.4	10.7
C. Systems integrating work criteria and personal characteristics	55.8	50.8	45.4	40.9	48.8	46.7
Total of all firms	100.0	100.0	100.0	100.0	100.0	100.0

II. Relation among Various Components of the Woge Package
(Kyūyō Kōsei Chōsa)

A. Structure of the Total Wage Package: 1949

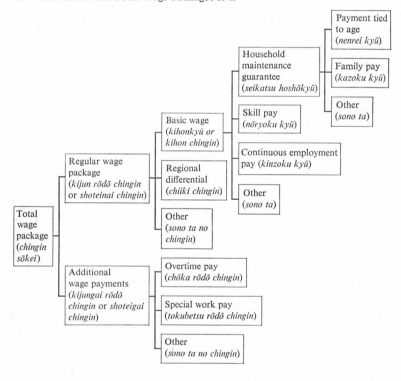

B. Structure of Criteria Commonly Used for the "Old" Wage Package: Through
1962

  A. Basic pay (*kihonkyū*)
    1. Age (*nenrei*)
    2. Educational background (*gakureki*)
    3. Experience or length of employment (*kinzoku, keiken*)
    4. Job skill (*nōryoku*)
    5. Title (*yakutsuki*)
    6. Occupation (*shokumu*)
    7. Special work (*tokushū sagyō*)
    8. Across the board (*ittei gaku*)
    9. Combination of criteria (*sōgō kettei*)

  B. Incentive pay (*shigeki kyū*)
    1. Attendance (*seikaikin kyū*)
    2. Efficiency (*nōritsu*)

  C. Livelihood maintenance pay (*seikatsu hojo kyū*
    1. Family maintenance (*kazoku*)
    2. Commutation (*tsūkin*)
    3. Geographic differential (*chiiki*)
    4. Other

  D. Overtime pay (*chōka kinmukyū*)
    1. Overtime (*jikangai*)
    2. Night work (*shin'ya*)
    3. Vacation work (*kyūjitsu shukkin*)
    4. Other

  E. Pay not related to work (*fushūgyō kyū*)
    1. Vacation pay for annual leave
    2. Pay for leave taken at the employee's own convenience
    3. Pay for leave taken not at the employee's own convenience

  F. Other pay

C. Structure of Criteria Commonly
    Used in the "New" Wage
    Package: Since 1963

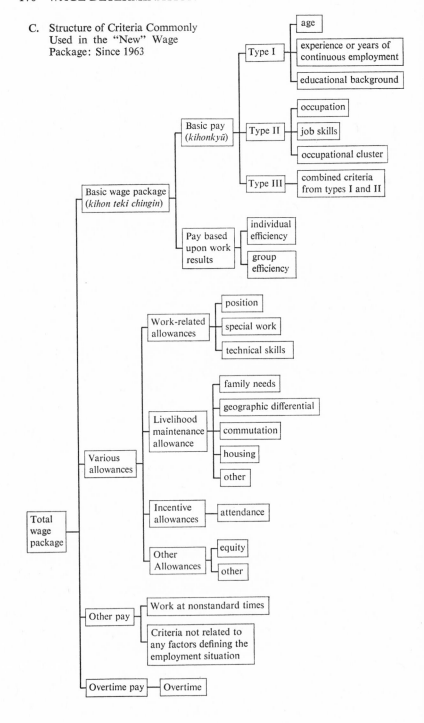

III. Distribution of Firms by Size and Type of Wage System (1949 *Chingin Kōsei Chōsa Hōkoku*)

A. Prewar and Postwar Comparisons: 1939 and 1949

Year	Industry	Unit of measurement and total number	Percentage of total wage package tied to basic pay										
			Total	0–10	10–20	20–30	30–40	40–50	50–60	60–70	70–80	80–90	90–100
1939	Machine manufacturing	Workers =499	100.0			1.8			10.6	23.0	23.5	21.6	19.5
1948	Machine manufacturing	Firms =121	100.0	8.2	29.7	20.7	11.6	11.6	5.8	3.3	1.7	6.6	0.8
1948	All manufacturing	Firms =556	100.0	5.6	23.6	15.5	11.7	12.1	11.3	7.0	5.6	6.5	1.1

B. Breakdown For Machine Manufacturing: 1948

Firm size (number of employees)	50–99			100–499			500–999			1000+			All Firms (50+)		
Number of firms surveyed	27			40			10			7			84		
Sex	Males	Fe-males	Males and Females	Males	Fe-males	Males and females	Males	Fe-males	Males and females	Males	Fe-males	Males and females	Males	Fe-males	Males and females
Basic pay	63	77	64	64	67	65	68	75	68	53	65	57	63	71	65
Wages in the form of subcontracting (piece rates)	21	15	21	17	15	16	15	14	15	28	26	28	19	16	18
Various allowances (for family maintenance, work at nonstandard times, etc).	7	5	7	7	9	8	9	5	9	4	5	4	7	7	7
Overtime	9	3	8	12	9	11	8	6	8	13	6	11	11	6	10
Total	100	100	100	100	100	100	100	100	100	100	100	100	100	100	100

C. Breakdown For Metal Processing Industries: 1948

Firm size (number of employees)	50–99			100–499			500–999			1000+			All firms (50+)		
Number of firms surveyed	9			16			0			6			31		
Sex	Male	Female	Both	Male	Female	Both	Male	Female	Both	Male	Female	Both	Male	Female	Both
Basic pay	58	72	63	57	74	6				54	70	57	57	74	63
Wages in the form of subcontracting (piece rates)	28	19	23	16	10	12				25	12	22	21	13	18
Various allowances (for family maintenance, work at non-standard times)	3	2	3	10	8	9				8	11	9	8	6	7
Overtime	11	7	11	17	8	12				13	7	12	14	7	12
Total	100	100	100	100	100	100				100	100	100	100	100	100

D.   Percentage Distribution of Firms Having Various Wage Package Components: 1949

Percentage of the total wage package accounted for	Type of Wage Component								
	Basic pay	Job pay	Incentive pay	Family maintenance pay	Price inflation pay	Geographic differential pay	Overtime pay	Special job pay	Other types of pay
0–10	5.6	89.4	34.4	61.9	21.3	4.54	85.5	99.2	100.0
10–20	23.6	5.5	22.4	34.4	11.2	34.7	12.3	0.9	
20–30	15.5	2.9	15.9	2.6	18.6	12.4	2.0		
30–40	11.7	1.0	12.6	1.1	12.8	5.0	0.2		
40–50	12.1	1.0	6.5		13.2	2.5			
50–60	11.3	0.2	4.1		10.8				
60–70	7.0		2.6		6.6				
70–80	5.6		1.0		4.0				
80–90	6.5		0.5		1.5				
90–100	1.1								
TOTAL	100.0	100.0	100.0	100.0	100.0	100.0	100.0	100.0	100.0
Number of firms	556	382	389	541	453	121	472	241	4
Percentage of surveyed firms (=556) with the component	100.0	68.7	70.0	97.3	81.5	21.8	84.9	43.3	0.7
Average percentage of each component in total wage package	38.9	6.9	21.8	9.4	31.9	13.5	6.7	5.0	5.0

IV. Various Subsystems within the Overall System of Remuneration (*Nikkeiren Chōsa*)

A. Composition of the Wage Payment Package (*chingin taikei*): Percentage of Firms with Various Items

Item	Year			
	1958	1963	1968	1974
I. Basic pay				
1. Age	20.5	30.8	31.5 ⎫	
2. Educational background	10.3	20.7	17.1 ⎬	37.4
3. Experience and/or length of employment with the same firm	27.6	33.1	39.5 ⎭	
4. Job skills	25.9	28.0	38.1 ⎫	32.5
5. Qualifications	10.0	12.1	15.9 ⎭	
6. Occupation	10.3	14.8	14.2	9.6
II. Incentive pay				
1. Pay for actually working without absenteeism	27.6	26.6	29.5	25.4
2. Pay for reporting-in	18.6	9.4	6.2	—
3. Commission	—	—	3.8	3.2
4. Individual efficiency	20.9	8.9	7.0	5.6
5. Group efficiency	23.3	13.8	10.9	7.5
III. Livelihood maintenance allowances				
1. Family maintenance	90.8	90.0	94.3	90.0
2. Commutation	82.2	77.6	93.8	89.7
3. Housing	24.2	37.0	58.4	67.1
4. Geographic differential	38.7	34.1	42.6	43.3
5. Tax assistance	⎧ 19.3	2.9	2.6	9.9
6. Insurance fees	⎩ 19.3	28.0	30.4	
7. Price inflation	5.1	4.2	4.7	5.2
IV. Other allowances				
1. Position	63.4	88.0	91.3	83.9
2. Special work	46.2	67.6	74.2	52.3
3. Shift work	15.0	24.7	39.0	43.3
4. Round-the-clock operations	—	3.5	4.1	—
5. Lay-off or non-work at the convenience of management	—	13.9	14.4	—
6. Technical skill	—	19.3	28.7	30.2

B.   System for Calculating Labor Costs (*chingin shiharai keitai*): Percentage of Firms Using Various Approaches

Item	Year			
	1958	1963	1968	1974
A. Time-tied payment				
1. Hourly rates	8.3	4.1	5.9	10.0
2. Daily rates	36.7	22.6	18.4	12.8
3. Weekly wage	0.8	0.6	0.7	0.4
4. Daily rates and monthly salary	43.5	44.9	52.2	70.1
5. Monthly salary	84.7	79.1	83.8	70.1
B. Incentive pay				
1. Straight piece rates	11.3	6.2	4.2	2.3
2. Progressive piece rates	2.8	2.0	1.4	0.4
3. Standard hour rates	4.3	4.2	2.3	0.8
4. Halsey premium	2.0	1.0	0.8	—
5. Rowan premium	1.0	0.2	0.5	0.1

C.   System for Wage Increases: Percentage of Firms Using Various Systems

Item	Year			
	1958	1963	1968	1974
I. System of annual increments				
A. Automatic increment	23.6	28.4	25.0	22.9
B. Increment after examination	87.7	82.4	87.3	80.0
II. System of increments as they occur				
A. Due to promotion or change in status	32.7	30.8	41.0	n.a
B. Due to distinguished service commendation	19.5	12.3	14.3	n.a
C. Due to occasional adjustments	28.6	24.7	26.6	n.a
III. System of established achievement criteria	51.0	58.3	61.5	n.a

D.   Bonus System: Percentage of Firms Paying Bonuses at Various Times or in Various Ways

Item	Year			
	1958	1963	1968	1974
A. At the end of accounting period	34.8	24.6	19.8	n.a
B. At the end of the calendar year	78.8	78.2	83.5	n.a
C. During the summer	75.3	78.3	79.8	n.a
D. Occasionally during the summer	5.1	13.8	12.3	44.6
E. Occasionally during the winter			14.9	54.4
F. Profit sharing			5.6	12.4
G. Production			9.7	

E. System of Retirement Pay: Percentage of Firms Subscribing to Different Systems

Item	Year			
	1958	1963	1968	1974
A. Lump sum payment	97.5	95.0	94.5	93.9
B. Lump sum paid as an annuity	4.6	8.0	22.6	20.6
C. Payment through a system operated by a "mutual aid society" for small and medium-sized enterprises	—	0.8	2.4	.2.4
D. National welfare pension scheme				
1. On an adjusted basis	—	—	7.8	12.3
2. On a fully-qualified basis	—	—	10.9	17.1
3. With some combination of both	—	—	1.1	1.3
E. Approved private pension fund				
1. Contributing system	—	4.6	9.6	8.8
2. Non-contributing system	—	3.7	16.0	26.6
F. Non-approved private pension scheme				
1. Contributing system	—	4.9	5.9	3.6
2. Non-contributing system	—	6.4	5.6	2.0
3. System with reserves held in the company	—	7.9	6.5	3.7
4. Systems with reserves held in a body other than the company	—	2.8	3.8	1.5

F. Productivity Arrangements: Percentage of Firms Having Various Systems

Item	Year			
	1958	1963	1968	1974
Sharing system based on value added	—	3.1	3.3	19.4
Sharing system linked to total sales	—	0.4	1.0	5.4
Other system	—	1.6	1.5	n.a.

G. Other Aspects of Wage Administration: Percentage of Firms Involved

Item	Year			
	1958	1963	1968	1974
Survey of employee's living expenses	—	5.4	5.6	1.7
Long-term wage planning	—	13.9	18.9	4.3
Long-term wage agreements	—	2.2	2.6	1.2

The Seniority-Merit Wage System in Japan

Umemura Mataji

1. The Nature of the Seniority-Merit Wage System

In recent years the seniority-merit wage system *(nenkō chingin seido)* has come under fire from all quarters: wage system theorists, labor union leaders, management groups, and most recently even the government. Opinions and proposals are as numerous as the number of participants in the debate. However, despite the fact that everyone seems to arrive at a conclusion which is critical of the existing system, curiously there is little agreement as to what actually constitutes the seniority-merit wage system. It is indeed odd that so many different starting points, each with its own subtle uniqueness in approach, can lead to the same conclusion. Nevertheless, a survey of the different viewpoints suggests that there is common agreement on five characteristics associated with the seniority-merit wage system[1]:

1. There are no recognized occupational wage rates which extend across the whole economy. Rather, wages for different occupational groupings exist only within the firm. The absolute and relative size of occupational wage differentials thus varies from firm to firm, being

This paper first appeared as "Nenkō Chingin ni Tsuite," *Keizai Kenkyū* (vol. 18, no. 2: April 1967), pp. 160–163. The author is Professor of Economics at Hitotsubashi University.

[1] This summary relies heavily on Koike Kazuo, "Kigyōnai Chingin Kōzō" [The Structure of Wages within the Firm], *Bunken Kenkyū: Nihon no Rōdō Mondai* [Bibliographic Research: The Labor Problem in Japan], ed. by Rōdō Mondai Bunken Kenkyū Kai (The Study Group on Literature Relating to the Labor Problem) (Tokyo: Sōgō Rōdō Kenkyūjo, 1966), pp. 130–140.

decided upon independently within the framework of each individual enterprise.

2. Because the overall real wage is low, attention is focused on the need to guarantee each worker a minimum standard of living. Accordingly, wages are tied to the individual's life-cycle needs, which in turn means the age of each individual (male employee) or the number of years of continuous employment at the same firm. One result is the great weight given to seniority as a factor determining wage rates. This fact is reflected in the very low level of wages earned across the board by young employees just starting out in the work force. Because starting wages are so low, it becomes imperative that the individual's wages be raised as he ages and assumes added financial responsibilities after marriage. In this fashion, the system institutionalizes itself.

3. Given this emphasis on seniority, wage rates do not very well reflect the quantity or the quality of the labor supplied by each individual.

4. Within any given firm the wage differential between those in the top age group and those in the youngest group is much greater than that found in firms in other industrialized countries. The wage differentials existing within Japanese firms are therefore unique.

5. The seniority-merit wage curve is most prominent among white- and blue-collar workers in the large firms; these "unique" characteristics seem to become less important as the size of the firm decreases.

These are the general characteristics of the wage system in Japanese firms. To be sure, even on this level there are differences in nuance and emphasis when it comes to approach or definition. In looking for a common understanding by deducing from various viewpoints the five characteristics mentioned above, we are considering the literature in a general way in order to arrive at a definition and perhaps some built-in assumptions or hypotheses with which we can work. This no doubt results in our overlooking certain differences which are central to the arguments on various sides of the issue. However, our intention is not to enter the debate itself. Rather, our concern at this stage is with the general framework around which the various positions taken in the debate rotate.

2. The Development of Intra-firm Wage Structures

Before examining the appropriateness of the above summary of how the seniority-merit wage system is conceived, it is first necessary to consider the way in which we have conceptualized the general process by which the internal wage structure is derived within the individual enterprise. The next few paragraphs focus on this matter.

In considering the "internal wage structure within the firm" we are not talking about a structure which lies beyond the bounds of traditional wage theory. Rather than looking for another theory to replace "traditional" theory, I suggest that we are dealing with a problem requiring the careful application of existing theories. What is the process by which a generalized or abstract theory of wages is made useful on the concrete level? To be sure, the application of wage theory to existing realities is not as easy as it seems. For example, general wage theory is based upon the assumption that each person's labor is equivalent. In reality, however, we begin with the fact that the labor supplied by each person is different.

According to the traditional theory of wages, the amount of labor willingly supplied and demanded will naturally change when the wage rate changes in the labor market. The traditional approach to supply and demand shows how an equilibrium is derived from the competitive interaction of buyers and sellers in the market. However, this "macro approach" tends to minimize differences in the labor supply behavior of each individual worker and to overlook the unique properties of specific types of demand occurring in the production of specific commodities. These kinds of assumptions greatly simplify reality. Without becoming bogged down in this problem, I wish to take a closer look at the "micro level" by examining how wage rates are structured within the firm.

A. The Labor Supply and the Value of Labor

Labor's awareness of its own value in the labor market is in most cases the result of two types of knowledge. The first comes from comparisons among friends and others doing similar work in the neighborhood.[2] This is a major source of standards based on concepts of parity or fairness. The second is awareness of the level of expenses incurred in maintaining one's family at a given standard of living. There are thus relative and absolute standards involved in appraising the value of one's own labor.

In the process of establishing a given standard of living, individuals join together in various social activities. People within a given group

---

[2] On these comparisons, see Sano Yōko, Koike Kazuo and Ishida Hideo, eds., *Chingin Kōshō no Kōdō Kagaku* [A Behavioral Science Approach to Wage Bargaining] (Tokyo: Tōyō Keizai Shimpō Sha, 1969), Parts One and Two.

tend to form social strata based upon the fact that they share similar standards of living. Although the exact nature of these strata must still be examined empirically, for the time being we will work on the assumption that such strata do in fact exist. Accordingly, workers are thought to have a rather fixed notion of what their standard of living ought to be. In addition to this standard, we can further assume that most people also have some idea of the normal size and composition of families in their own strata. Given these two cognitive inputs, the worker is able to formulate his life-cycle needs. Once life-cycle needs are determined, the worker is able to arrive at some amount of income which will be necessary to guarantee that his family's needs are met at each point in his life cycle. That amount of income is called his "target income". Formulated in this way, the target income of each worker represents his "reproduction costs" as set forth in traditional Marxist theory.

In deciding upon the price at which he will supply his own labor, the individual makes constant reference to his target income and to the wages received by others. The individual's supply price will vary according to his social stratum and his access to information about wage rates in society at large. It should be pointed out that whereas the making of wage comparisons is a pragmatic exercise with rather stable or predictable results, the choice of an absolute amount as a target income is based upon a subjective judgment which is tied to the individual's own circumstances. The latter is thus more subject to change. For example, continued unemployment may cause an individual to lower his target income and seek previously unacceptable employment in order to make ends meet on a day-to-day basis. His concept of reproduction costs is thus narrowed to his minimum physical needs, and cultural activity becomes a luxury.

B. The Demand for Labor and the Value of Labor

Once a business firm has decided upon a technology and how best to organize its human resources to utilize that technology, the next task is deciding on the types of persons who will best fit the needs of that organization. If the organization itself is a given, with various employment practices and customs having already been institutionalized, as is usually the case, consideration of these traditions must also be brought into the picture. Management will tend to think of roles in terms of categories. Each type of role is then assigned a value based upon its relative importance. The demand price for different types of labor is in principle based upon the marginal productivity of each job category. In reality, however, it is often necessary to simplify the measurement of marginal productivity, and most firms today no doubt use only a rough rule of thumb, such as job analysis or job evaluation, to determine the demand price for each type of labor required.

C. Wage Bargaining

There is little reason to expect that the supply and demand prices for various types of labor will coincide with each other. Accordingly, labor and management derive a commonly agreed-upon price through a complex process of bargaining. If a "going rate" has been fairly well established in the labor market for a given type of labor, it often becomes the guideline for labor and management in their negotiations. When the value of labor for the firm, as measured in terms of its own job criteria, falls below the going rate, it is common in the United States for the going rate to be used.[3]

Wage bargaining results in the structuring of wage rates for various job categories. The resultant wage structure is a function of (1) the supply and demand prices for labor, (2) the bargaining power of labor and management, and (3) the sensitivity of labor and management to the going rates. When there is an excess supply of labor or the bargaining power of the firm is otherwise increased, the structuring of wage rates will move closer to the various demand prices offered by management. Conversely, a labor shortage or other change which enhances labor's bargaining power will tend to result in a wage structure closer to the supply prices sought by labor.

In small enterprises with only a few employees, the firm can negotiate directly with each individual employee and can implement its personnel policies in that way. Indeed, it is not uncommon for small firms to operate according to an unwritten set of practices or customs. The wage system in such firms becomes an institution unto itself, thereby limiting the sphere for personal discretion in the allocation of wages to individual employees. In larger firms, it is necessary to formalize the wage system to ensure an atmosphere in which a sense of parity or fairness prevails. The details of how much is to be paid for each type of labor are usually set down in a written document. The document specifies how much each individual employee is to receive. Total income will be based upon some mix of personal characteristics (such as age and level of education), job performance, and various allowances. Accordingly, a variety of detailed schedules are combined to give each individual a unique value.

[3] Kaneko Yoshio, ed. *Amerika no Chingin Kettei* [Wage Determination in the United States], Part II (Tokyo: Nihon Seisansei Honbu, 1961), p. 149.

The preceding paragraphs have described only a most general theoretical outline for understanding how wage rates are determined; the actual details will vary from firm to firm. It might seem that labor and management spend their time in collective bargaining arguing about the composition of the various wage schedules and how they ought to be combined. This is partially because the actual distribution of wage payments and the composite schedule of wage rates (which results from adjustments in the specific schedules themselves or their relative weighing) have already been institutionalized as a result of collective bargaining sessions in the past. Consequently, the negotiations which are conducted today are concerned only with small changes or adjustments in specific components. It simply is not necessary or even possible to redo the whole system at each bargaining session. Collective bargaining is fundamentally a discussion of priorities as to which parts of the overall system should be changed in which ways, with careful attention being given to how changes in particular schedules will affect the actual amount of income received by each individual performing a specific job or functionally defined role. Accordingly, although the demand prices of management and the supply prices of labor remain as the basic starting point, it is the above process which results in a formula for synthesizing the two positions.

3.   Some Questions about the Seniority-Merit Wage System

The discussion in the preceding section on how a system of wage differentials is derived through collective bargaining within the firm leads us to entertain certain doubts about the logic embedded in the discussion of the seniority-merit wage system. In the remainder of this essay I wish to consider briefly some common questions generally raised about the concept of the seniority-merit wage system.

A.   The Absence of Uniform Occupational Wage Rates

Looking at the first characteristic described at the beginning of this chapter, one undeniable fact would seem to be that occupational wage rates are not uniform throughout the labor market in Japan. Furthermore, the great majority of observers seem to agree that this is a basic characteristic of the Japanese wage structure. However, there is an error in the logic. If we are talking about the absence of uniform occupational wage rates as a characteristic of the seniority-merit wage system there is no problem. The problem comes in trying to generalize for the economy or the labor market as a whole. First, the seniority-merit wage system is an institution which has been established and maintained within each firm. Its existence reflects power relationships and other factors which come into play within the confines of the individual enterprise. On the other hand, occupational wage differentials result from general conditions in the labor market as a whole. Another problem with the first generalization is that it makes it difficult for the second, third, and fourth characteristics mentioned above to be reconciled with the fifth. Given this problem, the question of whether common occupational wage rates exist throughout the whole economy should be considered separately from our analysis of seniority-merit wage systems within individual firms.

B. The Low Standard of Living as a Source of the Seniority-Merit Wage System

The second characteristic associated with the seniority-merit wage system seems to embody simultaneously two rather different kinds of explanations. The true essence of the system is seen as being both (1) in the overall wage system which is built around an age component and various kinds of allowances including the family allowance and (2) in the functions which such a system fills in terms of guaranteeing a minimum standard of living.

The emphasis on the various wage payment schedules tends to suggest that wages have lost their importance as a price mechanism for regulating the flow of labor in the labor market. It also implies that the resultant system of wage rates is only indirectly tied to any notion of broader society-wide occupational wage rates. In contrast to that interpretation, however, wage schedules are in fact composed so as to preserve occupational wage rates prevailing in a much broader labor market. The use of a seniority-merit wage payment scheme is only a means to that end. One corollary which results from too much emphasis on the seniority-merit wage payment scheme is the tendency to exaggerate the importance of changes in the scheme within the firm even when no major changes are occurring in the economy as a whole. In opposition to that position, I suggest that, without changes in the external economic realities, changes of any type in the various payment schedules are insignificant. Without important changes in the macro-economy it is unlikely that there will be any significant change in the actual distribution of wages. On this point, we inadvertently come to question the impact of the union movement on the structure of actual wage payments.

C.   Reproduction Costs, Labor Supply, and Wage Rates

The emphasis on the importance of life-cycle needs as a consideration in determining wage rates is linked with the third characteristic which suggests that wages are not tied to the quantity or quality of labor. The second section of this chapter suggested that the internal wage structure, which results from the interaction of labor and management, is closer to meeting the needs of labor than to meeting the needs of management. For this to happen, however, one of three situations is envisioned: (1) there must be a labor shortage or an exceptionally strong demand for labor in the labor market; (2) the bargaining power of the unions must be stronger than that of management; or (3) both of these trends must be present together.

Unfortunately, the facts do not validate these hypotheses. Japan is characterized by a labor surplus, not a shortage. This is true in spite of the shortage of new graduates in the youngest age brackets in recent years. Moreover, there is common agreement among the debaters that the present standard of living cannot cover the reproductive costs of an excessive population. On this point, then, a large number of participants in the debate contradict themselves.[4] Nevertheless, it is still difficult to deny that the seniority-merit wage system to some extent works to fill the function of guaranteeing life-cycle needs. In dealing with this paradox, there is another line of attack which posits that management is happy to go along with the supply prices desired by labor as long as doing so is not contrary to its own interests. At the extreme, one might even argue that the demand prices offered by management closely resemble the supply prices offered by labor. To accept this reasoning, however, it is necessary to reexamine the demand behavior of management.

D.   On-the-job Training, Technological Change, and Seniority Wages

Here we deal specifically with the third characteristic associated with the seniority-merit wage system—the lack of correspondence between

---

[4] On the contradictions built into the second and fifth characteristics of the seniority-merit wage system, see Koike Kazuo, *Chingin: Riron to Genjō Bunseki* [Wages: Theory and Current Analysis] (Tokyo: Daiyamondo Sha, 1966), pp. 125–126.

wage and skill levels. In looking at the demand side of the labor market, we must ask why management gives priority to employees who stay with the same firm for a long time. A small number of people have looked at the history of industrial wage labor in Japan and, in partial answer to this question, stressed the importance of Japan's approach to technological innovation and on-the-job training.[5]

The major thrust of their approach is as follows. Most of Japan's industrial labor force has been supplied from agricultural villages throughout Japan. Workers were not organized in any way, nor did they have very accurate information about the labor market. Often they came to the urban industrial areas without any positive plan to enter a specific line of work. Only rarely did one of them take the initiative in looking for a specific job. Given their nearly total ignorance and the lack of any organization, the buyers soon came to hold the upper hand in the labor market. Finally, new entrants to the labor force did not have even an elementary knowledge of factory life. Accordingly, management had to train the new recruits in every aspect involving the operation of the plant and the types of social organization necessary for industrial production. It was thus necessary for management to give employees a considerable education. In this process, the use of older workers to pass on their acquired skills to younger workers was an economy. One result was the transferral of a technology and training which was built around the needs of a specific firm. Another result was a high correlation between one's years with a given firm, one's age, and one's acquired skills. The close correlation between wages and years with the same firm meant that wages were also closely tied to the acquisition of skills. To the extent that wage rates are tied to skills, the third characteristic generally associated with the seniority-merit system becomes further removed from reality.

E. Some Problems with the Emphasis on Technological Change

Research stressing the development of a peculiarly Japanese approach to technological change and job training within the firm has done much to boost the stock of those who have stressed the unique importance of seniority-based wage rates in the Japanese context. However, a number of issues have not yet been resolved. In the remaining paragraphs four are mentioned.

[5] See for example Ujihara Shōjirō, *Nihon Rōdō Mondai Kenkyū* [Research on the Labor Problem in Japan] (Tokyo: University of Tokyo Press, 1966), Part III, Chapters One and Three.

First, although it now seems clear that the type of on-the-job training described above provided a solid base for the seniority-merit wage system, no one has yet proved that a causal link did in fact exist between the two. It is an explanation of causality which may be logically consistent, but one which nevertheless has not yet been proven. The Japanese approach to on-the-job training provided a necessary but not sufficient condition for the emergence of the seniority-merit wage system. In order to prove that a causal link did in fact exist, it must be proved that the transmission of technical skills in firms disadvantaged by a tremendous gap between the modern technology imported from Western Europe and Japan's own traditional technology necessitated such a system. This in turn requires that, despite the large reserves of unskilled labor, there has been a very limited supply of skilled workers able to utilize the newly imported technology. Consequently, there must have existed a great difference in the elasticity of different types of labor.[6]

Second, one doubts whether the kind of on-the-job training and education given in Japanese firms is uniquely Japanese.[7] If there is anything special or different about Japan, it is the gap between the modern technology imported from abroad and the traditional technology indigenous to Japan. This reflects Japan's relatively late start in the race to industrialize. International comparisons require careful isolation of the variables involved and acquisition of all the facts; armchair speculation will not do.

Third, it is natural that the influence of technological innovation on skills which are taught on the job in the traditional fashion is given considerable weight by those emphasizing the importance of a uniquely Japanese approach to industrialization. However, technological innovation in Japan has varied greatly by industry and by firm. It is thus dangerous to simplify the facts by generalizing about all of Japan from a few more-or-less isolated examples.[8]

Finally, given the fifth characteristic associated with the seniority-

[6] Chingin Kenkyūkai Rōdōryoku Ryūdōsei Shōiinkai (Subcommittee on Labor Mobility, Wage Research Group), *Chingin Seido to Rōdōryoku no Ryūdōsei ni Tsuite (Chūkan Hōkoku)* [The Wage System and Labor Mobility: An Interim Report] (Tokyo: Rōdō Shō, 1964), mimeographed, p. 4. However, the report did not go so far as to deal with the gap between newly imported technology and traditional technology.

[7] Koike suggests that it is not. See his *Chingin: Sono Riron to Genjō Bunseki*, pp. 130 and 140.

[8] Chingin Kenkyūkai Rōdō Seisansei Kankei Shōiinkai (Subcommittee on Labor Productivity, Wage Research Group), *Rōdō Seisansei Kōjō to Chingin Seido ni Tsuite* [Improved Labor Productivity and the Wage System] (Tokyo: Rōdō Shō, 1967), mimeographed, pp. 3–23, and the research materials which appeared in a

merit wage system (the fact that this system is found primarily in the large firms), how should we account for the rapid technological change which has occurred in small and medium-sized firms? This is the most important shortcoming of explanations which link the emergence of the seniority-merit wage system with Japan's peculiar pattern of job training. Do proponents of such theories believe that the smaller firms did not employ any skilled labor? Did employees in these firms acquire skill through on-the-job taining in a manner which was not practiced in the large firms which seemed to require a seniority-merit wage system? If similar training did exist, then one must indicate where and how such training was implemented in the smaller firms which did not have the seniority-merit wage system. Also, how did the smaller firms go about recruiting such skilled labor? Before we can accept any theory about the impact of technological innovation, we must explain how labor came to be stratified in the process of acquiring such skills. Given these difficulties, it seems to me that another approach is necessary.

companion volume, *Sangyōbetsu ni Mita Gijutsu Kakushin to Chingin Seido no Dōkō* [Technological Change and Revisions in the Wage System for Various Industries] (Tokyo: Rōdō Shō, 1967), mimeographed.

An Analysis of Factors Determining Starting Pay

Tanaka Hirohide

1. Introduction

In recent years it has become increasingly difficult for firms to recruit the number of new graduates they desire. This tightening of the labor market results in market forces playing a more important role in determining the starting pay for graduates who are entering the labor market for the first time. In deciding the starting wage rates for these graduates, each firm must consider two things: First, how has the firm been performing and how is its wage system presently organized to provide for those currently employed? Second, what are other firms paying to obtain the services of graduates?

A look at any of several recent surveys on factors determining the starting pay for graduates clearly indicates that market factors, including both the structure of supply of and demand for labor in particular industries and more comprehensive structural changes in the national economy itself, are extremely important.[1] However, the surveys also suggest that the initial wage rate is shaped by institutionalized norms and practices which define the whole process of employment. Although many people seem to be aware of these various influences, it is interesting to note that discussions of the labor market and the various market

This paper first appeared as "Shoninkyū Kettei No Mekanizumu ni Kansuru Ichibunseki," *Rōdō Tōkei Chōsa Geppō* (vol. 16, no. 11: November 1964), pp. 4–9. The author is Chief of the Labor Policy Section in the Minister's Secretariat, Ministry of Labour.

[1] Rōdō Shō (Ministry of Labour), *Sanjūhachi Nen Rōdō Keizai No Bunseki* [The 1963 White Paper on Labor] (Tokyo: Ōkura Shō Insatsu Kyoku, 1964), p. 168.

forces are seldom clear on how these various forces actually interact to determine the starting pay for new graduates.

This study focuses on the mechanism determining starting pay for graduates by examining shifts in the offers made to them through the Public Employment Security Office. In analyzing the wage mechanism two approaches are commonly used. The first involves a macro analysis. This approach seeks to explain movements in the national average of starting salaries by considering correlations with various quantitative economic indicators. The result of such research is usually a mathematical model. This approach has been promoted considerably in recent years by the interest in intermediate-range economic planning. Using this type of model, the Economic Research Institute attached to the Economic Planning Agency has produced some interesting analyses. The second approach considers the problem on a microeconomic level. By examining the behavior of each individual firm, its advocates seek to reveal a rationale for the system of starting salaries. In addition to a solid understanding, some idea of future trends can be deduced. This study adopts the second approach.

2.   The Dispersion of Starting Salaries for New Graduates

A.   The Process of Forming a Market Rate for New Graduates

Applications indicating the desire of firms to employ students who graduate in March are accepted by the Public Employment Security Office from June or July of the preceding year. We are interested initially in how the going wage rate changes over time as the applications come in, and how strictly employers adhere to the going rate. Here we are interested in two criteria which define the state of the market: (1) the amount of dispersion in offers to new graduates (meaning nonconformity) and (2) the degree of stability exhibited in the standard or going rate (the mode). The amount of dispersion or deviation from the mode does not change much over time (see Tables 1, 2, and 3).

Looking first at high-school graduates, Table 1 shows how many manufacturing firms sought to hire males graduating from high school in March 1965 through the Public Employment Security Office and the starting salaries these firms offered. The offers are grouped together by the Public Employment Security Office every two weeks starting

Table 1:   The Coefficient of Dispersion for the Starting Salaries Offered in
Manufacturing to High-school Males Graduating in March 1965

Round	The average starting salary	The 25th percentile in terms of the amount offered	The 75th percentile in terms of the amount offered	Coefficient of dispersion	Number of firms
1	¥16,000	¥15,000	¥16,750	0.109	24
2				0.113	91
3	16,132	15,372	16,908	0.095	118
4				0.095	336
5	16,063	15,317	16,942	0.101	197
6				0.093	197
7	16,010	15,254	16,838	0.099	169
8				0.096	144
9	16,056	15,313	17,045	0.108	140
10				0.104	79
11	15,963	15,222	16,704	0.093	80
12				0.115	98
13	16,000	15,261	16,739	0.092	68
14				0.086	72
15	15,950	15,285	16,788	0.094	133

Notes: (1)   The coefficient of dispersion (CD) is calculated as follows:

$$CD = \frac{\left(\begin{array}{l}\text{the 75th percentile in terms}\\\text{of the amount offered}\end{array}\right) - \left(\begin{array}{l}\text{the 25th percentile in terms}\\\text{of the amount offered}\end{array}\right)}{\left(\begin{array}{l}\text{the 50th percentile in terms}\\\text{of the amount offered}\end{array}\right)}$$

(2)   The figures are for all employment security offices in Tokyo.

(3)   A "round" refers to the set of offers received from firms in a two-week period.

Source: Tokyo Tō Rōdō Kyoku (Bureau of Labor, Tokyo Metropolitan Government), *Gakusotsu Kyūjin Ichiranhyō* (*Kōkō*) [Reference Tables on the Demand for Graduates: High Schools], undated and mimeographed.

the summer before the students graduate. The coefficient of dispersion is low for each individual lot. It is also low for the averages taken for each of the 15 lots at successive two-week intervals. Accordingly, the market does not develop over time as firms feel out the supply and demand and then gradually enter the market themselves. Rather, the stability of the coefficient of dispersion over time and its relatively small value suggest that the market is already established before the first applications are even received. If we divide the sample into firm-size groupings, it is interesting to note that the average offer is ever so slightly inversely related to firm size (Table 4).

The formation of the labor market for middle-school graduates is somewhat different. Although the amount of dispersion shown in

Table 2:   The Coefficient of Dispersion for the Starting Salaries Offered in
Manufacturing to Middle-school Males Graduating in March 1965

Period in which the offer was made	Location of the Employment Security Office					
	Gotanda		Kamata		Ōmori	
	Coefficient of dispersion	Number of firms	Coefficient of dispersion	Number of firms	Coefficient of dispersion	Number of firms
Through June 1964	0.117	59	0.098	779	0.110	398
First half of July 1964	0.094	302	0.111	246		
Second half of July 1964	0.106	216	0.091	144	0.095	333
First half of August 1964	0.112	87	0.075	14	0.1031	150
Second half of August 1964	0.094	98	0.128	134	0.123	105
First half of September 1964	0.119	46	0.114	46		

Notes: (1)   The coefficient of dispersion is calculated as in Table 1.
(2)   The figures are only for jobs offered to those who will become
live-in employees in some local area.

Source: The above table was calculated by the author from the applications
for employees submitted to the above three Employment Security
Offices.

Table 3:   The Coefficient of Dispersion for the Starting Salaries Offered in
Manufacturing to Middle-school Males Graduating in March 1964

Month in which offer is made		Employment Security Office			
		Gotanda		Ōmori	
		Coefficient of dispersion	Number of firms	Coefficient of dispersion	Number of firms
June	1963	0.132	81	0.109	275
July	1963	0.108	313	0.103	14
August	1963	0.119	192	0.1159	284
September	1963	0.145	175	0.125	237
October	1963	0.116	124	0.148	382
November	1963	0.126	87	0.145	172
December	1963	0.158	30	0.149	116
January	1964	0.223	19	0.138	57
February	1964	0.199	14	0.133	76
March	1964	0.034	5	0.121	58

Notes: Same as for Table 2.
Source: Same as for Table 2.

Table 3 is small and rather stable, much like the behavior regarding
high school graduates, the data in Tables 5 and 6 suggest that the
average offer rises over time. In other words, employers are penalized

Table 4:   The Average Starting Salary Offered in Manufacturing to High-school Males Graduating in March 1965 by Firm Size   (unit: yen)

Period in which the offer is made	Firm size (number of employees)		
	500 or more employees	100–499 employees	30–99 employees
1	15,667	16,200	—
3	16,077	15,938	16,273
5	15,750	15,738	16,652
7	15,333	15,757	16,523
9	15,400	15,719	16,500
11	15,333	16,000	15,917
13	15,833	15,583	16,350
15	15,600	15,981	15,853

Source: Same as for Table 1.

Table 5:   The Average Starting Pay Offered in Manufacturing to Middle-school Males Graduating in March 1964   (unit: yen)

Month in which offer was made	Employment Security Office	
	Ōmori	Gotanda
June	10,895	10,661
August	10,971	11,094
October	11,125	11,293
December	11,275	12,000

Source: Same as for Table 3.

Table 6:   The Average Starting Pay Offered in Manufacturing to Middle-school Males Graduating in March 1965

Month when the application was received	Employment Security Office		
	Gotanda	Kamata	Ōmori
Through June 1964	12,581	12,949	12,871
First half of July	12,868		
Second half of July	13,000	13,048	13,175
First half of August	12,821	13,292	13,140
Second half of August	12,991	13,375	13,250
First half of September	13,550	13,326	
Second half of September		13,550	

Note: The Ōmori office did not keep clear records of when the original applications were received. Thus we must rely on the number of times firms contacted the local offices. The first batch was published on July 28, and the others appeared at two-week intervals.

Source: Same as for Table 2.

for late entry into the market for middle-school graduates by higher prices. This fact is even clearer if we look at the total distribution of wage offers made in June and December 1963 for middle-school graduates appearing on the market in late March 1964 (Figure 1). The demand for male graduates from middle schools is very stand-ardized in the first few months, and then the amount of dispersion increases while the amount of starting pay offered increases slightly over time. One explanation seems plausible. A large number of firms, considering the fact that the shortage of new graduates is worsening year by year and realizing that they will have to pay more in the coming year, make early offers. In reality, however, the offers are quite similar: the going rate for the preceding year plus alpha. Since alpha tends to be the same for all firms, firms must come back and make a second offer in order to be competitive. As individual firms seek to establish their superiority over their competitors even in the short term, the offers to the prospective graduates are given a further boost as the months pass. The extent to which the amount offered to the potential graduates rises depends upon such factors as the general state of the economy at the time and the relative balance between the supply of and demand for the graduates. For example, when entre-preneurs are not confident where the economy is headed following a recession, few firms will make applications for personnel reinforce-ments. Moreover, tending to believe that the competition for labor will not become that acute, many probably feel that they can secure the

Figure 1:   The Distribution of Wage Offers at the Ōmori Employment Security Office for Prospective Middle-school
Graduates, June and December 1963.

Note: The percentages are calculated for the number of firms
in each salary class by dividing that number by the total
of all firms filing applications in each respective month.

Source: Same as for Table 3.

necessary labor by simply going along with the market rate. Even if it is necessary later to raise the amount one is offering, it is unlikely that the increase will have to be very large.

If the offers rise in the manner described above, the firms which put in their offers early are at a disadvantage, and will find it necessary to revise their offers upwards. It is difficult to carefully verify this point since the necessary data are not available. Nonetheless, by going through the old forms which the various offices have not thrown away, one can piece together some supporting evidence. Table 7 tells us about the behavior of firms which made offers early and then later revised those offers so that they would be on a par with the going rate toward the end of the year. Eighty percent of the revisions came from firms which had initially made offers in June and July.

B.   The Characteristics of Firms Which Make Early Offers

Given the fact that the market rate for new graduates does not vary much once the first offers are made, and the fact that the dispersion in the amounts offered is very small, the next task is to examine how and why the firms making early offers decide on the initial amount to offer. To obtain answers to these kinds of questions, a small survey was taken among three hundred firms in the Tokyo area which had made offers to graduates through the Public Employment Security Office. Respondents were simply asked to fill in freely on an enclosed postcard (postage prepaid) the factors they considered in deciding upon an amount to offer graduates. The rate of return was 60 percent. The results of that survey are given in Table 8. Two features stand out in the behavior of these firms. One concerns the reasons for deciding upon a given amount to offer new graduates and the other has to do with the amount of increase occurring each year.

Table 7:   Revised Offers for Middle-school Students Graduating in March 1964   (unit: yen)

Offer	Employment Security Office		
	Ōmori	Gotanda	Kamata
Original offer	10,366	10,142	10,185
Revised offer	11,265	11,188	11,026

Note: The figures are only for firms for which the revised figure is clear. Some firms revised their offers, but the more recent figures are not available.

Source: Same as for Table 3.

If we look initially at the reasoning behind the firms' decision to offer a given amount (Table 8), the following facts seem to be clear. First, many firms had attended a meeting held by the Public Employment Security Office and the Labor Bureau of the Tokyo Metropolitan Government to provide information about the situation regarding the new crop of graduates. At such meetings some time is devoted to the discussion of appropriate wage rates. This seems to have influenced many firms. Second, the associations of businessmen in the same line of business or in the same geographic locale circulate such information, but this becomes the determining factor for only slightly over 10 percent of all firms. Third, many firms have come to feel it is simply in the natural course of events that starting pay will go up each year as prices rise and the shortage of new graduates is increasingly felt. Finally, as a kind of corollary, since the starting pay for new graduates must conform to wage schedules existing within the firm, it is only natural that the starting wage will rise in order to maintain an overall balance in terms of the earnings of all others presently employed.

It has been suggested that since the early 1960s the Public Employment Security Office has come to play an important role in setting the going rate. This observation is supported by the fact that nearly 30 percent explicitly mentioned the Office as a decisive factor in deciding upon the amount of their offer.[2] It is interesting to note that the average starting pay (¥12,700) offered by the firms which attended the explanation meeting (firms citing the importance of the information received at the meeting, *i.e.*, reason A in Table 8) was considerably below the average amount (¥13,400) offered by firms which acted more independently (those citing reasons B, D, E, and F in Table 8). It would seem that the former group of firms relied upon the Office's information precisely because they wanted to offer the lowest pay pos-

---

[2] Every year a general meeting open to all employers is held at each Public Employment Security Office branch before they open their doors for applications to hire new graduates the following year. The meeting serves as a forum where prospective employers can discuss trends for the coming year and ask questions. Those who attend are given two types of information. One consists of the average starting salaries paid in the year just completed and the rates of increase recorded in the past. From this kind of information it was estimated that the starting pay for graduates in March 1965 would be ¥12,800. The second type of information concerns the very minimum pay new graduates are likely to accept. Based upon the average paid by very small firms which were able to secure enough labor through group hiring the preceding year, it was recommended that ¥10,000 would be the minimum for graduates in March 1965. Here it should be pointed out that the going rate for starting wages and wage increases is set by the very large firms in April and May, and later followed by the smaller firms as the spillover effect begins to take place. See the article in this volume by Sano Yōko.

Table 8:   Factors Influencing the Amount Offered by the First Firms to Contact
the Office of Employment Security

Reason	Percent
All firms returning the survey	100
A. Information supplied by the Public Employment Security Office	27
B. Various kinds of survey data	6
C. The rate offered by other firms in the same line of business or an agreement by some group of businessmen	12
D. The market in general	15
E. Firm's need for labor	16
F. Price inflation	14
G. The wage situation within the firm	16
H. Other reasons	4
I. No response	9

Note: Because multiple answers were accepted, the percentages do not add up
to 100.

sible. Such firms were aware of the fact that they would have to pay
more as the entire pay scale shifted upwards, but sought the least
possible increase in personnel costs. On the other hand, firms more
likely to follow general trends in the economy and use various kinds
of statistical data for further reference tended to be firms which paid
higher wages for those already employed and therefore presumably
better able to pay. Such firms also sought to be as competitive as
possible in the market for new graduates. Even though some of those
firms could not pay enough to hire older workers, they no doubt felt
that they could afford slightly more in order to employ the better
graduates.

The behavior of firms belonging to employers' associations (firms
citing reason C in Table 8) is no doubt similar to that of those relying
on the guidelines set forth by the Employment Security Office. In
deciding upon an organizational minimum, there is a tendency for such
associations to cite a low figure which nearly all the affiliated members
can meet. Again, this type of standard is acceptable to the financially
weaker firms; with less ability to pay, they usually seek the minimum
rate which will secure the labor they need. Accordingly, the average
amount offered by this type of firm was also rather low (¥12,800).

The second characteristic of the early offers is the fact that they
represent an increase which is a rounded-off figure. As Table 9 shows,
over one-third of the firms simply added an even ¥1000 or ¥1500
to the amount they had offered the preceding year. Although the
¥1000–1500 range of offers is somewhat low according to the prevail-

Table 9:   The Percentage Distribution of Firms According to the Increase Offered in Starting Pay for Middle-school Males Graduating in March 1965

Amount of increase in starting pay (yen)	Results of the postcard survey	Results of a survey by the Aichi Employers' Association (Aichi Keikyō)	Results of a survey by the Fukuoka Employers' Association (Fukuoka Keikyō)
0	7	18	3
–499	3	1	—
500	3	10	12
500–999	5	12	
1000	25	21	36
1001–1499	10	8	
1500	11	11	24
1501–1999	8	5	
2000	11	8	17
2000–2499	2	2	
2500	8	1	8
2501–	7	3	
Total	100	100	100

ing rate of increase in recent years, there is a certain logic in this behavior if we consider (1) the fact that these are the first offers and can later be revised and (2) the fact that many of the firms offering a predetermined increase of ￥1000 are firms at the upper end of the pay scale overall. It seems logical that firms which already have a higher standard for starting pay in absolute terms could afford to offer less of a rise provided that they later augment their initial offer. Indeed, precisely because of their better standing overall, and thus their superior long-term earnings potential for the individual employee, they may well be better able to succeed in obtaining the labor they need early on before the high going rate is established. This certainly would be consistent with the fact that the larger firms as a whole offer slightly lower starting wages than the smaller firms and the fact that the most prestigious firms in Japan are usually the first to reach agreement with prospective graduates. Indeed, perhaps it is they who set the low rate which is then picked up by the first firms to make offers through the Public Employment Security Office.

In summary, the following three points stand out with regard to the first firms to make offers: First, the Public Employment Security Office is the most important source of information for the largest number of firms. Second, the group of firms depending on the Public Employment Security Office for information is the group offering the lowest starting salaries. Third, the difference between the amount offered for employees having graduated the past March and prospective graduates in the succeeding year is around ¥1,000–1,500, with a rounded-off figure being most common. In addition, it should be pointed out that the agreement reached by the Federation of Textile Workers (Zensen Dōmei), calling for an across-the-board starting salary of ¥13,000 for males graduating from middle school in March 1965, no doubt was also a factor influencing the market that year.

C. Differences in Starting Pay Offers by Firm Size and Industry

(1) *Firm size.* Two features characterize the distribution of wage offers made by large and small firms. First, the average amount offered varies inversely with firm size. Second, so too does the coefficient of dispersion for the amount offered. These facts are clearly evident in Figures 2 and 3. The coefficient of dispersion for the larger firms in Figure 2 is 0.106, whereas for the smaller firms it is 0.110; the respective figures for Figure 3 are 0.093 and 0.107. The difference is small but consistent. In addition to the factors given above, the large firms are no doubt more tightly bound by institutional factors than the smaller firms. If the offer is too high, for example, it may throw the whole seniority wage curve out of alignment and cause the firm's middle-aged employees to become dissatisfied. On the other hand, a relatively high standard of wages overall means that too low an offer may

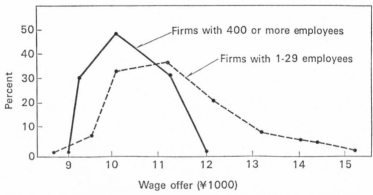

Figure 2: The Distributions of Wage Offers Lodged with the Gotanda Office for Middle-school Male Graduates (March 1965) to Work at Live-in Firms by Firm Size

Source: Calculated by the author from the application forms at the Gotanda Employment Security Office.

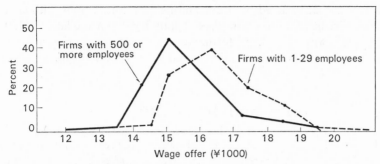

Figure 3: The Distribution of Wage Offers for High-school Male Graduates
(March 1965) by Firm Size
Source: Same as for Table 1.

result in a discontinuity at the lower end of the curve. Finally, the
larger firms will be more involved with the unions' annual spring wage
offensives and therefore be more likely to depress their offers as a
hedge against outside speculation on the firm's ability to pay wage
hikes in general. For example, the reference tables used to construct
Table 1 suggest that firms planning an overall upward shift in the pay
schedule *(bēsu appu)* made offers to new graduates which averaged
only about ¥15,000, considerably below the average of ¥16,000
registered for all firms.

(2) *Industry.* Figure 4 shows that there is very little difference in the

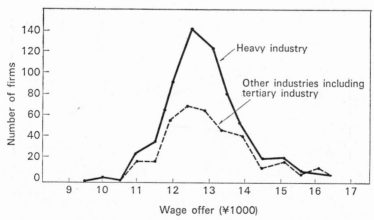

Figure 4: The Distribution of Wage Offers at the Ōmori Office for Middle-
school Graduates (March 1965) by Industry
Source: Calculated by the author from the application forms at the Ōmori
Employment Security Office.

average amount offered by heavy and light industrial firms, although the coefficient of dispersion will be slightly higher for the latter (0.120 compared with 0.099). Unfortunately, the data are primarily for small firms, and the classification of industries is very rough.

3. Offered Pay and Actual Pay

In this final section I wish to touch briefly on the relationship between the amount of pay offered to prospective graduates some six to nine months before they graduate and the pay they actually receive when they begin work the following April. First, the average pay offered by firms was ¥11,000, whereas graduates were employed in such a fashion as to result in the actual pay earned being below the average offered (Figure 5). In other words, the percentage of advertised positions which were actually filled was higher when the amount offered was either below or above the average offer or the modal offer.

These results are curiously unexpected in view of the commonly accepted theories of the labor market which posit that labor will rationally choose higher wages. One would have expected the graduates to choose a disproportionately larger percentage of the firms which

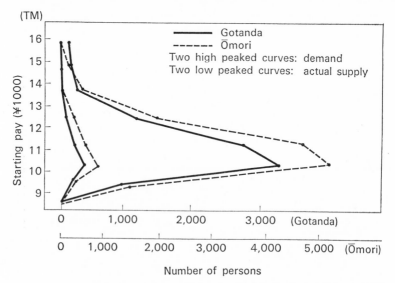

Figure 5: The Number of New Middle-school Male Graduates (March 1964) Sought and Actually Employed by the Amount of Starting Pay Involved

offered higher starting pay. Although a number of possible explanations come to mind, the fact that the larger firms are bunched at the lower end of the range of starting salaries offered suggests that the most feasible explanation will be related to firm size. It is likely that new graduates are aware that the starting pay does not reflect the total package of working conditions which include bonuses, future wage increases, promotion, and hours of work. Until about 1956 or 1957 the amount offered to new graduates varied directly with firm size and reflected fairly well the total package of working conditions. In recent years, however, the differential in the starting pay offered to prospective graduates has completely disappeared. Indeed, as Figures 2 and 3 suggest, the differentials have been reversed, and the amount offered has ceased to function as a barometer indicating the state of the labor market. Graduates today seem to be taking a longer-term view of things, and the larger firms are aware of this situation and perhaps have contributed to its creation. Putting aside considerations like the suitability of the work to be assigned and the environment at the place of work, it is clear that differences in the hours of work, pay hikes, and bonuses alone make the larger firms attractive places to work. Consequently, as these other considerations become more important, firms will be less able to secure the labor they desire simply by offering higher starting pay than their competitors.

Although limited in its scope, the above analysis clearly suggests that the labor market is rapidly changing. On the one hand, the dual structure associated with firm size has begun to appear in ways which make it difficult for the smaller firms to compete. At the same time, the stiffened competition has caused the smaller firms to bunch together. Only the firms which are considerably ahead of the others are able to offset their relative disadvantage in terms of other working conditions and thereby secure the labor they need. In the future the starting pay offered to prospective graduates will no doubt continue to be influenced strongly by (1) the macro-economic factors which shape the labor market and (2) the complicated process of pace-setting and spillover effects which underline the importance of information flows and the behavior of the firms which first approach the Public Employment Security Office. Reflecting various on-going changes in this environment, we can now see a new pattern emerging from this dynamic process.

Intra-firm Wage Differentials

Nakamura Atsushi

1. Introduction

The wage which each individual employee receives is known as the "individual wage rate" *(kobetsu chingin)*. Individual wage rates vary considerably depending upon two general sets of factors. One set is composed of the various characteristics or attributes peculiar to the individual employee. These include sex, educational background, age, and occupational responsibilities or job content. The second set is composed of characteristics associated with the firm to which the individual employee is attached. This set includes the firm's geographical location, its size, and its industrial classification.

This paper examines the factors which are usually cited as the most important sources of intra-firm wage differentials in Japan. Ascriptive factors such as years of employment with the same firm, age, and educational background are given special attention since they are most commonly associated with the seniority wage system. Attention is also given to firm size and occupational differentials and the way in which these relate to differentials based upon ascriptive criteria.

This study originally appeared as "Kigyōnai Chingin Kōzō no Bunseki," *Tōyō Keizai* (special issue no. 31: January 29, 1975), pp. 45–52. The regression analysis presented in this paper was performed with the kind assistance of the staff in the computer center at the Japan Productivity Center. For a full report on all the statistical results of the regression analysis, refer to Nihon Seisansei Honbu (The Japan Productivity Center), *JPC Kobetsu Chingin Yosoku Shihyō: Shōwa 49 Nen* [JPC Projections on Individual Wage Rates: 1974] (Tokyo: Nihon Seisansei Honbu, 1974), pp. 573–612. The author is Professor of Economics at Gakushūin University.

Firm size is particularly emphasized since it is commonly believed that it accounts for larger differentials in Japan than in other similarly industrialized countries. Although the inter-firm wage structure *per se* is not analyzed in this paper, effects of firm size on the relative importance of the aforementioned individual, ascriptive factors will be studied, and the contrast between large and small firms will be discussed. From one perspective, occupational differentials may also be considered ascriptive in that various costs, pecuniary and non-pecuniary, are involved in attaining the necessary levels of skill and knowledge required for each occupation. Furthermore, an element of seniority will also be built into occupational differentials.

Although this paper is concerned with delineating the structure of intra-firm wage differentials, it is also concerned with methodology. It is commonly said that American and European wage systems emphasize achievement-oriented criteria such as productivity, skills, and experience. Economic sociologists have for some time contrasted those factors with the more ascriptive criteria, such as age, which they believe to be characteristic of the Japanese wage system. The following analysis of occupational differentials suggests that the apparent differences between Japan and the West perhaps arise more out of differences in the methodology used than from differences in the actual distributions.

2. Characteristics of the Seniority Wage System

A. The Data

The results of various annual surveys on individual wage rates are now available. They supply personnel managers with reliable information relevant to the revision of their own wage systems. In addition to specialized surveys which focus on wages for particular occupations, there are surveys which concentrate wholly on model wage schedules. However, because these surveys lack the comprehensiveness needed for our study, we have used the Ministry of Labour's Chingin Kōzō Kihon Tōkei Chōsa (Basic Survey on the Wage Structure) which is taken every year, with a larger sample being used every third year. The most recent of the larger surveys, which was taken in June 1973, is utilized in this analysis.

The survey gives two different figures on earnings: (1) the contracted monthly salary and (2) the actual monthly cash earnings. Both figures represent nominal amounts before taxes are withheld. This study considers only the monthly salary of regular employees. Although the hourly rate for overtime is proportional to the hourly rate calculated from the monthly salary (with a 25 percent premium), the existing differential in the amount of overtime worked in firms of different sizes results in total monthly cash earnings which do not truly reflect firm-size wage differentials.

Table 1 gives the average monthly salary by age and years of employment for male middle-school graduates in manufacturing. Similar data are available for either males or females with different levels of education for each industry, for the two major occupational categories (blue and white collar), and for firm-size groupings. Firms with fewer than ten employees are excluded from the survey.

Moving diagonally from the upper left-hand corner to the lower

Table 1: Monthly Salaries by Age and Years of Employment with the Same Firm for Male Middle-school Graduates in Manufacturing: June 1973
(Unit: ¥1000 yen)

Age	Years of employment with the same firm								
	0	1	2	3–4	5–9	10–14	15–19	20–29	30+
–17	44.0	47.8	48.6 (15)	—	—	—	—	—	—
18–19	51.1	51.7	51.8	54.8 (15)	—	—	—	—	—
20–24	60.3	63.0	61.6	63.1	67.8 (15)	—	—	—	—
25–29	68.5	71.5	73.3 (25)	74.9 (25)	78.9 (20)	84.9 (15)	—	—	—
30–34	73.5	78.2	80.2	81.2 (30)	86.9 (25)	91.6 (20)	100.4 (15)		
35–39	75.6	81.3	83.0	83.7 (35)	92.7 (30)	96.9 (25)	105.5 (20)	111.3 (15)	
40–44	75.3	79.8	81.5	84.4 (40)	91.0 (35)	97.9 (30)	109.3 (25)	120.8	127.7 (15)
45–49	74.3	75.9	80.3	81.3 (40)	88.8 (35)	99.0 (30)	108.6	121.2	137.5
50–54	69.5	72.4	76.5	80.6 (40)	85.6 (35)	99.6	108.7	122.9	137.3

Note: The figures within the parentheses indicate the age at which the individuals in a given category (matching the salaries immediately above) entered the firm with which they were employed at the time of the survey.

Source: Rōdō Shō (Ministry of Labour), *Chingin Kōzō Kihon Tōkei Chōsa* [Basic Survey on the Wage Structure] (Tokyo: Ōkura Shō Insatsu Kyoku, 1974).

right-hand corner in Table 1, we can gain some idea of the pay expected by the standard employee who finds employment immediately upon graduation from middle school and plans to follow through the normal progression of promotions within one firm until retirement.[1] This schedule of wage payments is shown by curve AC in Figure 1 and may be called the "standard seniority wage schedule".

On the other hand, curve AB can be drawn by plotting the amount paid to newly hired employees in each age group. The figures are arrayed vertically in the leftmost column of Table 1. The curve is hereafter referred to as the "starting salary schedule". The employee with some years of experience elsewhere (or who has spent some time either unemployed or otherwise outside the labor force following graduation) is usually identified as a non-standard employee. When a middle-school graduate aged 25 is hired, it is assumed that he

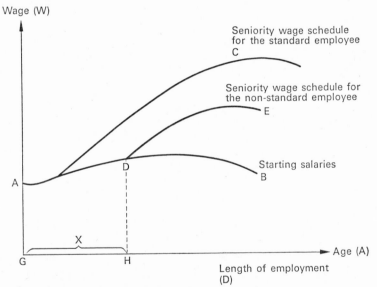

Figure 1: The Seniority Wage Schedules and Starting Salaries for Male Middle-school Graduates Employed in Manufacturing

[1] In Japan those who enter a firm upon graduation and stay with the same firm until the fixed age for retirement (usually age 55, although this has changed somewhat in recent years) are known as "standard employees" (*hyōjun rōdōsha*). Those who enter after having worked somewhere else are known as "mid-career transfers" or "non-standard employees" (*chūto saiyōsha*). A middle-school education is compulsory. Students usually complete their compulsory education at age 15. The likely earnings at each age for the standard employee with a middle-school education are indicated in Table 1.

has spent ten years working elsewhere. His starting salary would be at a point like D in Figure 1. If he thereafter remains with the same firm, his salary is likely to rise in the manner denoted by curve DE. Note that the curve is different from that for the standard employee. A non-standard seniority wage curve is tailored for each non-standard employee. Its shape will depend upon the starting age (the value of X in Figure 1) and other ascriptive factors related to each non-standard employee.

B. A Formulation

The above observations for males suggest that the individual's salary (W_i) is a function of his age (A_i) and length of employment with the firm (D_i), where i denotes a particular employee.

Expressed mathematically,

$$W_i = f(D_i, A_i).$$

If we concern ourselves only with the standard employee, we could use either D_i or A_i since the latter term is merely the sum of D_i and the individual's age at graduation (which is fixed and equal to G in Figure 1). The value of G will remain fixed for any group of age cohorts with the same level of education. However, to incorporate the "non-standard employee, a slightly different formulation is required. If we let H_i denote the age of the individual when he was first employed by his present employer, and X_i denotes the number of years between graduation and assumption of the present employment, the above formula may be rewritten as follows:

$$W_i = f(D_i, X_i, G_i) \text{ where } X_i = H_i - G_i.$$

The value of X_i will always be zero for the standard employee and will take on a positive and constant value for any given non-standard employee. The second formula is clearly the more flexible. Returning briefly to Figure I, we can see that the initial income of the standard employee (with $X_i = 0$) is denoted by the value of AG. Additional increments will move his earnings upwards over time as indicated by curve AC. The initial income of the non-standard employee (with $D_i = 0$) is denoted by the value of DH. Additional increments will move his earnings upwards over time in a manner indicated by curve DE. The values on a curve such as DE occur when the values of both D_i and X_i are positive. The initial income earned by successively older entrants to the firm is denoted by curve AB. All three curves (AC, DE, and AB) fit the shape of a parabola, and can be expressed with the following quadratic equation:

$$W_i = a_0 + a_1 D_i + a_2 D_i{}^2 + a_3 X_i + a_4 X_i{}^2 + a_5 D_i X_i .$$

The constant a_0 represents the starting salary of the standard employee. The second and third terms describe the standard seniority wage schedule. When X_i is zero, a_2 will determine the shape of the curve AC (in Figure 1). A positive value for a_2 will result in the parabola being convex (see Figure 2).[2] In a similar manner, the value of a_4 will determine the shape of curve AB, which represents the starting salary of the non-standard employee. The last term with a_5 will make the function sensitive to any interaction between D_i and X_i. Even without the last term, the equation will reasonably approximate the actual seniority wage schedule for non-standard employees.

The next section will examine the results obtained by using conventional regression techniques to fit the above equation to several sets of data differentiated by sex, level of education, and firm size. A comparison of the estimated coefficients $(a_0, \ldots, a_5)$ for each specific set of employees reveals some interesting facts about the structure of the seniority wage system. Before considering the results, it should be mentioned that the median is used to describe age and length of employment, although these variables originally appear in the data as continuous values on an interval scale. Accordingly, the figures in parentheses in Table 1 represent the differences between D_i and A_i (i.e., they equal G_i or $A_i - D_i - X_i$). The values for X_i are obtained by subtracting the value of G_i (the age at graduation for a given group of

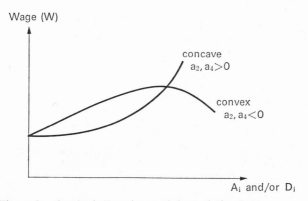

Figure 2: Quadratic Functions and the Seniority Curve

[2] Actually it is commonly agreed that the curve is convex (or "concave downwards", in the terminology of some) with the peak of the parabola coming before the retirement age of 55. As shown below, the exact location of the peak, however, will depend upon firm size, the individual's level of education, and numerous other factors.

middle-school graduates from the median age at which members of the group were employed with their current employer (H_i) (*i.e.*, $X_i = H_i - G_i$ which equals $A_i - D_i - G_i$).

3.   Comparison of the Coefficients

A. Sex and Level of Education

The regression coefficients for a_0 through a_5 are given in Table 2 for groups differentiated both by sex and by level of education. Looking initially at the effect of education on the wage earnings of males, four observations should be made.

First, the coefficient of determination, which shows the extent to which the regression equation fits the data, indicates that there is a good fit for each set of data. For middle-school graduates the fit is particularly good (0.997). The coefficient is slightly lower for high-school graduates (0.986).

Second, as one might expect, the starting salary (a_0) varies with the level of education, rising from ¥38,985 for middle-school graduates to ¥58,663 for college and university graduates.

Third, the relation of length of employment to wage income varies considerably according to the level of education. This is particularly true if we look at the values for a_2 (coefficient of $D_i{}^2$). The estimated values for a_2 suggest that the standard seniority wage schedules for graduates of both tertiary institutions and high schools are concavely parabolic, whereas those for middle-school graduates are convexly parabolic. In other words, the extent to which seniority is remunerated tends to vary directly with the level of education. The value of a_1 has definite consequences for wage differentials among the three groups differentiated by level of education. The value of a_1 for graduates of tertiary institutions is larger than the values obtained for the other two groups. Again, it would seem that higher education tends to be remunerated by a seniority wage curve which is higher at all points.

Fourth, the values for a_3 and a_4 suggest that the starting salary schedule for middle-school and tertiary graduates is convexly parabolic, whereas that for high-school graduates is concave. This suggests that high-school graduates are penalized relatively more for shifting jobs. It is not clear why this occurs, but it is a phenomenon requiring further investigation.

Considering briefly the differences between men and women, we

Table 2:   Regression Coefficients for Seniority Wage Functions for Groups by Sex and the Level of Education for Employees in Manufacturing: June 1973

(Units defined to give values in yen)

Sex	Level of education	a_0	a_1	a_2	a_3	a_4	a_5	Standard deviation	Coefficient of determination
					Coefficients				
Males	Middle school	38,985	3,946 (40.0)	−29.5 (−10.5)	3,312 (18.9)	−71.3 (−7.1)	−91.5 (−16.6)	1,330	0.997
Males	High school	50,344	3,627 (10.2)	20.8 (2.0)	2,182 (2.8)	30.1 (0.5)	−106.9 (−4.4)	4,486	0.986
Males	Tertiary	58,663	5,323 (9.3)	57.2 (3.2)	3,366 (1.9)	−25.3 (−0.2)	39.0 (0.7)	5,789	0.993
Females	Middle school	42,637	1,773 (11.8)	−7.9 (1.9)	197 (0.7)	−25.5 (−1.7)	31.5 (−3.7)	2,027	0.981
Females	Tertiary	48,797	1,880 (10.7)	1.8 (0.3)	362 (0.9)	−58.1 (−2.2)	−28.7 (−2.4)	2,210	0.987

Note: The figures in parentheses are the respective t values.

are first impressed by the fact that the overall fit of the equation is not as good for women as for men. Moreover the estimated values for each coefficient are much smaller for women. Indeed, the value of a_2 can almost be ignored. This means that age and length of employment have less effect on the earnings of females. In other words, the salary paid to females does not rise much with their age, and there is more nearly a going rate common to all women, whereas age and length of employment seem to divide men into a number of different income strata.

B. Firm Size

The firm-size differential has been discussed frequently in studies on the Japanese economy. However, only crude averages are commonly given for each firm-size grouping. The connection with differences in age, length of employment, educational background, and occupation are scarcely noted.

Although our data are not grouped according to occupational categories, level of education tends to parallel the general distinctions made among broadly defined occupational categories such as blue collar and white collar. Table 3 gives the values obtained for different groupings based upon firm size and level of education. First, the equation fits the situation in the large firms better. This suggests that factors such as age and length of employment are still major determinants of the overall distribution of salaries in the large firms despite the introduction of pay schemes tied to job content.

Second, the starting salary (a_0) is higher in the larger firms. Although this is consistent with our expectations, the firm-size differential is greater than that derived from averaged data. This means either that the bend in the seniority wage curve given by our equation is more pronounced for the smaller firms than would actually be the case, or that the distribution of the population into different age or length-of-employment groups is such as to give weighted averages which seem to differ from the schedules as originally conceived in Figure 1.

Third, the coefficients for length of employment (a_1 and a_2) vary greatly according to firm size. For middle-school graduates the curve is convex regardless of firm size, although the curvature is greater in the smaller firms. For the other two groupings by level of education, the curve is concave for both groups in the larger firms and convex for both groups in the smaller firms.

Finally, the coefficients for the starting-salary curve (a_3 and a_4) also vary considerably by firm size. The starting-salary curve for

Table 3: Regression Coefficients for Seniority Wage Function for Groups Differentiated by Firm Size and the Level of Education for All Male Employees in Manufacturing Industries: June 1973

(Units defined to give values in yen)

Level of education	Firm size (number of employees)	Coefficients						Standard deviation	Coefficient of determination
		a_0	a_1	a_2	a_3	a_4	a_5		
Middle school	1000+	43,384	3,514 (23.3)	−16.7 (−3.9)	2,625 (9.8)	−47.8 (−3.0)	−63.9 (−7.5)	2,032	0.995
	100–999	35,143	5,008 (24.1)	−72.3 (−12.3)	3,423 (9.3)	−71.8 (−3.4)	−93.3 (8.0)	2,801	0.989
High school	1000+	53,722	3,133 (8.7)	36.3 (3.4)	1,033 (1.3)	84.9 (1.6)	−52.3	4,566	0.987
	100–999	47,249	4,317 (10.4)	−15.2 (−1.3)	2,533 (2.8)	6.0 (0.1)	−89.5 (−3.2)	5,227	0.979
Tertiary institution	1000+	60,058	4,850 (6.7)	87.7 (3.9)	4,173 (1.9)	−139.3 (−0.7)	102.5 (1.5)	7,325	0.990
	100–999	54,342	7,640 (11.2)	−71.2 (−3.4)	1,774 (0.6)	279.9 (1.4)	−134.9 (−2.1)	6,888	0.983

Note: The figures in parentheses are the respective t values.

middle-school graduates is convex in both larger and smaller firms. For high-school graduates the curve is consistently concave. For graduates from tertiary institutions, however, the curve seems to be convex in the larger firms and concave in the smaller firms. It is particularly interesting to note that the curvature is greater for the smaller firms. In other words, the inter-firm wage differential is relatively small for the young and those new to the firm, but grows larger over time for the older employees and those who have been employed for a long period.

In order to better understand the significance of the above analysis, the following explanation of the convex parabola is perhaps useful. If we examine the convex parabola used to express the seniority wage schedule, the value of X_i is zero and we have the following equation:

$$W_i^1 = a_0 + a_1 D_i + a_2 D_i^2.$$

By setting the first derivative equal to zero, we can obtain the length of employment (D_i^*) which will maximize the individual's salary. In other words, $a_1 + 2a_2 D_i = 0$ and $D_i^* = -a_1/2a_2$. D_i^* is positive since $a_2 < 0$ in the convex curve. Adding to it the individual's age at graduation, we have the age for which his salary peaks. We can thus estimate that the value of D_i^* for middle-school graduates is 105 years in the large firm. This contrasts with an estimated value of 35 years in the smaller firms. This means that the middle-school graduate who enters a large firm directly upon graduation will enjoy a fairly good annual increase in his wages through to retirement at the age of 55 whereas in a smaller firm his income would perhaps peak at the age of 50 and actually decrease at an accelerating rate thereafter.

As long as the starting salary schedule is convex, we can estimate the age at which the starting salary peaks as follows:

$$X_i^* = A_i - D_i^* = -a_3/2a_4.$$

Therefore,

$$A_i^* = D_i^* - (a_3/2a_4).$$

Here the firm-size difference is smaller, the age at which starting salaries peak for middle-school graduates being 42 in the larger firms and 39 in the smaller firms. We should also note that the age at which starting salaries peak is lower than that for the seniority wage curve and is less sensitive to firm-size variation. Generally speaking, the starting salary schedule is determined by changes in the labor market. Particularly important are the supply of new graduates and the existing levels of salary paid to those currently employed (especially to the standard employees).

Finally, it should be pointed out that the conclusions on firm size seem to hold throughout each industry over time. Accordingly, it might be reasonable to conclude that the starting salary schedule indicates the lowest value at which labor will be supplied by members of each age group.

C. Occupation and the Seniority Wage Curve

The Basic Survey of the Wage Structure breaks down the data for more than a hundred occupational groups; the same data are also broken down for various age groups. However, information on length of employment is unavailable for these occupational sets. For this reason we are forced to use a simplified formula:

$$W_i = b_0 + b_1 A_i + b_2 A_i^2.$$

The constant b_0 denotes the starting salary paid to the workers in different age groups. The role of b_1 and b_2 is analogous to that of the a_i's in the preceding formula. The formula serves as only a rough estimate of the age profile for salaries in each occupation, but does not give an exactly drawn seniority wage schedule in terms of the length of employment. Although the equation was used to analyze 106 different occupational groupings, limitations of space prevent us from presenting all the results.[3]

For every occupational grouping, the coefficient (b_1) for the linear element is positive. Moreover, for nearly every occupation the value of the coefficient is large enough to result in a rising age-wage curve. For only six occupations is the coefficient (b_2) for the quadratic element positive. Accordingly, for most occupational groupings the age-wage relationship results in a convex parabola. Although the salary for males aged 25 (b_0) is somewhere between ¥70,000 and ¥80,000 per month, there is considerable variation in the value of the other two coefficients (b_1 and b_2) and hence in male salaries as the men age. Looking at the age for which salaries peak in each occupation, we found that it came before the age of 40 in six occupations and after 50 for twenty-eight occupations. In other words, the peak occurs before the age of 50 for three-fourths of all occupations. It is interesting to observe that the data give a peak which is over 50 for most industries when all occupations are averaged together.

[3] For these results see my "Chingin Kōzō no Bunseki to Shin Chingin Keikō Chihyō" [An Analysis of the Wage Structure and Tables on New Wage Trends], *Rōsei Jihō* (no. 2249: December 13, 1974).

4.   Conclusion: Some Unanswered Questions

The findings in the two preceding sections are somewhat at odds. The apparent paradox no doubt results from the fact that the data for industries are broken down by both age and length of employment whereas the occupational data are classified only by age. In other words, the use of A_i and the use of D_i have given us slightly different results. This phenomenon no doubt reflects the fact that a certain amount of occupational mobility exists.

Speculating on the nature of the data and commonly accepted notions of job or occupational mobility, we can imagine the situation depicted in Figure 3. First, assume that there are three occupations in industry J, denoted by curves X_j, Y_j, and Z_j. Mobility (or promotion) from occupations with lower earnings (such as Z_j) to those with higher earnings (such as X_j) no doubt occurs as individuals age. Moreover, such mobility (or promotion) does not occur simultaneously for all age cohorts. As cohorts age, the more able members move first and then others follow. As we go out along the age axis and consider successively older age groups and calculate their average for the industry, we find that the relative weightings of each occupational group change as the proportion of cohorts in the higher occupations gradually increases. In order for the phenomenon described above to occur, inter-occupational mobility must continue beyond age P at which the maximum earnings are realized by an individual occupational

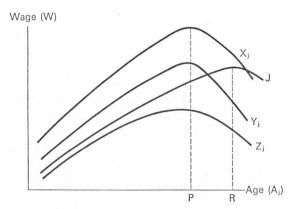

Figure 3:   Differences in the Seniority-Merit Wage Curve By Industry and Occupation

grouping, otherwise the averaged peak for the industry could not mathematically be further to the left, as is shown in Figure 3.

This raises a number of interesting questions about the rates of inter-occupational mobility. On the one hand, it would seem possible that the averaged distance (or some other measure of the distance) between the peaks of the occupational curves and the industry curve might serve as one kind of index of occupational mobility in an industry. The findings suggest that it would be fruitful to examine more closely career patterns and the extent to which occupational or job clusters exist. In this connection, particular attention needs to be paid to the concept of internal labor markets.[4] Further research along these lines is certainly called for before more precise statements of a comparative nature can be made. It is hoped that this exploratory excursion will promote such research.[5]

Selected Bibliography on the Japanese Wage System

Nakayama Ichirō, ed. *Chingin Kihon Chōsa* [Basic Studies on Wages] (Tokyo: Tōyō Keizai Shimpō Sha, 1956).

Shōwa Dōjin Kai (The Shōwa Club), *Wagakuni Chingin Kōzō no Shiteki Kōsatsu* [The Japanese Wage System in Historical Perspective] (Tokyo: Shiseidō, 1960).

Ono Akira, *Sengo Nihon no Chingin Kettei* [Wage Determination in Postwar Japan] (Tokyo: Shiseidō, 1960).

Mizuno Asao, *Chingin Kōzō Hendō Ron* [The Theory of Changes in the Wage Structure] (Tokyo: Shin Hyōron Sha, 1973).

Sumiya Mikio, "Nihonteki Rōshi Kankei Ron no Saikentō" [A Reappraisal of the Theories of Japanese-style Labor-Management Relations], *Nihon Rōdō Kyōkai Zasshi* (No. 185: August 1974), pp. 2–10 and (No. 187: October 1974), pp. 2–11.

---

[4] On the concept of internal labor markets, see P. B. Doeringer, "Determinants of the Structure of Industrial Type Internal Labor Markets," *Industrial and Labor Relations Review* (vol. 20, no. 2: January 1967), pp. 206–220.

[5] This paper focused primarily on explaining an analytical approach and was limited to a consideration of the data for June 1973. For a longitudinal analysis, including a more detailed explanation of the analytical methods used, see the author's "Kobetsu Chingin Kōzō to Sono Hendō Patan ni Kansuru Ruikeiteki Haaku ni Tsuite" [An Approach to Understanding the Structure of Individual Wages and the Pattern of Change in that Structure], in Nihon Seisansei Honbu (The Japan Productivity Center), *Kobetsu Chingin Yosoku Shihyō, Shōwa 49-Nen, Kaisetsu Hen* [Individual Wage Rates, 1974: Explanation] (Tokyo: Nihon Seisansei Honbu, 1974), pp. 1–25.

A Quantitative Analysis of Factors Determining the Rate of Increase in Wage Levels during the Spring Wage Offensive

Sano Yōko

1. Introduction

The Phillips Curve expresses the way in which the rate of unemployment and a few other variables are related to changes in wage levels. Nevertheless, a relatively simple set of relationships may be interpreted in a great variety of ways.[1] For example, if we focus our attention on the unemployment rate, then the emphasis will be on the supply of or demand for labor as the major variables determining the rate at which wages increase. Accordingly, there is little room for unions to influence wage rates in the dynamic economy. However, if emphasis is placed upon the variables which cause the curve showing the relationship between wages and unemployment to shift, then the price level (inflation) and profit margins become important. Accordingly, forces working within the context of collective bargaining must be analyzed. Indeed, taken to the one extreme, we might say that the price level and company profits determine the bargaining power of the union.

This essay presents one approach to the study of these problems, a model which is still in the process of being developed. This paper reports on the development and use of a quantitative model for understanding the factors which shape the outcome of the spring wage offensive as measured by the resultant change in the wage rates.

This study was first published as "Shuntō Sōba no Keiryō Bunseki" in *Gendai Rōdō* (no. 1: July 1975), pp. 55–70. The author is Professor of Labor Economics at Keio University.
[1] Nishikawa Shunsaku and Shimada Haruo, "Rōdō Shijō Kikō to Chingin Kettei" [The Labor Market Mechanism and the Determination of Wage Rates], *Kikan Gendai Keizai* (no. 15: Winter 1974), pp. 88–105.

Rather than use a simple economic model or a psychological approach, the author seeks to introduce a behavioral model which introduces as independent variables several aspects of the decision-making process. An attempt is thus made to build a model which will center on the subjective behavior of the two main actors, labor and management.

2. Criteria Determining the Increase in Wage Levels

In order to ascertain the views of labor and management on the criteria determining the amount of increase in wage levels, a survey was sent in 1966 to managements in 630 large companies and to the leadership of 675 important unit unions associated with the same firms. In 1969 a similar survey was also sent to managements in an additional 347 small and medium-sized firms (of which 127 had unions) and to the leadership of 150 unit unions in Nagano Prefecture.[2] The same format was used to investigate the attitudes of labor and management. To the knowledge of this author, it is the only survey of its type.

Table 1 summarizes the results of the four survey sets. Comparing the results for management in the large firms with those for management in the small and medium-sized firms, one immediately notices the relative importance of the demand for labor and the relative unimportance of the firm's economic position (ability to pay). However, price inflation was significantly more important for the large firms. Looking at the views of union leaders, firm size does not seem to account for much variation, although the demand for labor seems to be an important consideration in the smaller firms whereas the firm's economic position seems to be more important in the large firms. It should be emphasized that within each firm-size grouping both labor and management tended to emphasize the same variables. The only exception is the weight given by the union leaders to "the intensity of wage demands among the rank and file".[3]

[2] For a more detailed explanation of these surveys, see Sano Yōko, Koike Kazuo, and Ishida Hideo, eds., *Chingin Kōshō no Kōdō Kagaku* [A Behavioral Science Approach to Wage Bargaining] (Tokyo: Tōyō Keizai Shimpō Sha, 1969), Chapter Six, "Chingin Kettei Kijun to Rōdō Shijō" [The Labor Market and Criteria Determining Wage Rates], pp. 151–180; and Sano Yōko, Ishida Hideo, and Inoue Shōzō, eds., *Chūshō Kigyō no Chingin Kettei* [Wage Determination in Small and Medium-Sized Firms] (Tokyo: Tōyō Keizai Shimpō Sha, 1971), Chapter Three, "Rōdō Shijō to Chingin Kettei Kijun" [The Labor Market and Criteria Determining Wage Rates], pp. 41–60.

[3] In other words, the sixth most frequently cited factor by labor leaders in the large-firm sector was "general economic conditions". The sixth most frequently

Table 1:   The Most Important Criteria Determining Wage Increases as Identified by Union Leadership and Management from among Thirteen Criteria

	Rank order	For management	Percent	For labor unions	Percent
For large firms employing over 1000 persons (1966)	1	The going rate: increases being paid by other firms	25.2%	Price inflation	22.1%
	2	Price inflation	24.3	The going rate: increases being paid by other firms	19.0
	3	Economic position of the firm	14.8	Intensity of wage demands among the rank and file	14.0
	4	Rise in wage rates for new graduates	14.2	Rise in wage rates for new graduates	11.5
	5	General economic conditions (related to the business cycle)	6.0	Economic position of the firm	11.1
Medium-sized and small firms in Nagano Prefecture (answers for management only at firms with no unions) (1969)	1	The going rate: increases being paid by other firms	27.5	Price inflation	20.0
	2	The need to maintain personnel levels	17.9	The going rate: increases being paid by other firms	17.5
	3	Rise in wage rates for new graduates	17.1	The need to maintain personnel levels	14.0
	4	Price inflation	16.2	Intensity of wage demands among the rank and file	12.7
	5	Rise in the standard of living	7.8	Rise in wage rates for new graduates	9.5

Note: Respondents were asked to list the three most important criteria determining wage increases at their firm.

The percentage figures refer to the percentage of firms which listed a particular item among the top three. Accordingly, the total number of answers (=100%) would be three times the total number of firms surveyed.

Source: Adapted from Sano Yōko, Koike Kazuo and Ishida Hideo, ed., *Chingin Kōshō no Kōdō Kagaku* [A Behavioral Science Approach to Wage Bargaining] (Tokyo: Tōyō Keizai Shimpō Sha, 1969), pp. 168–169; and Sano Yōko, Ishida Hideo and Inoue Shōzō, *Chūshō Kigyō no Chingin Kettei* [Wage Determination in Small and Medium-sized Firms] (Tokyo: Tōyō Keizai Shimpō Sha, 1971), p. 50.

cited factor by their counterparts in the smaller firms was the rise in the standard of living. If we removed "intensity of wage demands" from the list of criteria, the five most important factors would be the same for labor and management in a given firm-size sector, although the ordering would be slightly different. The top five criteria are then mentioned in the large-firm sector by 78.5 percent of management and 63.7 percent of union leaders. In the medium-sized and small firms, the figures are 78.7 and 61.0 percent, respectively.

Because the questions and the choice of answers were slightly different in the surveys taken in 1966 and 1969, it is difficult to make longitudinal comparisons with our data. However, the survey of conditions determining wage increases taken among management at 2500 firms with more than thirty employees by the Ministry of Labour does allows us to make such a study from the viewpoint of management. Although the format of the survey differs from that of ours,[4] changes in the importance of criteria determining wage increases are highlighted by the Ministry's survey. The results are given in Table 2, which shows that the importance of "firm performance" decreased over time, while that of the "going rate" and "price inflation" increased. The influence of the "need to secure labor" varied from year to year. The "going rate" and "price inflation" were particularly important in 1974 when the largest wage increases were obtained. In 1971 and 1972, when wage increases were relatively smaller, "firm performance" was more significant and the "going rate" less so. In

Table 2:   The Single Most Important Criteria Determining Wage Increases as Identified by Management from Among Six Criteria

	1970	1971	1972	1973	1974
Firm performance	41.2	43.0	40.1	30.4	26.6
The going rate	32.5	25.3	29.1	34.8	37.5
The need to secure labor	15.6	16.5	11.2	18.2	8.6
Price inflation	6.3	10.5	11.0	12.9	24.0
The maintenance of stable labor-management relations	3.8	3.8	7.6	3.2	2.7
Other factors	0.4	0.9	1.0	0.5	0.6
Total	100.0	100.0	100.0	100.0	100.0
Average wage increase among large firms in the private sector	18.5	16.9	15.3	20.1	32.9

Source: Rōdō Shō, Rōsei Kyoku (Bureau of Labour Administration, Ministry of Labour), *Chingin Hikiage Nado no Jittai ni Kansuru Chōsa Kekka Hōkoku Sho* [Report on the Survey of Conditions Concerning Wage Increases] (Tokyo: Ōkura Shō Insatsu Kyoku, annually beginning in 1971).

[4] Whereas our survey asked about the factors explaining the difference in the rate of increase in wages between the current and the preceding year, the survey by the Ministry of Labour asked about the most important consideration determining wage hikes in general. In contrast to our instructions asking for the three most important items among thirteen, the Ministry of Labour has asked respondents to indicate the single most important factor among six items. The results are given in Tables 1 and 2. The greater weight given to price inflation in our survey perhaps reflects our interest in explaining changes in the amount of the wage increase over a two-year period. However, Table 2 is intended to show longitudinal changes rather than to make comparisons between the two surveys.

other words, poor firm performance tends to constrain wage increases whereas the going rate tends to push wages up. Actually, the fact that a going rate is established may well reflect the improved performance of all firms so that all are willing to pay. However, in years like 1971 or 1972, when the economy grew at a slower rate, the difference in performance among firms meant that the overall average was lower and that there was no going rate (signifying a small standard deviation or other coefficient of dispersion). In other words, wage differentials widened since firms which initially have higher wage rates usually perform relatively better when the pace of economic activity slows down.[5]

Summarizing the results of the three surveys mentioned above, it is clear that during the decade after 1965 the going rate, firm performance, the supply of and demand for labor, and price inflation were important considerations determining wage rates. Second, in the large-scale sector the going rate played a relatively more important role; for the small and medium-sized enterprises the supply of and demand for labor was relatively more influential. Third, in periods of slower growth, enterprise performance was more significant; in periods of high growth, the going rate was more important. Fourth, in small and medium-sized enterprises, the presence of a union increased the importance of the going rate but did not seem to affect the extent to which price inflation was considered. Finally, given a particular firm size, union leadership and management gave similar appraisals of the criteria.

---

[5] Although the survey of the Ministry of Labour is the only survey amenable to comparisons over time, a few comments need to be made on the choice of answers given in the questionnaire. First, in our survey we distinguish between "the rise in wages for new graduates" and "the need to maintain personnel levels" as indicators showing the state of supply and demand in the labor market; the Ministry of Labour's survey uses only one variable, "the rise in wages for new graduates". A second difference is the Ministry's inclusion of "the maintenance of stable labor-management relations". In designing a questionnaire, each category must be theoretically significant in terms of the variable it represents, and each of the categories must clearly be mutually exclusive. However, a term like "the maintenance of stable labor-management relations" is extremely ambiguous, and perhaps increases the likelihood that respondents will choose one of the other four categories. Since the weight given this item is rather small, one imagines that the respondents interpreted it as a factor affecting labor-management relations but unrelated to the other four more important items. One wonders how the answers might have been affected had "stable labor-management relations" been at the top of the list of possible answers. See Ishida Hideo, "Chingin Kettei no Kijun" [Criteria Determining Wages], *Kikan Rōdō Hō* (no. 94: Winter 1974), p. 187.

3. The Extent of the Spillover Effect from Labor and Management in the Large Firms

The choice of the "going rate" from among the various criteria affecting wage rates is indicative of behavior which is based upon the actions of others. In the realm of wage negotiations this means that labor and management in one firm will take their cue from labor and management in another firm. In our research, we sought to make a theoretical distinction between market conformity based purely upon supply and demand factors in the labor market and market conformity which also gives consideration to collective bargaining and related institutions. Thus, in talking about the going rate, it is entirely possible that in the case of the large firms we are referring to market conformity which arises out of institutional factors, whereas in the smaller firms reference is to a common wage rate determined by forces in the labor market.[6]

We thus have an interest in examining separately the spillover effect from large to small firms.[7] In the 1969 survey mentioned above (see note 3), we asked labor and management at the large firms who had cited "going rate" as one of the three most important factors to indicate the other unions or firms whose lead they followed. Our analysis of the answers suggests that both labor and management sought to follow trends within their own industry, but that consideration of trends in other industries was also important (although it is more difficult to generalize for all firms in all industries about the second type of influence). The 1968 survey suggested that labor and management at small and medium-sized firms were eager to know about trends in the large firms. To be sure, since the answers to this question were often not complete, and some didn't even respond, it is difficult to draw an accurate "sociogram".

Table 3 summarizes for each industry the behavioral patterns involved in market conformity with regard to wages. The patterns are

[6] See Sano, Ishida, and Inoue, *Chūshō Kigyō no Chingin Kettei*, Preface, pp. 3–22, and Chapter Six, "Chūshō Kigyō Sekutā ni Okeru Seken Sōba" [The Going Rate in Small and Medium-Sized Firms], pp. 41–60.

[7] On this aspect of the analysis, see the following three items by Inoue Shōzō: "Chingin Hakyū no Kōzō—Tekkōgyō to Shokuhin Kōgyō" [The Structure of the Spillover Effect: An Analysis of the Steel and Food Processing Industries], in *Chingin Kōshō no Kōdō Kagaku*, ed. by Sano, Koike, and Ishida, pp. 231–276; "Chingin Hikaku to Chingin Hakyū" [Wage Comparisons and the Spillover Effect], *Nihon Rōdō Kyōkai Zasshi* (vol. 13, no. 10: October 1971), pp. 20–29; and "Chingin Shijō no Seidoteki Sokumen" [Institutional Factors in Wage Determination], *Mita Gakkai Zasshi* (vol. 65, no. 1: January 1972), pp. 41–64.

Table 3: The Spillover Effect in Eleven Industries (from the Survey in 1966)

A Industry	B Intra-industry spillover	C Differences in patterns of intra-industry reference for labor and for management	D Inter-industry spillover
Processed food	Flour, sugar, confections, dairy products, oils and foodstuffs form their own sub-groups. Smaller firms are linked to large firms but there is no single large firm which dominates the market.	Almost no difference	Seldom does union leadership or management look to trends outside the industry. When cited, the chemical industry is mentioned most frequently, followed by steel and private railways. Smaller firms are concerned with industries important in the local economy.
Steel	The five major firms form the major subgroup. Other firms form sub-groups around products such as ferro alloys and other basic iron and steel products.	Among management there is a subgroup for firms with smaller furnaces. The link with Tekkō Rōren (Steel Worker's Federation) provides other linkages.	Fairly independent of other industries. Union more concerned than management with inter-industry comparisons. Concern with firm's external financial ties and the local economy—particularly among smaller firms.
Chemicals	Sub-groups exist for ammonium sulphate, carbon, soil and fats, paints, pharmaceuticals, oxygen and film. The ammonium sulphate sub-group follows the industry as a whole. The ammonium sulphate sub-group is then watched by the other major sub-groups. The others watch the major firms in the chemical industry as a whole. Film and plate glass tend to be independent. They have high wages, but do not seem to affect the other sub-groups.	Both have similar sub-group patterns. Unions considering settlements are concentrated primarily in general chemicals.	Both labor and management are concerned with trends in other industries. Management in the largest firms looks at the results of about 80 other large firms which are leaders in their own industries. Steel and private railways are mentioned most often. Unions consider steel, private railways, electrical goods, shipbuilding, and public employees.

A Industry	B Intra-industry spillover	C Differences in patterns of intra-industry reference for labor and for management	D Inter-industry spillover
Electrical machinery	Sub-groups: 1. general electrical machinery, 2. heavy electrical machinery, 3. light electrical appliances, and 4. automatic electrical equipment. The large manufacturers take the lead for the first three sub-groups.	Unions and management behave similarly. Federation of Electrical Workers plays a leading role.	Management in the large firms takes a look at trends in other industries. Labor is concerned primarily with steel, shipbuilding, and rolling stock.
Railway equipment	Uses the industry as a whole for comparisons.	No significant differences between labor and management.	Management considers major firms in shipbuilding most frequently, then the major firms in steel, private railways, and electrical machinery. Labor looks at these plus the public enterprises.
Automobiles	Sub-groups exist for complete assembly makers, sub-contracting parts makers, and independent parts makers. Among the "complete assembly" makers, two large firms making both passenger cars and trucks are predominant.	No significant differences between labor and management.	Management for the "complete assembly" firms considers major firms in steel, heavy electrical machinery, shipbuilding, and manufacturing in general. Management in the other sub-groups looks broadly at industries having some relationship to the auto industry. Unions consider steel, private railways, chemicals, electrical machinery, shipbuilding, and others. They also look at settlements obtained by other major unions.
Shipbuilding	Large firms form a core group. Smaller firms are dependent on the major firms.		Two largest manufacturers consider steel and heavy electrical machinery as most important. Unions take a broader view, considering mainly steel, automobiles, private railways, and the machine industry in general.

A Industry	B Intra-industry spillover	C Differences in patterns of intra-industry reference for labor and for management	D Inter-industry spillover
Aircraft	Major firms form the core.	No significant differences between labor and management.	Management considers steel, private railways, shipbuilding, electrical machinery, railway equipment, and automobiles. Unions also include chemicals and the machine industry in general.
Private railways	Major firms form a cohesive sub-group. Other sub-groups include related services, bus companies, and bus companies engaged in other activities as well.	No significant differences between labor and management.	Both consider steel, representative firms in chemicals, all firms with over 1000 employees, and the decisions of the labor-relations commissions.
Road transport	Large firms have close ties on a local or regional basis.		One large firm looks at the National Railways. Another considers steel and the private railways. Unions do the same.
Ocean transport	Two groups exist, each with very strong ties: large firms and medium-sized firms.	No significant differences between labor and management.	Consider several dozen "first-class" firms.

Source: From an analysis of the 1966 Survey given in Sano, Koike, and Ishida, eds., *Chingin Kōshō no Kōdō Kagaku*, pp. 78–81.

drawn from the responses of both labor and management at the large firms surveyed in 1966. Industries influenced from the outside register similar patterns for labor and for management; however, the patterns of intra-industry reference sometimes differ for labor and management (see column C). The concern with conformity within industries and industry subgroups is particularly strong among management. Whether this is due to the competitive influences within the product market is discussed below. Since unions are organized on a similar industrial and subgroup basis, their consciousness also tends to fit this pattern. Unions not conforming to the behavior of others in their industry may be organized differently: they seem to formulate their own comparisons on an individual basis.

Some large firms do refer to events outside their own industry. In particular, such behavior seems to characterize the large firms in the leading industries and the most important unions and firms within a given industry or subgroup. The transport equipment industry is taken as one example in Figure 1. It is an industry in which market conformity reflects considerable similarity from firm to firm in terms of production inputs and outputs. Concern with other industries arises from a number of specific considerations: product relationships for firms diversified into several lines of production; financial ties; and, in the non-manufacturing industries, interaction with the local economy.

The industries most frequently studied were steel, chemicals, private railways, electrical goods, and shipbuilding. With these industries as the leaders, spillover to other industries is shown in Figure 2. Large firms in other industries follow settlements in the leading industries, and they in turn then set the norm for small and medium-sized firms in their own industries.

The survey of small and medium-sized firms in Nagano Prefecture was also used to identify differences between two types of firm groupings: the group of firms which depended upon making constant

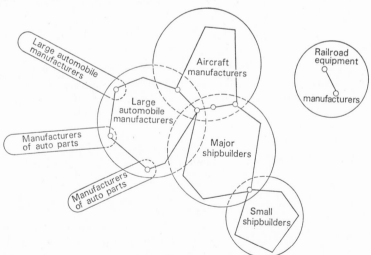

Figure 1:   The Spillover Effect in the Transport Equipment Manufacturing Industries (1966).

Source: Inoue Shōzō, "Chingin Hikaku to Chingin Hakyū" [Wage Comparisons and the Spillover Effect], *Nihon Rōdō Kyōkai Zasshi* (vol. 13, no. 10: October 1971), p. 27.

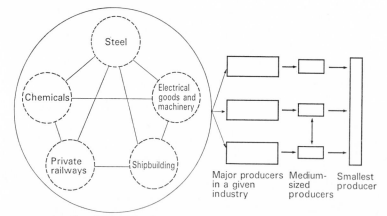

Major producers Medium- Smallest
in a given   sized   producer
industry   producers

Leading firms and unions
in the major industries

Figure 2: The Spillover Effect Throughout All Industries (1966)
Source: Inoue Shōzō, "Chingin Hikaku to Chingin Hakyū" [Wage Comparisons and the Spillover Effect], *Nihon Rōdō Kyōkai Zasshi* (vol. 13, No. 10: October 1971), p. 29.

references to other firms and the group of firms characterized as product competitors. In industries characterized by the presence of large-scale producers, the reference group for the firm consisted primarily of those firms which were most competitive in the product market.[8] In industries characterized by the presence of small-scale producers, however, only 6 percent of the firms with unions and 12 percent of the firms without unions used product competitors in their industry as their main reference. For the vast majority of the firms surveyed, the product competitors in their own industry did not form the major reference group.

To shed light on this problem, the survey in 1966 of large firms throughout the country asked why respondents decided to follow the behavior of another firm or union.[9] In making intra-industry comparisons, management cited the following considerations in order of importance: (1) similar firm size, (2) competitive considerations, and (3) the reality of dealing with the same industrial labor federation. Unions cited the following: (1) affiliation with the same industrial labor federation, (2) similar firm size, and (3) competitive considerations. Although the order of importance is different, labor and management seem to agree that market competition is not the main criterion determining the reference group. Viewing the large-scale sector more

[8] See Sano, Ishida, and Inoue, eds., *Chūshō Kigyō no Chingin Kettei*, pp. 78–81.
[9] Sano, Koike, and Ishida, eds., *Chingin Kōshō no Kōdō Kagaku*, pp. 103–109.

closely in terms of firm size, it is clear that the larger firms are less concerned with problems of labor mobility and forces directly affecting the firm such as competition, firm size, revenue, or capital assets. Rather, as size increases, there seems to be more concern with the structure of union organization and, on the part of both labor and management, with their firm's role as pattern setter for the industry as a whole. To be sure, the overall weight of factors related to the performance of the firm is considerable (accounting for 50 percent of the responses from management and 45 percent from the unions). However, such criteria are not always the sole or even the overwhelming consideration; moreover, the importance of such criteria varies inversely with firm size. This fact suggests that perhaps the causal connection between the product market and the pattern of wage conformity is not so strong. In other words, although wage increase settlements tend to be structured around the product market, considerations of competition within the product market are not necessarily the most important factor shaping the pattern of wage conformity. Finally, it is important to underline the fact that this survey was taken in 1966.

4. Factors Determining the Going Rate in the Spring Wage Offensive

Based upon the foregoing discussion, we might legitimately inquire about the type of model which can be built with these kinds of variables.[10] For the dependent variable (the increase in wages), we use

---

[10] The discussion in this section is based upon the following research:

(1) Sano Yōko, "Yonjūninen no Shuntō Sōba Yosoku" [A Projection on the Going Rate in the 1967 Spring Offensive], *Rōsei Jihō* (no. 1876: January 6, 1967), pp. 2–25;

(2) Sano, "Shōwa Yonjūsannen Shuntō Chinagegaku no Yosoku Kekka" [The Accuracy of Predicted Wage Increases for the 1968 Spring Offensive], *Rōsei Jihō* (no. 1924: January 19, 1968), pp. 2–14;

(3) Sano Yōko, Ishida Hideo, and Shimada Haruo, "Shuntō Sōba no Yosoku Hōhō to Kekka" [The Method and Accuracy of Predictions for the Spring Wage Offensives], *Rōsei Jihō* (no. 1987: March 14, 1969), pp. 2–29;

(4) Sano Yōko and Minotani Chiohiko, "Shuntō Sōba no Yosoku Shōwa Yonjūgonen" [Predictions for the 1970 Spring Wage Offensive], *Rōsei Jihō* (no. 2026: March 20, 1970), pp. 2–28;

(5) The same for 1971 in *Rōsei Jihō* (no. 2072: March 12, 1971), pp. 2–20;

(6) The same for 1972 in *Rōsei Jihō* (no. 2119: March 10, 1972), pp. 2–24;

(7) The same for 1973 in *Rōsei Jihō* (no. 2166: March 9, 1973), pp. 2–29;

(8) The same for 1974 in *Rōsei Jihō* (no. 2213: March 8, 1974), pp. 2–27;

(9) Sano Yōko and Minotani Chiohiko, "Shuntō Sōba Kettei Mekanizumu no Tokuchō to Sono Henka" [The Special Characteristics of the Spring Offensive Mechanism for Wage Determination and Some New Changes], *Rōsei Jihō* (no. 2259: March 7, 1975), pp. 2–30.

the average absolute amount of increase. Previous use of (1) the average percentage increase, (2) the absolute increase in wage rates for new graduates entering the labor market, (3) the average percentage increase of those rates, and (4) changes in individual wage rates in both our own research and that of the Ministry of Labour suggests that the average amount of the absolute increase in wages is the most viable indicator for this variable when studying the behavior of labor and management.[11] Although the difference between the performance of this proxy and that of the other candidate proxies narrows over time, the average amount of the absolute increase in wages continues to provide us with the best fit.

As stated above, the most important factors affecting wage rates during the ten years since 1965 have been the going rate, the performance of the firm, the supply of and demand for labor, and the price level. In seeking to explain the movement of our independent variable, the average absolute increase in wages, we obtained our best results with a simple linear equation. The specifics of the equation are found in the explanation of our projections for the years 1968 through 1974 and the more general discussion appearing in 1975 (see item (9) in footnote 10). Here a brief summary will suffice. The two most important variables explaining change in the level of wages are the going rate and firm performance. The variable representing the supply and demand situation for labor has some effect, but its weight is very small. In the case of the large firms, it can be omitted altogether. The variable for the price level does not register as significant for the eight-year period beginning in 1966 but suddenly becomes important in 1974. We might reason that there is a threshold effect: if price inflation is kept below a certain rate it seems to have little effect; however, once over a certain level, it begins to have a noticeable effect.

The most difficult variable to quantify is the going rate. The proxy which best expresses this variable is the amount of the wage increases decided at an earlier date by labor and management in the pace-setting firms (as defined by labor and management at firms which are relatively late in determining their wage packages). The difficulty with this formulation is obvious: we are forced to explain wage hikes with wage hikes. The very high correlation for the amount of wage in-

---

[11] See Sano, Koike, and Ishida, eds., *Chingin Kōshō no Kōdō Kagaku*, p. 141; Sano, Ishida, and Inoue, eds., *Chūshō Kigyō no Chingin Kettei*, pp. 68–71; and Rōdō Shō Rōsei Kyoku (Bureau of Labor Administration, Ministry of Labor), *Chingin Hikiage Nado no Jittai ni Kansuru Chōsa Hōkoku* [Report on the Survey of Conditions Concerning Wage Increases] (Tokyo: Ōkura Shō Insatsu Kyoku) for the years 1966 through 1975.

creases among firms means that we can explain nearly 100 percent of the shift in wage rates with this one variable. Theoretically we are left with an indeterminate equation; it becomes impossible to sort out the real causes from the superficial ones.

To circumvent this problem we used a proxy to indicate firm profits. Considering the fact that decisions on wage rates are made on the level of the individual firm, firm profits reflect the firm's ability to pay and thereby the economic performance of the firm. Price inflation and the supply of and demand for labor are constants defined at the national level; they are givens in the general economic picture which affect everyone. Accordingly, is it not possible to argue that the influence of other settlements is the result of the greater ability of the pace-setters to pay? An index showing the ability to pay of one firm or sector as opposed to that of all other firms or sectors was constructed to show the relative likelihood of one influencing the other. In other words, the ability to pay in one firm or sector is always relative to the ability of others to pay; some firms or industries are always in a better position to pay, and a look at wage movements suggests that there is always a connection between the wage increases in a given industry and the earnings in the economy's major industries, regardless of the earnings for that particular industry.

The best earnings data are for industries, not individual firms; they are supplied by the Bank of Japan.[12] Accordingly, we take the average wage increase for each industry as the dependent variable. In the preceding section we briefly explained how the spillover effect or the trend toward conformity in wages was based upon inter-industry and intra-industry comparisons, with various weights being given to one or the other depending upon the individual industry (see Table 3 and Figures 1 and 2).

Differences in the impact of price inflation, the supply-demand situation in the labor market, and the ability to pay can best be understood on an industry basis since labor-management relations and personnel composition also vary considerably according to industry. In concrete terms, the ability to pay is defined as the per-capita net profits in an industry, an approach which treats all firms within an industry together. Actually, a full understanding requires that we consider a second type of intra-industry spillover. The analysis is again complicated by the great variety of intra-industry patterns from industries in which the dual structure is important, such as steel and

[12] Nihon Ginkō (Bank of Japan), *Shūyō Kigyō Keiei Bunseki* [Analyses of Business Conditions at Major Firms] (Tokyo: Ōkura Shō Insatsu Kyoku, for the years 1959 through 1973).

private railways, to those in which product subgroupings are important, such as in foodstuffs. On an industry basis, however, we are left with thirteen industries for which the Bank of Japan has data on profits and the Ministry of Labour had data on the average increase in wages. Ignoring differences in standard deviation, the two averages are calculated for each industry. Strictly speaking, a test of the hypotheses developed out of the research introduced above in the preceding section ought to involve a comparison of each industry's profitability only with those industries which were cited as being influential. However, such data are unavailable. Accordingly, the spillover effect of other industries upon the industry concerned is measured by comparing the per-capita profits of that industry with the average for the other twelve industries. The above surveys are such that the data for all industries are gathered at the same point in time. Moreover, the coverage of the surveys varies from industry to industry, and just one value for the variable is given: the average per-capita net profits for all industries taken from a survey of 452 major firms. Since the weight of any one industry is small, the average of the other twelve is for all intents and purposes the same as the average for all industries. Looking back on the research, it would perhaps have been better to use a smaller number of leading (pattern-setting) industries. Nevertheless, we used the simple average of per-capita profitability for each industry in order to calculate the extent to which it deviated from the averaged per-capita profit for all other industries. The rationale for doing this lies in the belief that labor and management are concerned with comparisons which indicated how their firm stacks up in the economy as a whole. The mechanism determining wage increases during the annual spring wage offensive is expressed by the following formula:

$$\Delta W_{it} = a_0 + a_1 \left\{ \left(\frac{\pi}{L} \right)_{at} - \left(\frac{\pi}{L} \right)_{it} \right\} + a_2 \left(\frac{\pi}{L} \right)_{it} + a_3 CPI_{t-1} + a_4 U_{t-1}.$$

The variables are defined as follows:

ΔW_{it} The average wage increases for each industry.

                  $i = 01, \ldots, 13$ (data for 150 large firms)

                  $t = 1960, \ldots, 1974$

$\left(\dfrac{\pi}{L} \right)_{at}$ The average per-capita net profits for all industries for each year. The same figure is used for all industries.

$\left(\dfrac{\pi}{L} \right)_{it}$ The average per-capita net profits for each industry for each year.

CPI_{t-1} The annual percentage change in the consumer price index as measured one year earlier. The same value is used for every industry.

U_{t-1} The percentage of people receiving unemployment benefits in the previous year. The‚same value is used for every industry.

Plugging the data for the years 1960 through 1974 into the above equation, the coefficient (a_3) for CPI_{t-1} was insignificant, and U_{t-1} could be left out completely. The two major variables—firm performance (the ability to pay) and the spillover effect (the differentials in ability to pay)—seem to vary in their relative importance from one industry to another.

Examining the different combinations of variable weightings, we tried to identify stable patterns built around the value of the parameters. The results of that exercise are given in Table 4. Among the thirteen industries, the parameters for both variables in six industries responded according to our hypotheses. These are listed as A-type industries. In private railways and transport equipment (B-type industries), however, wage increases were tied to profit rates in other industries rather than to profits within the industry. In C-type industries (steel, metals, chemicals, pulp and paper, and electric power) the influence of other industries did not seem to be great; the importance

Table 4: A Comparison of Results for Each Industry: The Stability of Parameters for Each Variable (1960–1972)

	Industry	The spillover effect $\left\{\left(\dfrac{\pi}{L}\right)_{at} - \left(\dfrac{\pi}{L}\right)_{it}\right\}$	Ability to pay (performance of the firm) $\left(\dfrac{\pi}{L}\right)_{it}$	Type
1	Private railways	○	×	B
2	Steel	×	○	C
3	Electrical machinery	○	○	A
4	Shipbuilding	○	○	A
5	Metals	×	○	C
6	Electric wire	○	○	A
7	Transportation equipment	○	×	B
8	Chemicals	×	○	C
9	Petroleum	○	○	A
10	Cement	○	○	A
11	Pulp and paper	×	○	C
12	Coal	○	○	A
13	Electric power	×	○	C

Note: ○ Significant
     × Not significant

Source: Taken from Sano Yōko and Minotani Chiohiko, "Shuntō Sōba Yosoku Shōwa Yonjūhachinen" [Predictions for the 1973 Spring Wage Offensive], *Rōsei Jihō* (no. 2166: March 9, 1973), pp. 18–20.

of profits within the industry was clearly decisive. The C-type industries, no doubt, include both the pattern-setters and those which simply act independently.

In measuring the spillover effect, it is desirable to use comparative time series data to estimate the effect in each industry. Unfortunately, as is explained above, because the data for all industries are pooled, we must assume that the derived values are constant for each industry. This in turn requires that we use a larger sample.

The correlation coefficient for each of the values of the corresponding parameters for each variable used in the work done to data (1960–1974) is given in Table 5. Looking at the period 1965–1974, the correlation of parameters for the two most important independent variables when used alone increases until about 1970 and then decreases. To improve the fit, in more recent years we tried to add other variables as proxies for the change in wages in the past so as to obtain a trend effect. Also, we could not rely on only the above-mentioned two variables to explain the wage hikes in 1974. For that year changes in the consumer price index must be included in the equation. Here there is also a problem in changing our sample. The earlier estimates, for 1960–1973, were based upon data for 13 industries and 150 firms. The newer estimates for 1965–1974 use data for 21 industries and 260 firms. There is thus a discontinuity in the estimates.

Finally, in Table 6 we give the percentage error in our predictions for the spring wage offensives from 1967 through 1973. At the bottom of the table, the variables used in the equation for making the predictions and the overall simple average of the percentage error are given. Owing to a change in the data in 1974, the results for that year are not comparable with the earlier results. The change did provide us with an opportunity to revise our model. Nevertheless, the extent to which the model underestimates the actual results is greater than in 1970. There is no consistent movement, however, in the overall measure of error. In particular, attention is directed to the large error in 1971.

5. Conclusions

Summarizing the results of our research, four facts seem clear. First, from 1965 to 1970 the importance of per-capita net profits as indicators of the spillover effect and the ability to pay was relatively greater. In the 1970s, however, their significance decreases, and it is necessary to introduce other variables. Second, among the other variables, there are the anticipation of higher wages on the basis of wage hikes in the

Table 5:   The Correlation Coefficient (R) Adjusted for the Degree of Freedom for Each Combination of Independent Variables

Years for which observations were made	Number of observations	Combination of variables used						
		$[(\pi/L)_{at}-(\pi/L)_{it}]$, $(\pi/L)_{it}$, U_{t-1}, Basic formula	$[(\pi/L)_{at}-(\pi/L)_{it}]$, $(\pi/L)_{it}$, U_{t-1}	$[(\pi/L)_{at}-(\pi/L)_{it}]$, U_{t-1}, $\Delta W_{i,\,t-1}$	$[(\pi/L)_{at}-(\pi/L)_{it}]$, $-(\pi/L)_{it}$, $(\pi/L)_{it}$, U_{t-1}, ΔW_{i*t}	$[(\pi/L)_{at}-(\pi/L)_{it}]$, $-(\pi/L)_{it}$, $(\pi/L)_{it}$, CPI_{t-1}	$[(\pi/L)_{at}-(\pi/L)_{it}]$, $-(\pi/L)_{it}$, $(\pi/L)_{it}$, ΔW_{i*t}	$[(\pi/L)_{at}-(\pi/L)_{it}]$, $-(\pi/L)_{it}$, $(\pi/L)_{it}$, RE_{t-1}
1960–1966	91					0.675		
1960–1967	104					0.775		
1960–1968	117	0.852	0.862					
1960–1969	130	0.908	0.916					
1960–1970	143	0.940	0.945					
1960–1971	156	0.917	0.931	0.973				
1960–1972	169	0.889	0.910	0.979				
1963–1972	130			0.986	0.987			
1966–1972	91	0.784	0.875	0.983				
1963–1973	132	0.933					0.983	0.838
1965–1973	108	0.917					0.991	0.986
1968–1973	126	0.851					0.991	0.921
1965–1974	201					0.875	0.936	
1968–1974	147	0.852				0.975	0.933	

Note: The top part of the table is based upon the older data for 13 industries, the lower part of the table upon the newer data for 22 industries. $\Delta_{i*t}=0.5\Delta W_{1,t-1}+0.3\Delta W_{1,t-2}+0.2\Delta W_{1,t-3}$. RE_{t-1} denotes the ratio of effective job openings.

Source: Sano Yōko and Minotani Chiohiko, "Shuntō Sōba Kettei Mekanizumu no Tokuchō to Sono Henkō" [The Special Characteristics of the Spring Offensive Mechanism for Wage Determination and Some New Changes], Rōsei Jihō (no. 2259: March 7, 1975), pp. 5 and 15.

Table 6: The Wage Increase Predicted for Each Industry and the Percentage Error

Industry	1967		1969		1969	
	Predicted wage increase	Percentage-error	Predicted wage increase	Percentage error	Predicted wage increase	Percentage error
1 Private railways	4,021	7.2	4,698	6.8	5,356	20.6
2 Steel	4,720	−10.1	5,119	−17.8	5,816	−11.0
3 Electric machinery	4,218	5.5	5,056	11.0	5,858	17.3
4 Shipbuilding	4,105	8.2	4,798	8.4	5,563	23.0
5 Metals	4,307	6.4	5,063	18.0	5,845	23.8
6 Electric wire	4,329	−4.7	5,189	−5.0	5,783	4.8
7 Transportation equipment	3,936	8.4	4,586	13.9	5,299	25.9
8 Chemicals	4,407	3.2	6,263	7.8	6,018	10.1
9 Petroleum	4,800	−6.0	5,655	1.4	6,279	9.4
10 Cement	5,007	−14.6	6,391	−22.2	7,010	−1.9
11 Paper, pulp	4,106	−15.5	4,791	−19.8	5,499	11.5
12 Coal	3,466	−95.0	5,473	1.1	4,620	12.7
13 Electric power	4,724	3.5	4,069	−27.2	6,384	11.8
Average amount of error		−1.8		−1.8		12.8
Time period used to estimate	1959–66		1940–47		1959–66	
Coefficient of correlation (R) adjusted for degree of freedom	0.767		0.776		0.852	
Variables used in the equation	$(\pi/L)_{at}$ $(\pi/L)_{lt}$		$(\pi/L)_{at}$ $(\pi/L)_{lt}$		$(\pi/L)_{at}$ $(\pi/L)_{lt}$	

Note: The percentage error is calculated as

$$\frac{\text{Actual increase} - \text{Predicted increase}}{\text{Actual increase}}.$$

past and, in 1974, the rise in the consumer price index. Third, taking the period 1960 to 1974 as a whole, the variables showing consistent significance are the ability to pay and the spillover effect as measured with figures on per-capita net profits. Finally, leaving aside 1974 as a special year, the weightings of these two variables are about the same, with past wage hikes having half their individual weights. If we include 1974, the weightings again would be roughly 1.0, 1.0, and 0.5 respectively, but with the price level then having a relative weighting of 0.7.

1970		1971		1972		1973	
Pre-dicted wage increase	Percent-age error	Pre-dicted wage increase	Percent-age error	Pre-dicted wage increase	Percent-age error	Pre-dicted wage increase	Percent-age error
7,305	18.8	6,748	30.7	9,542	6.8	13,342	8.6
8,120	−9.4	6,841	8.9	7,872	−3.6	—	—
7,874	9.0	7,013	19.3	8,989	5.3	13,092	6.8
7,558	36.2	7,019	36.2	10,381	7.4	14,964	8.2
7,748	23.3	7,020	34.4	9,097	7.8	14,608	6.2
7,687	5.5	6,868	24.5	8,649	−0.1	13,002	7.9
7,042	17.2	6,211	30.0	10,020	13.0	13,306	11.3
8,130	17.6	7,239	20.4	10,490	3.1	14,130	9.7
8,806	11.9	8,344	20.6	9,575	7.4	15,539	1.0
8,666	−8.3	7,584	15.9	8,534	3.8	13,740	12.4
7,656	15.0	6,561	22.2	6,038	3.7	12,778	13.7
6,639	−31.5	6,006	−22.9	10,414	1.8	9,803	9.2
8,444	7.8	7,882	21.7		−3.4	14,025	7.1
	7.5		20.8		4.1		7.9
1940–69		1960–70		1960–71		1966–72	
0.916		0.945		0.973		0.983	
$(\pi/L)_{at}$		$(\pi/L)_{at}$		$(\pi/L)_{at}$		$(\pi/L)_{at}$	
$(\pi/L)_{lt}$		$(\pi/L)_{lt}$		$(\pi/L)_{lt}$		$(\pi/L)_{lt}$	
U_{t-1}		U_{t-1}		ΔW_{t-1}		ΔW_{it}	

Source: See the annual reports listed in footnote 10.

The Economic Impact of Labor Disputes in the Public Sector

Kōshiro Kazutoshi

1. Introduction

The public sector has a particular importance in the Japanese system of industrial relations, and employees in the public sector play a leading role in determining the direction of the labor movement. Although public employees accounted for only 13.9 percent of all employees in 1975, they represented 27.1 percent of all union members (see Table 1). Moreover, 86.2 percent of the union members in the public sector are affiliated with Sōhyō, the largest national federation of labor in Japan. They account for 64.2 percent of Sōhyō's total membership. Public sector employees account for only 7.1 percent of the membership in Dōmei, the second largest national federation.

Since 1957, disputes focusing on the right to organize and the right to strike in the public sector have increased. In 1965 the Japanese Diet ratified I.L.O. Convention No. 87, but the disputes have continued to the present.[1] In 1973 the government accepted the report of the Advisory Council on the Public Personnel System (Kōmuin Seido Shingi Kai), which had deliberated for eight years,[2] and since then has

Adapted from "Kōkyō Bumon ni Okeru Sōgi Kōi to Sono Shoeikyō (The Effects of Labor Disputes in the Public Sector), in Komiya Ryōtarō, Hyōdō Tsutomu, *et al.*, eds., *Kōkyō Bumon no Sōgiken* [The Right to Strike in the Public Sector] (Tokyo: University of Tokyo Press, 1977), pp. 88–111. The author is Professor of Labor Economics at Yokohama National University.

[1] For an account of the events leading up to the ratification of I.L.O. Convention 87 by the Japanese Diet, see Ehud Harari, *The Politics of Labor Legislation in Japan* (Berkeley: University of California Press, 1973).

[2] Kōmuin Seido Shingikai (the Advisory Council on the Public Service), "Tō-shin" [Report and Recommendations to the Cabinet], *Kanpō* [Bulletin of the Government] (no. 14038: October 11, 1973); see the appendix.

Table 1: Employees and Union Membership by Sector and Applicable Labor Law and by Major National Labor Federation

(Unit: 1000 persons)

Legal status of employees	Total number	Number in labor unions	Rate of organization (percentage)	Affiliation with national center				Other nonaffiliated unions
				Sōhyo	Dōmei	Shinsanbetsu	Chūritsurōren	
All employees	36460	12590	34.5	4573	2266	70	1369	4705
Private sector	31379	9183	29.3	1635	2106	70	1368	4195
(to which the Trade Union Law applies)								
Public sector	5081	3410	67.1	2938	161	—	1	310
a. Public Corporation and National Enterprise Labor Relations Law	1153	1020	88.5	⎫ 1037 ⎬	140	—	1	73
b. Local Public Enterprise Labor Relations Law	328	229	69.8	⎭				
c. National Public Service Law	827	287	34.7	⎫				
1. Salary Law employees	500	287	57.4	⎬ 1901	21	—	—	237
2. Special job categories	327	0	0.0	⎪				
d. Local Public Service Law	2773	1871	67.5	⎭				

Note: Because of dual affiliation, the totals in the five columns on the right do not correspond precisely with the totals in the second column.

Source: Sōrifu (Prime Ministers Office), *Nihon Tōkei Nenkan* [Yearbook of Japanese Statistics], No. 26 (Tokyo: Ōkura Shō Insatsu Kyoku, 1976), pp. 594–595; Jichi Shō (Ministry of Home Affairs), *Chihō Kōei Kigyō Nenkan* [Yearbook of Local Public Enterprises] (Tokyo: Chihō Zaimu Kyōkai, 1976), p. 145; Rōdō Shō (Ministry of Labour), *Rōdō Kumiai Kihon Chōsa* [Basic Survey of Trade Unions] (Tokyo: Rōdō Shō Tōkei Jōhō Bu, 1976), pp. 36–37; and Jinjiin (National Personnel Authority), *Nenji Hōkoku Sho* [Annual Report for Fiscal 1975] (Tokyo: Jinjiin, 1976), p. 2.

focused its efforts on resolving issues concerning the right to strike in public enterprises.[3]

In August 1974, the Advisory Committee (Semmon Iin Kondan Kai) of the Ministerial Council on Public Corporations and National Enterprises was established; its views were presented to the government in November 1975.[4] The group advised that simple revision of the system of labor-management relations in public enterprises would not suffice. It recommended that the enterprises be reorganized, with some of them being transformed into private bodies. Finally, it called for a more comprehensive review which would consider the very nature of the public corporation and the public interest in general.

Dissatisfied with the views of the "specialists", the Council of the Public Corporation Labor Unions (Kōrōkyō), a body representing employees of the public enterprises, conducted an eight-day strike from November 26 through December 3, 1975. In the negotiations which followed, the government agreed (1) to give serious consideration to the body's views and (2) to set up a new body to implement the report. Following this line, in September 1976 the government set up another committee of specialists (The Council on the Basic Problems of the Public Corporations and National Enterprises) with eight subcommittees and three consultative boards.[5] The Council is to draft a final proposal within two years.

---

[3] Here the terms "public corporations" and "public enterprises" refer to the three public corporations (the Japan National Railways, the Public Telephone and Telegraph Corporation, and the Tobacco Monopoly) and the five public enterprises (the Postal Service, the Mint, the Government Printing Office, the State Forest Authority, and the Alcohol Monopoly). The problems of the right to strike and the right to organize in the non-industrial civil service were not discussed by the Committee of Experts (Semmon Iinkai), thereby postponing consideration of such issues to the report of the Advisory Council on the Public Service. See Kōshiro Kazutoshi, "Wage Determination in the Public Service in Japan: Changes and Prospects," in *Public Employment Labor Relations: An Overview of Eleven Nations*, ed. by Charles M. Rehmus (Ann Arbor: Institute of Labor and Industrial Relations, University of Michigan, 1975), pp. 43–61.

[4] Kōkyō Kigyōtai tō Kankei Kakuryō Kyōgi Kai Semmon Iin Kondan Kai (The Advisory Committee of the Ministerial Council on Public Corporations and National Enterprises), *Sankōsha Gogengyō tō no Arubeki Seikaku to Rōdō Kihon Ken Mondai ni Tsuite (Iken Sho)* [Views on the Optimal Organization of the Public Enterprises and the Basic Rights of Labor] (Tokyo: Sōrifu, mimeographed, November 1975).

[5] This group was officially called the "Kōkyō Kigyōtai Tō Kihon Mondai Kaigi" (Council on the Basic Problems of Public Corporations and National Enterprises). A consultative board was organized to consider each of the following three areas: (a) the managerial structure of the public enterprises, (b) the autonomy of each of the enterprises or corporations, and (c) more general legal reforms. Nakayama Ichirō was asked to coordinate these boards. The author of this paper is a member of the sub-board on wages which is under the third board considering legal reform.

This paper was prepared with the above developments in mind, and seeks to apply a quantitative approach to measuring the economic costs of strikes by employees of the Japan National Railways.

2. Methods of Estimating the Impact of Labor Disputes

As the division of labor becomes more refined, the various economic sectors become more interdependent. New technologies allow for economies of scale, which in turn require high rates of utilization. Accordingly, industrial societies have become increasingly concerned with the public costs incurred by strikes even when they occur in the private sector. Although this paper seeks to analyze in a quantitative fashion the impact of labor disputes in the Japan National Railways, it is useful to begin with a survey of the literature on measuring the impact of strikes in general.

A. Previous Research on the External Impact of Industrial Disputes

A standard starting point in this field is provided by Chamberlain and Schilling.[6] They use a number of indices to measure the public cost of strikes, including costs which are borne not directly by the parties to the dispute but by employees in related industries and by consumers. The first concerns the cultural necessity of the product or service being produced. Here two measures are relevant, one being the "dispensability" of the product or service and the other being its "deferrability". A second set of measures concerns the availability of stocks. The third set focuses on whether other products or services supplied by sectors not directly engaged in the dispute can be substituted. Using such concepts, the two constructed an "urgency index" with a scale of ten grades. The actual implementation of the index involves fairly subjective processes, and therefore does not necessarily provide the most suitable method for approaching the problem. Nevertheless, it is useful to bear these three sets of concerns in mind even though the methods of quantification [used by Chamberlain and Schilling are not used in this study.

[6] Neil W. Chamberlain and Jane Metzger Schilling, *The Impact of Strikes: Their Economic and Social Costs* (New York: Harper and Brothers, 1954). A Japanese translation by Kuronuma Minoru was published as *Sutoraiki no Son'eki Keisan* (Tokyo: Daiyamondo Sha, 1957).

Two approaches have been used to measure the impact of strikes at the macro-economic level. One is to take the "source approach" and measure the negative effect which strikes have on the economic growth rate. Denison, for example, estimates that the annual rate of economic growth in the United States would have been 0.01 percentage points higher had there not been any loss in the hours of work due to strike activity.[7] Compared with a loss of 0.1 percentage points owing to hours of work lost through illness and industrial accidents, the impact of strikes would not seem to have been very great.

A second approach emphasizing the macro-economic level of analysis focuses on the wage-price inflationary spiral caused by the latent ability of the unions to engage in disputative activities. As an issue central to the analytical framework associated with the Phillips curve, this aspect has already been examined by many persons, including Phillips, Lipsey, Hines, and Holt.[8] In Japan the Phillips curve has also been studied by a number of scholars, including Watanabe and Ono.[9] Using a regression analysis, the fourth section of this paper argues that the rate at which stikes occur in the public sector is one variable explaining the rate of change in money wages.[10]

[7] E. F. Denison, *The Sources of Economic Growth in the United States*, supplementary paper no. 3 (New York: Committee for Economic Development, 1962), pp. 276–277.

[8] A. W. Phillips, "The Relation between Unemployment and the Rate of Change of Money Wage Rates in the United Kingdom, 1861–1957," *Economica* (November 1958), pp. 283–299; Richard G. Lipsey, "The Relation Between Unemployment and The Rate of Change of Money Wage Rates in the United Kingdom, 1862–1957; A Further Analysis," *Economica* (February 1960), pp. 1–31; A. G. Hines, "Trade Unions and Wage Inflation in the United Kingdom, 1893–1961," *Review of Economic Studies* (vol. 31: no. 4: October 1964), pp. 221–252; and Charles C. Holt, "Job Search, Phillips' Wage Relation and Union Influence: Theory and Evidence," in *Microeconomic Foundation of Employment and Inflation Theory*, ed. by E. S. Phelps *et al.* (New York: W. W. Norton and Company, Inc., 1970), pp. 53–123.

[9] Watanabe Tsunehiko, "Chingin Kakaku no Kankei to Sono Seisakuteki Igi" [Wages and Their Relation to Value: Some Policy Implications], in *Nihon no Bukka* [Prices in Japan], ed. by Kumagai Hisao and Watanabe Tsunehiko (Tokyo: Nihon Keizai Shimbun Sha, 1966), pp. 52–67; and Ono Akira, *Sengo Nihon no Chingin Kettei* [Wage Determination in Postwar Japan] (Tokyo: Tōyō Keizai Shimpō Sha, 1973).

[10] For the details on this approach see Kōshiro Kazutoshi, Sano Yōko, and Shimada Haruo, *Kōshōryoku Moderu ni Yoru Shuntō Chinage no Bunseki—Shuntō Chinage ni Oyobosu Kankōrō no Eikyō no Sūryōteki Kenkyū* [An Analysis of the Spring Wage Hikes Using a Bargaining Power Model: Quantitative Research on the Impact of Kankōrō on the Spring Wage Hikes] (Tokyo: Tōkei Kenkyū Kai, March 1975).

B. Measurement of the Impact of Disputes in the Public Sector

The preceding discussion has focused on concepts relevant to the impact of strikes in general. The above-mentioned research did not give special attention to the different nature of disputes in the public sector. The literature on the impact of these disputes has focused on the concept of "essentiality" and how to quantify such criteria.

There is no consensus on whether to give public employees the right to strike. The arguments for and against usually depend upon a subjective evaluation of the costs and benefits of doing so. Accordingly, a careful appraisal of the arguments requires an assessment of the different assumptions behind each person's comparative criteria.[11] For example, in the final analysis do we limit our concern to a concept of public "essentiality" based on the notion of endangering public safety or public health, or do we take a broader view by considering the various distortions which strikes by public employees introduce into the democratic process itself?[12] The need to differentiate between these two interpretations of "essentiality" has been stressed in America by Wellington and Winter.[13] In particular, the broader interpretation of "essentiality" implies that we must give careful consideration to the elasticity of demand for public services and the lack of market constraints.

The incompatibility of these two views can also be seen in the ruling on the right to strike which was handed down by the Supreme Court in the 1966 case involving Zentei and the Tokyo Central Post Office.[14] The court argued that "although restrictions on the basic rights of labor ought to be conceived so as to maintain a healthy balance between the need for protecting and paying due respect to the basic rights of labor on the one hand and the need to promote the overall well-being of all citizens on the other, ... such restrictions must not go beyond the very minimum necessitated by considerations of overall efficiency." It proceeded to argue that consideration be

---

[11] Kojo Toshimarō, "Amerika ni Okeru Kōmuin no Sutoraiki Ken Ronsō" [The American Debate on The Right to Strike for Public Employees], *Kōkirō Kenkyū* (no. 10: 1972), pp. 42–53.

[12] *Ibid.*, pp. 51–53.

[13] H. W. Wellington and R. K. Winter, Jr., "Structuring Collective Bargaining in Public Employment," *Yale Law Journal* (vol. 79, no. 5: April 1970), pp. 805–870.

[14] The decision appears in *Saikōsai Daihōtei Hanketsu: Shōwa 39 Nen*, Case No. A-296, October 26, 1966. Quoted from *Jurisuto* (no. 359: December 1, 1966), pp. 72–81.

given to limiting the basic rights of labor only "in situations where it is absolutely necessary in order to avoid a serious conflict with national interest or where there is fear that the discontinuation of public services would seriously threaten the well-being of the people."[15] The meaning of the phrase "well-being of the people" is extremely ambiguous, but the idea of there being "a serious conflict with national interest" seems to imply the narrower meaning of "essentiality": is there or is there not a direct danger to the safety and health of the people?

In contrast to the 1966 decision of the Supreme Court stands its ruling in 1973 on the Zennōrin case involving a protest against the Protective Services Law (Keishoku Hō).[16] The court adopted the broader interpretation in this case, arguing that the disputative activity by civil servants tended "to warp the democratic procedural processes which ought to determine the working conditions of public employees". It emphasized the absence of market constraints in the public sector, and sharply criticized the Supreme Court's earlier judgments in 1966 and 1969. The decision in 1973 argued that in its earlier decisions the Court had evaluated the effects of disputes in the public service simply in terms of the various inconveniences felt by the people in their daily lives. The earlier decisions were thus criticized for ignoring the broader impact of such disputes upon the democratic processes of the nation.[17]

Although the pros and cons of the right to strike for public employees have been debated over the past twenty-five years, there has been very little careful consideration of the actual economic costs borne by the public. Such consideration is limited primarily to the exiguous materials on reductions in passenger or freight transport, the backlog of undelivered postal items, or the loss of revenue which are appended to the reports of the Advisory Committee (Semmon Iin Kondan Kai) of the Ministerial Council on Public Corporations and National Enterprises.

This paper seeks to evaluate the broad impact of strikes in the public sector as objectively as possible. In doing so, there is no reason to neglect the implication of the broader meaning of "essentiality", including the undesirable effects on the democratic political process mentioned above. However, it is extremely difficult to quantify these more ephemeral concepts. Accordingly, our measures of the social impact of disputes in the public sector will be limited to (1) the economic costs imposed in terms of the daily inconveniences suffered by the

---

[15] *Ibid.*, p. 73.

[16] The decision appears in *Saikōsai Daihōtei Hanketsu: Shōwa 43 Nen* Case No. A-2780, April 25, 1973. Quoted from *Jurisuto* (no. 536: June 15, 1973), pp. 84–111.

[17] *Ibid.*, p. 85.

public and (2) the inelasticity of demand for public services (meaning the extent to which suitable substitutes for such public services do not exist). The following section explains an attempt to measure these two types of impact during the eight-day "right-to-strike strike" in late 1975. Although the original analysis dealt with (1) the national railways, (2) the telephone and telegraph services, and (3) the postal service, the limited space in this volume requires that we focus our discussion on the national railways, with only brief mention being given to the other two. The fourth section will evaluate the impact of strikes in the public sector on the national economy by considering their connection with the wage hikes obtained through the annual spring wage offensive. Again, the space necessary for a detailed discussion is not available and only a skeletal outline is given.

3. Economic Costs of Strikes in the National Railways

During the eight-day strike in late 1975, 143,111 scheduled runs were canceled for passenger trains and 43,915 for freight trains. As Table 2 shows, the Japan National Railways forfeited ¥26,165 million in revenue. The secondary losses in directly related industries (including electric power, station shops and kiosks, dining-car services, box lunches, and various other services provided within the station buildings) are estimated at ¥13,719 million. The costs to potential passengers are equivalent to the revenue foregone by the Japan National Railways; they should be added to the losses borne by those in related industries. Accordingly, the total cost of the strike to the public would be a minimum of about 5 billion yen per day. In addition to the "secondary effects" (in directly related industries) there are also "tertiary effects", which means that the actual costs borne by the national economy are some multiple of the estimates given in Table 2. Clearly it is impossible to measure the full effects of the strike in a precise fashion. For this study a rough estimate is calculated by interpolating from an input-output matrix for the various industries of the economy and using the inverse matrix and adjusting the figures showing a drop in transportation services supplied by the national railways to take account of the shift to the private railways. However, it is extremely difficult to measure the increase in income accruing to other sectors of the transport industry resulting from the strike during this period, even if we can obtain figures on increases in the private railways. Here we will estimate the tertiary effects by taking the cross-tabulations

Table 2: The Impact of the "Right-to-strike Strikes" in the National Railways

Item		Estimated loss	Comment
Loss in revenue	Passengers	￥20,231 million	From estimates given in Ryokyaku Kyoku (Bureau of Passenger Services), *Ryokyaku Eigyō Seiseki Nenpō* [Annual Report on Passenger Sales]
	Freight	￥ 5,934 million	Estimates from Kamotsu Kyoku (Bureau of Freight Services), *Unyū Jōkyō Geppō* [Monthly Report on Transport Services]
Drop in the volume of services	Passengers	15.12 million passengers	
	Freight	3.95 million tons	includes: tangerines 50,000 tons; apples 4,000 tons; potatoes 18,000 tons; onions 9,000 tons; frozen fish 34,000 tons
Number of canceled trains	Passenger	143,111	
	Freight	43,915	
Revenue lost in related industries	Electric power	￥1,228 million	*Denryoku Chōsa Tōkei Geppō* [Monthly Statistics on Electric Power Surveys]
	Kiosks	￥6,378 million	
	Dining services	￥1,312 million	From a survey conducted on 6 January 1976
	Box lunch companies	￥1,844 million	
	Station building services	￥2,957 million	From surveys conducted on 1 December and 22 December 1975
	Subtotal	￥13,719 million	
Reduction in wages	Monetary value	￥ 993 million	
	Persons laid off	197,283 persons	
	Total man-hours	1,288,571 hours	
Saved expenses	Personnel costs	￥ 457 million	Travel allowance for drivers and conductors
	Power costs	￥1,819 million	Includes electric power
	Running expenses	￥1,615 million	Includes costs of making other arrangements for freight, parcels and passengers; cleaning of trains; etc.
	Maintenance costs	￥1,041 million	

Source: Calculated from data supplied by the Kokutetsu Shokuin Kyoku (Japan National Railways, Bureau of Personnel Affairs).

in the input-output table for 1970.[18] This gives us the following results:

$$
\begin{pmatrix}
\text{direct economic costs} \\
\text{or losses occurring} \\
\text{during the 8-day} \\
\text{strike in the Japan} \\
\text{National Railways}
\end{pmatrix}
\times
\begin{pmatrix}
\text{sum of coefficients} \\
\text{for transport industry} \\
\text{taken by adding up} \\
\text{the rows in an inverse} \\
\text{input-output matrix}
\end{pmatrix}
=
\begin{pmatrix}
\text{total} \\
\text{loss} \\
\text{of} \\
\text{the} \\
\text{economy}
\end{pmatrix}
$$

(¥26.165 billion) × (3.467) = ¥90.71 billion

The total loss to the Japan National Railways should be adjusted to show the amount of business which shifted to some other form of transportation (meaning the private railways or nonrail transport). Nevertheless, it is likely that the losses generated in the national economy by the national railways strikes will be about 3.5 times those incurred by the national railways alone. To be sure, this is but the crudest of estimates; it is unlikely that an exact measure of all public costs resulting from a stoppage of transportation services run by the national railways can ever be made. To do so would require measurement of (1) the indispensability of the service, (2) the ability of firms to do without the service or to accumulate unsold stock, and (3) the ability of the public to substitute other services. In the next few paragraphs I wish to consider the problems of measuring each of these items.

A. Indispensability

Although there are a few private rail lines which offer service parallel to that of the national rail lines in the large urban areas, the largest number of lines run by the national railways are in rural areas where no other service exists. As Komiya Ryūtarō has suggested, the number of small shopowners and artisans depending upon the daily sale of fresh produce or materials is quite sizeable. For these people the service of the national railways is indispensable. There are also those cases which involve important human rights such as access to one's dying parents.[19] Furthermore, even when passengers can postpone their journeys or use other means of transportation, we must calculate the losses in utility and the mental stress which results from excessive crowding when the trip is eventually made. We must also keep in mind

[18] Gyōsei Kanri Chō (Administrative Management Agency), Keizai Kikaku Chō (The Economic Planning Agency) *et al.*, eds., *1970 Nen Sangyō Renkan Hyō* [Inter-industry Input-Output Tables: 1970], vol. I (Tokyo: Ōkura Shō Insatsu Kyoku, January 1974), p. 73.

[19] Komiya Ryūtarō, "Kōkyō Bumon no Sutoken to Kokumin Fukushi" [Public Welfare and the Right to Strike in the Public Sector], in the *Nihon Keizai Shimbun* (October 1, 1975).

seemingly less important inconveniences which are not recorded simply because people can do without. It is quite impossible to estimate the indispensability of the railways as we cannot know which portion of the undelivered goods or passengers truly represents an economic loss.

B. The Ability of the Public to Postpone Its Demand for Services and to Accumulate Stock

Although transportation services can seldom be stored, an extension in the period required for transportation in effect results in a type of cost not dissimilar to that incurred when inventories accrue. Even if slight delays present no real financial problems (due, for example, to the practice of billing on fixed dates), opportunity costs and other losses to utility from not having access to goods in transit do involve costs for someone. Moreover, there is some limit to the ability of those requiring transportation to postpone their needs. Even in offices there would seem to be a considerable amount of work which cannot be postponed. Whenever strikes occur, a fairly large number of white-collar employees "camp" either in their offices or in hotels near their offices. However, one can estimate neither the monetary nor the other intangible costs involved in these practices.

C. The Ability of Passengers to Use Other Means of Transportation

In the urban areas like Tokyo and Osaka which also have private rail service, the private rail service can be substituted for national rail service. Using statistics compiled by the Ministry of Transportation, we have estimated the extent to which passengers shifted from the national railways to the private railways during the two months when the strike occurred in late 1975 (Table 3). Using the ratio of increase in passenger volume derived by comparing the results for October 1975 with those for October 1974 as a multiplier and for interpolation, projections were calculated for November and December 1975. Our calculations suggest that about three out of ten persons used the private railways when the national railways were unavailable. However, because the behavior of those buying long-term passes (who account for a large portion of commuting passengers) was also influenced by the change in fares,[20] it is difficult to estimate accurately the substitutability of the private railways.

[20] Fares for the national railways were raised in October 1974; for the private railways they rose in July 1974 and again in December 1975.

Table 3:   Estimates of the Substitutability of Private Rail Service for National
Rail Service in the Transportation of Passengers

(unit: 1000s of passengers per day)

		National railways (in Tokyo)		Seven largest private railways (in Tokyo)	
		Ordinary passengers	Passengers using long-term passes	Ordinary passengers	Passengers using long-term passes
A.	Actual numbers of passengers				
	October 1974	3006	6877	2756	6530
	October 1975	3373	6625	2891	6401
	November 1975	3116	6263	3165	6458
	December 1975	3098	5911	3183	6052
B.	Ratio of October 1975 to October 1974	1.1221	0.9633	1.0490	0.9802
C.	Anticipated number of passengers using the ratio of October 1975/October 1974 as a multiplicand				
	November 1975	3450	6358	3018	6540
	December 1975	3652	5789	3053	5701
D.	Estimated effect of the strike ($=C-A$)				
	November 1975	-334	-95	$+147$	$+82$
	December 1975	-554	$+122$	$+130$	-351
	Both months	-888 N		$+277$ P	

E.   The rate of substitutability

$$\left(\frac{N}{P}\right) \quad \frac{\left(\begin{array}{l}\text{the rise in the} \\ \text{number of passengers} \\ \text{using the private railways}\end{array}\right)}{\left(\begin{array}{l}\text{the decline in the number of} \\ \text{passengers using the national} \\ \text{railways}\end{array}\right)} = \frac{277}{888} = 31.2\%$$

Source: Un'yu Shō (Ministry of Transportation), *Min'ei Tetsudō Yusō Tōkei Geppō* [Monthly Statistics on the Private Railways] (Tokyo: Un'yu Shō, mimeographed each month for internal distribution); and Nihon Kokuyū Tetsudō (Japan National Railways), *Jōhō Shisutemu Bu* (Department of Information Systems), *Densha Tokutei Kikan Densha Seiseki Geppō* [Monthly Report on Electrified Railways in Specified Areas] (Tokyo: Kokutetsu Jōhō Shisutemu Bu, mimeographed each month for internal distribution).

In addition to substituting service on the private railways, it is also quite clear that many passengers used taxis, air service, and their own private automobiles. Again, it is impossible to determine the number for whom the cost of a night in a hotel was the cost of not having public rail service. Finally, it is difficult to estimate the net impact of this kind of spending on the various other sectors of the economy; while experiencing rising marginal costs, they also benefited from a whole variety of incidental costs arising out of the efforts of each individual to cope with the strike.

The relative importance of rail transport declined during this period owing largely to the expanded use of automotive transport (Table 4). Although strikes in the rail industry no doubt stimulate the auto-transport industry, there is a longer-term trend which is not the result of such strikes.

D. The Ability to Use Other Means of Transport for Freight Traffic

The movement of freight shows a greater elasticity than does the flow of passengers. To some extent this reflects the fact that over the years Kokurō (Kokutetsu Rōdō Kumiai), the Japan National Railway Workers' Union with 240,000 members, and Dōrō (Dōryokusha Rōdō Kumiai), the Japan National Railway Engineers' Union with 47,000 members, have focused the major thrust of their strike activity on the freight trains in order to minimize public criticism of their "illegal" strikes.

Table 4: Relative Importance of Various Conveyances for Transporting Passengers   (unit: percentage of passenger kilometers)

Fiscal year	National railways	Private railways	Motor vehicle			Ship	Plane	Total
			Bus	Auto-mobile	Total			
1955	55.3	27.2	14.2	2.5	16.7	0.6	0.2	100
1960	51.0	24.8	18.1	4.7	22.8	1.1	0.3	100
1961	49.5	24.5	18.5	6.0	24.5	1.1	0.4	100
1962	48.8	24.1	18.8	6.8	25.6	1.0	0.6	100
1963	47.4	23.2	19.5	8.2	27.7	0.9	0.7	100
1964	46.2	21.8	21.4	9.0	30.4	0.9	0.8	100
1965	45.5	21.3	21.0	10.6	31.6	0.8	0.8	100
1966	43.5	20.6	20.8	13.5	34.3	0.9	0.7	100
1967	41.6	19.5	20.4	16.7	37.1	0.9	0.9	100
1968	38.3	18.4	19.8	21.5	41.3	0.9	1.1	100
1969	34.4	17.8	19.0	26.9	45.8	0.8	1.3	100
1970	32.3	16.9	17.5	30.9	48.4	0.8	1.6	100
1971	30.8	16.1	16.3	34.3	50.6	0.8	1.7	100
1972	30.5	15.8	16.7	34.0	50.7	1.0	2.0	100
1973	30.9	15.6	16.6	33.5	50.1	1.1	2.4	100
1974	31.1	15.7	16.7	32.9	49.6	1.1	2.5	100
1975	30.3	15.3	15.5	35.3	50.8	0.9	2.7	100

Source: Kokutetsu Ryokyaku Kyoku (Bureau of Passenger Services, Japan National Railways), *Ryokyaku Eigyō Seiseki Nenpō* [Yearbook of Business Results for Passenger Transportation] (Tokyo: Japan National Railways, 1975), p. 149.

As Table 5 suggests, the national railways' share of freight transport has dropped remarkably. The use of trucks has expanded very rapidly, while shipping has also grown at a slower pace. More detailed figures show that the volume carried by the national railways increased until 1970, but has since been declining. A number of factors have produced the sharp decline in rail transport and concomitant expansion of automotive transport. First is the building of better roads. The Meishin Expressway from Nagoya to Kobe was opened in 1964. In 1969 the Tōmei Expressway was opened between Tokyo and Nagoya. Second is the tremendous expansion of the automobile industry and the relative drop in the cost of trucks. Finally, there is the flexibility and convenience of automotive transport. There are no doubt many other reasons for the decline of railway freight transport. Again, we cannot throw all the blame on strikes. However, compared with the speed and reliability of automotive transport, the delays resulting from strikes and the drop in the quality of the shipment (particularly of fresh produce) which often accompanies such delays add noticeably to larger structural problems facing the railroads. Here it is interesting to

Table 5: Percentage of Freight Carried by Various Types of Carriers

(unit: percentage)

| Year | National railways | Private railways | Trucks | | | Shipping | Total | Total ton km. (100 million) |
			Owned by trucking firms	Owned by the private firms of self-employed entre-preneurs	Total			
1960	39	1	7	8	15	45	100	1,389
1965	30	0	12	14	26	43	100	1,863
1970	18	0	19	20	39	43	100	3,506
1971	17	0	20	20	40	43	100	3,621
1972	15	0	20	20	40	45	100	3,892
1973	14	0	18	17	35	51	100	4,072
1974	14	0	19	16	35	51	100	3,758
1975	13	0	19	17	36	51	100	3,613

Note: The figures for 1975 are preliminary estimates. These figures are from Un'yu Shō (Ministry of Transportation), *Rikuun Tōkei Yōran* [Statistical Tables on Land Transportation] (Tokyo: Un'yu Shō, annual).

Source: Kihon Mondai Kaigi Council on the Basic Problems of Public Corporations and National Enterprises), *Nihon Kokuyū Tetsudō Kankei Shiryō Shū* [Documentary Materials on the Japan National Railways] (published by the Kihon Mondai Kaigi as Document Keiretsu No. 10: November 5, 1976). p. 39.

note that truck transport is not always cheaper,[21] although the per-unit cost of sending freight by truck is lowered by excessive loading, which frequently goes beyond the legally defined capacity. Moreover, the amount of energy used to move one ton one kilometer by rail locomotive is one-sixth that used by trucks and about one-third that used by water transport.[22] Nevertheless, the market share of the "most inefficient" mover is increasing the most rapidly. If the expansion of strike activity in the national railways is shown to be one of the sources of that sector's decline, we are forced to conclude that the economic costs of such activity are much greater.

4. The Impact of Kōrōkyō's Strikes on Wage Rates

Although space prevents us from presenting a detailed analysis, brief consideration of the impact of strikes in the public sector on average wage hikes achieved during the spring wage offensive is instructive.[23] Accordingly, the results of a regression analysis for the years 1961–1975 are discussed in the following paragraph.

The analysis treats the average wage hike obtained between 1961 and 1975 as the dependent variable. The change in wage levels measured both as an absolute amount (ΔW) and in percentage terms ($\dot{W}$) is used to represent this variable. Here the discussion is confined to a consideration of the absolute amount of the increase in wages. The ratio of job applicants to effective job opening at the Public Employment Security Offices for the first three months of the calendar year is used as a proxy to indicate the balance of supply and demand in the labor market (UYS). The number of days lost during the spring in the manufacturing industry is used as the proxy to rep-

[21] Un'yu Shō (Ministry of Transportation), *Rikuun Tōkei Yōran* [Statistical Tables on Land Transportation]. If we use the figures in this volume to calculate the average freight rate per ton-kilometer, the figure for trucking is 6.6 times that for the national railways in 1968, and 6.3 times in 1974.

[22] Kokutetsu Kansa Iinkai (The Auditing Committee for the Japan National Railways), *1975 Nendo Nihon Kokuyū Tetsudō Kansa Hōkoku Sho* [The Auditor's Report on the Japan National Railways for Fiscal 1975] (Tokyo: Japan National Railways, August 1976), p. 45.

[23] For more detail on the analysis and data presented in this section, see the following two items: Kōshiro Kazutoshi, Sano Yōko, and Shimada Haruo, *Kōshō-ryoku Moderu ni Yoru Shuntō Chinage no Bunseki*, and Kōshiro Kazutoshi, "Nihon no Chingin Kettei to Kokusai Hikaku" [Wage Determination in Japan and International Comparisons] *Gendai Nihon no Chingin*, vol. I, ed. by Ujihara Shōjirō (Tokyo: Shakai Shisō Sha, 1977), pp. 169–209.

resent the union's organizational strength in the private sector (MLS), and the number of strikers in the national railways during the same period is used to measure the organizational strength of unions in the public sector (GLS). Using these variables, the change in wage rates during the spring wage offensive can be explained as follows:

$$\Delta W = -3081 \quad +6799 \text{ UYS} + 6494 \text{ MLS} + 229.8 \text{ GLS}$$
$$(-2.82) \, (+6.59) \qquad (+2.51) \qquad (+11.96)$$
$$R = 0.988, \, S = 1123, \, DW = 2.41$$

Figures given in parentheses are t-values for the respective coefficients.

The figures used for each variable are given in Table 6. The above formula gives us average figures for the entire period which suggest that the strikes in the national railways accounted for ¥3024 of the average hike, a figure equal to an average of 26.9 percent of the total increase obtained in each of the years from 1961 through 1975.[24]

Although it is impossible to use the above function and coefficient to make direct inferences about the exact extent of the influence of disputes in the national railways or of Kōrōkyō (which represents employees of the Japan National Railways), it is also extremely difficult to argue that there is no influence at all. Moreover, even if we were to assume that the impact of strikes and other disputative activity in the public sector exerted as much influence as the formula suggests, it would be difficult to know whether on the macro-economic level the higher wage rates have been a plus or a minus in terms of stimulating the national economy. On the one hand, it would seem likely that the resultant increase in individual consumption has been desirable; on the other, one might score the wage hikes as being excessive and thereby argue that they are one factor accelerating price inflation.

5.   Conclusion

The preceding discussion has sought to formulate an approach for examining whether or not the right to strike ought to be extended to employees in the five national enterprises and three public corporations. Two approaches were used to ascertain the effects of strikes by employees in these undertakings.

The first sought to present an objective means of quantifying the impact of illegal strike activity by employees of the Japan National Railways. In doing so, we examined (1) the direct loss of income to the national railways, (2) the secondary effects on directly related

---

[24] On the method used to calculate the effect of strikes in the national railways on wage increases, see the notes attached to Table 6.

Table 6:   Variables Used in a Collective Bargaining Model for Estimating the Wage Hikes during the Spring Wage Offensive

Year	Percentage change in wages during the spring wage offensive (W)	Absolute amount of the increase in wages during the spring wage offensive (ΔW)	The number of working days lost in manufacturing during the spring wage offensive (MLS)	Ratio of National Railway employees participating in strikes during the spring wage offensive (GLS)	Ratio of effective job seekers to job openings during January and March (UYS)
1961	13.8	2,970	0.4585	0.26	0.64
1962	10.7	2,515	0.2670	0.65	0.63
1963	9.1	2,237	0.1517	0.32	0.54
1964	12.4	3,305	0.1644	0.22	0.67
1965	10.6	3,150	0.4066	0.91	0.63
1966	10.6	3,403	0.2014	2.62	0.55
1967	12.5	4,371	0.1303	0.35	0.78
1968	13.6	5,296	0.1912	4.32	0.97
1969	15.8	6,865	0.2605	3.02	1.06
1970	18.5	9,166	0.2807	1.82	1.30
1971	16.9	9,727	0.4340	10.84	1.10
1972	15.3	10,138	0.3182	16.77	1.02
1973	20.1	15,159	0.2236	34.13	1.63
1974	32.9	28,918	0.6726	69.22	1.54
1975	13.1	15,279	0.3160	51.94	0.72
1976	8.8	11,596	—	—	0.62

Notes: 1. The data for estimating the change in wage rates comes from the Labor Union Section, Bureau of Labor Administration, Ministry of Labour (Rōdō Shō Rōsei Kyoku Rōdō Kumiai Ka).

2. MLS is calculated as follows for manufacturing firms with 30 or more employees:

$$MLS = \frac{\left(\begin{array}{l}\text{number of working days lost in manufacturing}\\\text{from February through May}\end{array}\right)}{\left(\begin{array}{l}\text{number of regular}\\\text{employees}\end{array}\right) \times \left(\begin{array}{l}\text{average number of}\\\text{days worked during}\\\text{the February-May}\\\text{period}\end{array}\right)}$$

3. GLS is calculated as follows without reference to the days lost or worked:

$$GLS = \frac{\left(\begin{array}{l}\text{number of national railway employees participating}\\\text{in strikes during the spring wage offensive}\end{array}\right)}{\left(\begin{array}{l}\text{the number of national railway employees at the}\\\text{end of the fiscal year, } i.e.,\text{ the end of March}\end{array}\right)}$$

4. The average values for each variable between 1961 and 1975 are as follows:

ΔW =   8,170
GLS = 13.1613
UYS =   0.9187
MLS =   0.3051

By multiplying the average value for each variable by the value of the respective coefficient in the wage function, we can estimate the contribution of each variable to the average increase in wages during this period.

industries, and (3) the tertiary effects on the economy as a whole by considering (a) the dispensability of services provided by the national railways, (b) the ability of the public to postpone demand for the services or to accumulate inventories during such strikes, and (c) the extent to which substitute services could be found for (i) passengers and (ii) freight. A comparison with employees in other public corporations and enterprises suggests (1) that the impact of strikes by employees of the Telephone and Telegraph Corporation is not so great and (2) that it is impossible to quantify the economic costs borne by the public when postal workers strike.[25]

One thing is clear: discussion of the impact of strikes in the public sector must go beyond a simple calculation of the apparent economic costs. However, if we can somehow gain a better idea of the economic costs, as we have done here in only the most sketchy fashion for strikes involving only the employees of the national railways, we will be taking one small but significant step in the direction of building a base for more accurate comparisons and more vigorous debate. Nevertheless, we will continue to be plagued by our inability to grasp a number of intangible dimensions. The intangibles would seem to be particularly important in evaluating the impact of strikes in the public sector because of the nature of the services provided and the fact that public corporations and enterprises operate as monopolies in most cases. Accordingly, although the impact on the public varies according to the technological nature of the service (such as the extent to which it is capital-intensive, the relative share of labor costs to total costs, and the degree of automation) and the degree to which similar services can be obtained from private firms, we are less likely to know the full amount of inconvenience felt by private households to the extent that monopolistic conditions exist. Corporations perhaps can minimize the impact of an interruption in postal services by using the telephone, telex, facsimile, or other communications media; families are financially less able to do so. In other words, any judgment about the essentiality of the various public services must recognize these problems in measuring the inelasticity of demand for public services and consider broadly the impact of strikes in the public sector on the entire democratic process of government. At the same time, this broad definition of essentiality must be tempered by an appreciation for the basic rights of labor.

The second approach used in this study focused on the extent to

[25] For more details on the analysis of the National Telephone and Telegraph Corporation and the Postal Service, see the author's original paper cited in the note at the foot of p. 236.

which strikes in the public sector affect wage determination. Relying upon a framework commonly associated with the Phillips Curve, we used a regression analysis to examine a number of variables. We are not fully satisfied with this approach, but we feel it is one way of looking at the macro-economic impact on the national economy. Where the collective determination of wages through the spring wage offensive plays a unique role, there is a certain rationale to adopting this approach as long as Kōrōkyō plays a significant role in the process.

Finally, it is well to bear in mind the fact that this paper has examined the impact of behavior which is defined as illegal by Article 17 of the National Enterprise and Public Corporation Law. Given this prohibition, the actual volume of strikes and other related disputative activity in the public sector is surprising indeed. Nevertheless, we ought not to overlook the fact that unions of employees in the public sector continue to be restrained by the above legislation. For example, unions affiliated with Kōrōkyō are forced to avoid an all-out strike by the financial costs accompanying the disciplinary action meted out by the authorities. Consequently, they have chosen to engage in more focused strikes aimed at creating disruptions at key bottlenecks. Beginning with the strikes for the right to strike, the disputative activities of Kōrōkyō in recent years have, perhaps unintentionally, given us a valuable opportunity to evaluate the influence of strikes in the public sector. However, we cannot rely only on the quantitative analysis of past data to give us all the answers. Just as some claim that legal changes will result in fewer strikes and other disruptions in the public sector as labor-management relations improve, so too do some underline the possibility that more lenient legislation will usher in a period of increased disruption. In the end, the final solution will require a considerable amount of shrewd political judgment.

Comparative Perspectives on Labor's Share

Ono Akira

1. A Definition of Functional Shares and Some Major Issues

A. Types of Income Distribution

Generally speaking, two approaches are used to study the distribution of income. One is concerned with the functional distribution of income: the allocation of wages to labor, rent to land, and interest to capital. The focus is on how much return each of the factors of production receives for its contribution to total economic output. The second approach is concerned with the size distribution of income: the relative equality or inequality of distribution among individuals who may earn various combinations of wages, rent, and interest.

In this short essay attention is focused on the first approach with an emphasis on the share which labor receives. If we represent the wages paid to labor as W and the total amount of income distributed (national income or the value added) as Y, labor's share is defined in percentages as the following fraction: $\frac{100W}{Y}$. Although the basic concept is very simple, the actual measurement of W and Y presents a number of problems. This is particularly true when using data for several different

This study first appeared as "Wagakuni no Rōdō Bumpairitsu no Suii to Kokusai Hikaku," *Tōyō Keizai*, a special issue on income distribution (no. 3764: October 4, 1973), pp. 60–68. The author is Professor of Economics at Hitotsubashi University.

industries or for several points in time. International comparisons add further complications. It is thus important to define briefly the terms used in this essay.

B. Wage Income

Looking first at the numerator (W), one must decide whether "wages" will refer only to the income of "production workers" and ordinary employees, or whether the term will also include remuneration paid to staff members of management as well. This problem arose in the prewar period when some people concerned with the topic argued that the latter type of payment was merely a distribution of profits accruing to the owners of capital and their representatives. We take a different view here, and argue that even staff members of management receive a certain fixed income to cover their reproduction costs (*i.e.*, their living costs). Accordingly, we include the incomes and various allowances of managers in our definition of wage income. We exclude, however, any bonuses paid to such personnel out of the accrued profits of the business firm. Given our concern with the functional distribution of income, this is a sound approach. It is also the definition of employee income used in the national income accounts.

C. Income or Value Added

The definition of the denominator is a simple matter when dealing with the nation as a unit of analysis. It is equal to national income. However, when focusing on just one industry, it is important to distinguish between income produced by the industry and income accruing to the industry. This does not become a problem with national income accounts, but must not be overlooked in calculating income for a single industry. For example, although insurance premiums, advertising costs, and storage charges are included in the income earned by manufacturers, they are not part of the actual income produced by the industry. To avoid double counting, it is important to deduct all intermediate costs from the revenue earned by the industry. Other considerations must also be kept in mind. For example, in using national income accounts, labor's share will vary according to the definition of national income. Does one use the figures for gross income or for net income? How are indirect sales taxes handled? The pitfalls are many, and extreme care is required in these seemingly trivial matters.

D. Wages and Profits

Marxist economists often refer to the rate of surplus value or the rate of exploitation. If we accept the proposition that national income consists of two components, wage income (W) and profits (P), the relationship of labor's share to profits can be expressed as follows:

$$\frac{W}{Y}=\frac{W}{W+P}=1\Big/\Big(1+\frac{P}{W}\Big)$$

The percentage ratio of profits (P) to variable capital (W) is the rate of surplus value. As the rate of surplus value $\frac{P}{W}$ increases, labor's share $\frac{W}{P}$ decreases.

2. Accounting for Labor and Capital in the Calculation of Labor's Share

A. The Composition of the Labor Force and Labor's Share

One widely recognized index of an economy's stage of development is the composition of its labor force. In the early stages of development the percentage of the labor force in agriculture and, consequently, the percentage of self-employed (meaning "entrepreneurs" and family employees) in the labor force is high. As economic development occurs, the number of the self-employed diminishes rapidly as many enter secondary and tertiary industries and become employees. In the early stages, however, the widespread existence of cottage industry tends to blur the line between worker and capitalist, or employee and employer.

One problem is that statistics on income include all the income of the self-employed as being earned by the individual entrepreneur. In other words, entrepreneurial income includes wages, rent, and interest. It is a kind of "mixed income" which is not broken down into its functional components. In introducing the Marxist division of national income into wages and profits, a third component, the mixed income of individual entrepreneurs, was initially omitted. Accordingly, national income is expressed more precisely in the following manner: Y= W+P+Z.

Since the percentage of "self-employed entrepreneurs" in the labor force is generally quite high in the early stages of development, so too is the percentage of national income accounted for by the mixed income of individual entrepreneurs. Conversely, because the percentage of the labor force occupied by employees is low, the percentage of national income associated with wage income is also low. The fact is that labor's share (W/Y) is affected by shifts in the composition of the labor force. Indeed, at the one extreme the complete absence of any employees would result in labor's share being zero. Accordingly, although the simpler indices of labor's share may have heuristic value for studying the dynamics of economic growth, their use as an index of exploitation is unjustified. We must develop the concept further if it is to be used to study the functional distribution of income.

There are several ways to cancel out the effect of changes in the composition of the work force on labor's share. One limits the analysis to sectors of the economy which are sufficiently "modernized" for the composition of the work force to have stabilized. This is the line of reasoning followed by many who have limited their analysis to manufacturing. However, even in the manufacturing industry in Japan many small firms continue to be run largely by family members. Because of this dual structure in the economy, rather than entire industries which are fully "modernized", we are likely to find only a few large firms in each industry which meet the requirements of this approach.

Another approach often used calls for a breakdown of the "mixed income" of self-employed entrepreneurs into its functional components: the returns to labor and the returns to non-labor inputs (e.g. the ownership of land and capital). There are two ways to do this. One is to calculate values in terms of the labor input; the other calls for calculations based on the returns to capital. The first method requires that we assign a market value to the labor of the self-employed entrepreneur and other family members working with him. This is then subtracted from the family's total entrepreneurial income and treated as wage income. Let the market wage rate be "w"; the number of employees, "L"; and the total number gainfully employed (the work force), "N". The number of individual entrepreneurs and their family members is N−L. The amount of wage income is wL. Calculated in the simple manner described above, labor's share is wL/Y. If we add on the return to labor for the enterpreneur and his family, w(N-L), labor's share can be expressed as follows:

$$\frac{W}{Y} = \frac{wN}{Y} = \frac{wL + w(N-L)}{Y}.$$

Rewritten, this reads

$$\frac{W}{Y}=\frac{wN}{Y}=\frac{wL}{Y}\cdot\frac{N}{L}.$$

In other words, the earlier calculation of labor's share $\frac{wL}{Y}$ is multiplied by the ratio of the total labor force to employees. In economies where the distinction between employers and employees is clear, there is less problem in measuring labor's share as wL/Y. In less developed economies, however, the number of employees is often very small, resulting in a great difference between the values of wL/Y and wN/Y. Accordingly, as an index which is independent of changes in the composition of the labor force, and which can be used either to make comparisons over time or to make international comparisons, wN/Y should be used, not wL/Y.

The return-to-capital approach follows a similar process to calculate the average return to capital. The only problem is that labor's share will vary according to the approach as each uses different sets of statistical data.

B. Estimates of Labor's Share

In Figure 1 four different estimates of labor's share are given for the years 1953–1969. The first set of estimates (A) is based on the simple calculation most often used, with the quotient being derived by dividing employee income by national income. The return to the labor of the self-employed worker or entrepreneur is not included. Using this approach, labor's share is shown to have fluctuated, generally having remained stable at around 50 percent in the 1950s, then rising slightly during the 1960s. This pattern no doubt reflects the impact of postwar economic growth and the various changes occurring in the structure of the labor force. One proof of this can be found in the fact that labor's share falls when changes in the structure of the labor force are accounted for in the calculation. This can be seen in the fourth set of estimates (D). Labor's share dropped rapidly in the 1950s and then leveled off in the 1960s. The curve again kinks around 1960. Since labor must share in the distribution with capital, with the two shares totaling 100 percent, it is strange that labor's share should be over 100 percent in the 1950s.

This obviously results from the fact that the wage rates in small enterprises are far below those in the large firms. To avoid this anomaly, the wage rates in small firms should be used to calculate the income of entrepreneurs and their families. However, the choice of a wage rate

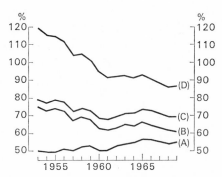

Figure 1:   Four Estimates of Labor's Share for All Industries: 1953–1969

Notes: $A = \left(\dfrac{wL}{Y}\right) \times (100)$. Data taken from Keizai Kikaku Chō (Economic
Planning Agency), *Kokumin Shotoku Tōkei Nenpō* [Annual Report on National Income Statistics] (Tokyo: Ōkura Shō Insatsu Kyoku, every year).

$B = \left[1 - \left(\dfrac{\pi_i(k_i + k_n)}{Y}\right)\right](100)$, where π_i is the rate of return on capital in incorporated firms, k_i is the capital stock in incorporated firms, and k_n is the capital stock in non-incorporated firms. The data are from Shionoya Yūichi, "Infureshon no Kaibōgaku, Kata to Gensen" [Anatomy of Inflation: Patterns and Courses], a mimeographed paper.

$C = \left(\dfrac{Y-Z}{wL}\right)(100)$, where Z is the income earned by non-incorporated firms or the self-employed. The data are from the source used for A above.

$D = \left(\dfrac{wL}{Y}\right) \times \left(\dfrac{N}{L}\right) \times (100)$. Data for the first multiplicand come from the source used for A and C. Data for the second multiplicand are from Sōrifu Tōkei Kyoku (Bureau of Statistics, Prime Minister's Office), *Rōdōryoku Chōsa* [Survey of the Labor Force] (Tokyo: Nippon Tōkei Kyōkai, every year).

for this sector is quite arbitrary. Moreover, even if we agree to consider the wages for family members as equal to the wages earned by employees in small firms, it is doubtful whether the same wage rate should be used for estimating the return to the labor of the entrepreneur.

The second set of estimates (B) in Figure 1 partially accounts for shifts in the composition of the labor force by providing estimates of the return to capital (profits) for entrepreneurs. The profit rate for incorporated enterprises is used as a rough estimate to interpolate for non-incorporated firms. In this case, however, the return to land is counted as wages, which means that the size of labor's share is overestimated. Labor's share drops from about 75 percent to the low 60s by about 1960, and thereafter fluctuates around that level. The behavior of the third set of estimates (C) is similar, although the estimates are persistently above those for the second set.

Reasoning from the standpoint of "economic man", it is likely that the switch from being self-employed to being an employee occurs when one is aware that his earning power in the labor market is greater than his marginal productivity when self-employed.

If the labor market is functioning properly (*i.e.*, is competitive), wage rates and marginal productivity should be the same for employees and self-employed workers. The use of the "going rate" in the labor market thus assumes that the distributive mechanism associated with competitive labor markets actually exists. Regardless of whether the return-to-labor or the return-to-capital approach is used, the problem of ascertaining the validity of these basic assumptions remains.

C. Circumventing the Problems of Ascertaining Market Competitiveness

When two methods for estimating the return to the labor of self-employed workers result in quite different estimates, as in Figure 1, most economists would compare the competitiveness of the labor and capital markets. We are thus left with having to define and measure market competitiveness. The presence of labor unions is a commonly cited example of a non-competitive factor in the Japanese labor market. On the other hand, Shinohara Miyohei has shown how the dual structure extends into the financial markets of Japan.

The estimates represented by line C in Figure 1 represent an attempt to circumvent the problem of changes in the composition of the labor force. In this case, the following formula was used:

$$\text{Labor's share} = \frac{W}{Y-Z}.$$

The income of non-incorporated firms (self-employed workers) is simply removed from the picture altogether. However, for some reason this approach is not used as frequently as either the return-to-labor or the return-to-capital approaches described above. Perhaps this merely reflects the fact that the debate has traditionally focused on the other indices. Moreover, the concept does not have the backing of the more established theoretical framework which assumes that the labor market is for the most part competitive. Nevertheless, the remainder of this study uses the third measure of labor's share (line C in Table 1) in order to avoid the problems associated with the changing composition of the labor force. The discussion below focuses primarily on the incorporated sector of the economy.

There are three reasons for using this index to estimate labor's share. First, it avoids the necessity of having to make judgments about market competitiveness. This is important in Japan where the so-called "modern economists" and Marxist economists stand in such rigid opposition to each other. From a scientific point of view, one would like to avoid interjecting one's own subjective assessment of the labor and capital markets. This is a big advantage. Second, this index is much easier to calculate from the data. This is particularly true when compared with the return-to-capital approach which requires that we know the level of profits for the incorporated sector and the capital stock for both incorporated and unincorporated firms. Finally, the available data allow us to obtain percentage returns to labor and capital which total 100 percent.

3. Some Long-term International Comparisons of Labor's Share

Using the third measure of labor's share introduced above (C in Figure 1), international comparisons of the relationship between labor's share and the level of economic development are of considerable interest. Figure 2 plots labor's share against per-capita income for nine countries in 1967. Although the simple measure of labor's share (W) suggests a very clear positive correlation between per-capita income and labor's share, the correlation nearly disappears when the income of self-employed workers is excluded. The next few paragraphs will discuss (1) the inevitable changes occurring in the composition of the labor force as a result of economic development and (2) the paradox of differentials in productivity.

A. Changes in the Composition of the Labor Force

The difference between the two estimates given in each country in Figure 2 is larger for the "less developed" countries than for the "more developed" ones. Labor's share would seem to be slightly lower in Japan than in other similarly industrialized countries. Although this may be due partially to differences in the data, examination of a few individual industries seems to substantiate that labor's share in Japan is indeed lower than in the other advanced countries. Taking the manufacturing

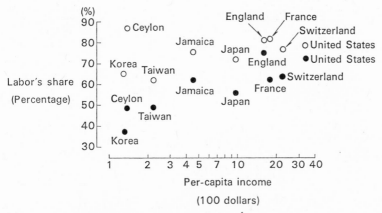

Figure 2: Labor's Share and Per-capita Income for Nine Countries: 1967

Notes: ● =Labor's share=$\dfrac{wL}{Y}$

○ =Labor's share=$\dfrac{wL}{Y-Z}$

Source: Sōrifu Tōkei Kyoku (Bureau of Statistics, Prime Minister's Office), *Kokusai Tōkei Yōran* [International Statistics Handbook] (Tokyo: Ōkura Shō Insatsu Kyoku, 1969).

sector, for example, Table 1 gives labor's share for differently sized enterprises in the United States and Japan. Regardless of firm size, labor's share is significantly lower in Japan. Moreover, if we consider (1) the fact that gross income figures for the United States include depreciation in the denominator whereas Japan's statistics are for net returns and (2) the fact that there is a ten-year gap in the information for the two countries (1958 for the United States and 1969 for Japan), there is even more reason to be confident that Japan's rate is relatively low. Another significant difference is the very large gap in Japan between the productivity of the labor-supply sector (agriculture being one typical industry) and the labor-demand industries like manufacturing. The continued low productivity in the labor-supply sector keeps the standard of living down for those in that sector, but also affects the pricing of labor going into more modern industries where technological change is occurring more rapidly. Accordingly, even though Japan has introduced modern technology into many of its industries, the increased ability to pay employees in those industries which have a strong demand for labor is not fully reflected in labor's share since these industries do not determine the going price for labor. Consequently, labor's share in Japanese industries is below that in similar

Table 1: Labor's Share in Manufacturing Industries by Firm Size

Firm size (number of employees)	Japan (1969)		United States of America (1958)	
	Productivity differential in terms of value added	Labor's share	Productivity differential in terms of value added	Labor's share
5–9	—	—	69.8	51.0
10–19	40.4	44.1	70.0	54.0
20–49	46.4	42.2	71.6	54.6
50–99	51.2	38.7	74.1	53.4
100–499	64.4	34.5	81.1	51.0
500–999	85.2	30.0	89.1	50.7
1000–	100.0	30.4	100.0	53.2

Note: Labor's share $=\dfrac{W}{Y}$

Source: Tsūsan Shō, Daijin Kanbō Tōkei Bu (Research and Statistics Bureau, Minister's Secretariat, Ministry of International Trade and Industry), *Kōgyō Tōkei Hyō* [Census of Manufacturers: Report by Industries: 1969]; and Bureau of Census, Department of Commerce (United States of America), *United States Census of Manufacturers* (Washington, D. C.: Government Printing Office, 1958).

American industries despite the fact that they share a similar standard of technology. In relatively less developed countries like Japan which import in a very short period vast amounts of technology from more advanced countries like the United States, the gap between productivity and wage rates is large. This is what makes labor's share in Japan low by international standards. Shinohara Miyohei draws similar conclusions in his studies on an even larger number of countries.

B. Productivity Differentials and Labor's Share

Table 1 also shows that labor's share is inversely correlated with firm size in Japan, whereas firm size does not much affect labor's share in America. The difference is linked to firm-size differentials in productivity. If we set value added per employee in firms with one thousand or more employees at 100, productivity in firms with ten to nineteen employees falls to 40.4 percent in Japan but to only 70.0 percent in America.

At the same time, however, the level of wages will also be based upon the going rate for unskilled labor. The differential between income and productivity varies directly with the amount of skill possessed by each occupational group. Given these differentials which arise because wages are pegged to the productivity of the lowest wage group (the unskilled), the overall supply curve for labor will reflect the traditional standard of living. In other words, quick improvements in productivity will not translate themselves into equally rapid increases in the wage rate. The difference instead goes to management. Management is a much smaller group and is usually better informed; it also has needs for money (such as further investment) which go beyond living styles and which tend to be tied to tradition and hence are slower to change (although the consumption and other behavior of the *nouveaux riches* suggest these patterns can change quickly when certain types of mobility occur). Nevertheless, management adjusts more quickly than the collective work force to the fact that a larger profit exists. Labor's share is thus smaller in firms with rapid technological change. Moreover, as the gap in productivity widens, so too does the differential in labor's share. Here it should be emphasized that labor's share in Japan varies inversely with the absolute level of wages. High labor productivity and concomitant high wages in Japan's large firms are the result of high investment in capital, which is then reflected in a lower share for labor. In the United States, this kind of variation in labor's share is minimal because the differentials in productivity are small. However, even in America a similar pattern can be found for individual industries in which productivity varies noticeably by firm size.

Across industries the same basic relationship also seems to hold between productivity and labor's share. Figure 3 shows that for both the United States and Japan, labor's share is highest in the industries with the lowest productivity. In both countries the petrochemical industries have by far the highest productivity, yet both clearly record the lowest shares for labor. At the other end of the extreme is the high share found in foodstuffs, clothing, and personal effects where productivity is low. The pattern of both productivity differentials and labor's share is very similar in the two countries.

C. The Stability of Labor's Share

A look at how labor's share has fluctuated in Japan's non-agricultural industries for most of this century (Figure 4) suggests four salient trends. First is the general rise in the bottom line which is influenced by shifts in the composition of the labor force. From 1906 to 1920 labor's share was about 40 percent; from 1920 to 1940, between 45 and 50 percent; and in the postwar years, somewhere around 60 percent. Second is the stability of labor's share when the influence of changes in the composition of the labor force are excluded (the upper

A. Japan (1969)

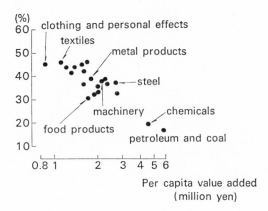

Per capita value added
(million yen)

B. United States (1967)

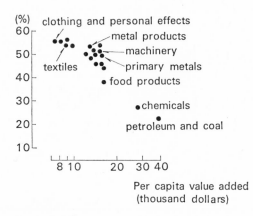

Per capita value added
(thousand dollars)

Figure 3:   Labor's Share and Productivity (Value Added) in Manufacturing
              Industries

Note: Labor's share $= \dfrac{\text{all cash payments to employees}}{\text{value added}}$

Source: The respective volumes of the sources listed for Table 1.

line in Figure 4). In both the prewar and postwar periods labor's
share has remained at approximately 70 percent. The division of income
between labor and capital thus appears to be fairly stable. Third,

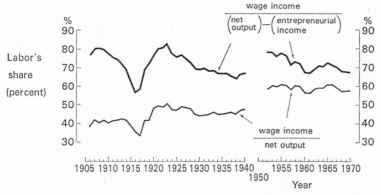

Figure 4: Labor's Share in Secondary and Tertiary Industries in Japan: 1960–1970

Source: Minami Ryōshin and Ono Akira, "Yōsoshotoku Bumpairitsu [Factor Incomes and Labor's Share in Secondary and Tertiary Industries], in Ohkawa Kazushi and Minami Ryōshin, eds., *Kindai Nihon no Keizai Hatten* [Economic Development in Modern Japan] (Tokyo: Tōyō Keizai Shimpō Sha, 1975), pp. 616–617.

Japan's experience in this regard closely parallels that of America and Great Britain, at least in the postwar period (Figure 5). Rough measures of labor's share show a slight increase (the lower lines) while the adjusted figures for labor's share (the upper lines) show considerable stability around 75 percent in Great Britain and 80 percent in the United States. Again, international differences in labor's share are partially due to the use of different definitions of income in the statistics of each country.

Fourth, in the case of Japan, in both Figure 1 for all industries and Figure 4 for secondary and tertiary industries the data show the same slight bend upwards in the late 1950s and early 1960s. Interestingly, Ohkawa Kazushi notes that a similar bend upwards can also be found in the prewar period, one which is linked with longer-term macro-economic trends. Comparing the time periods designated by Ohkawa and Rosovsky as periods of long-term expansion (namely, 1906–1919, 1931–1938, and 1954–1961) with the downward movement in labor's share, the impact of rapid capital formation which accompanies rapid growth is clearly evident. On the other hand, in periods of economic recession the share of labor rose. Briefly stated, labor's share moves in a cyclical fashion, but in the opposite direction to the economic growth rate. Furthermore, short-term fluctuations seem to occur not only in Japan but in other countries as well. In the case of Japan,

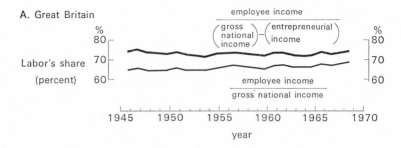

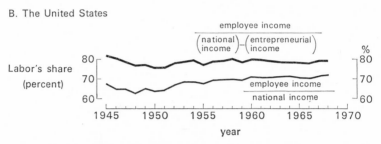

Figure 5: Labor's Share for all Industries in the United States and Great Britain in the Postwar Period

Source: For Great Britain, see the London and Cambridge Economic Service for the Times Newspapers, Ltd., *The British Economy Key Statistics: 1900–1970* (Cambridge: Department of Applied Economics, University of Cambridge, undated), p. 4.

For the United States, see Bureau of the Census, Department of Commerce, *Statistical Abstract of the United States* (Washington, D. C.: Government Printing Office, various years).

however, labor's share seems to be extremely sensitive to long-term changes in the growth rate, and will fluctuate up and down even with long-term movements in the economic growth rate.

4. The Mechanism Determining Labor's Share

Countries which are late in starting the process of industrialization share two characteristics. One is the borrowing or importation of foreign technologies. The second is the existence of surplus labor in agriculture. These two characteristics are considered briefly in the remaining paragraphs.

A. The Borrowing of Foreign Technology

In developing countries nearly all the technology used in the "modern" sectors is imported from the "advanced" countries. Entrepreneurs in the industrialized nations have developed technologies appropriate to the structure of comparative factor costs in their own country. However, in countries which lack a store of scientific knowledge and which are not blessed with the economic margin necessary for developing their own technologies, entrepreneurs are unable to choose the mode of production most suited to maximizing profits within the framework of their own country's endowment of the various factors of production. For them the only choice is the technology developed in the advanced countries: the development of any other technology or of accompanying production functions is beyond their capabilities. Moreover, entrepreneurs in the less developed countries have little leeway to adapt foreign technology which meets the relative factor prices domestically. As R. S. Eckaus suggests, whatever the actual production function may be, entrepreneurs are inclined to believe that the technology will not allow for factor substitution. The production functions which the less developed countries import from the more "advanced" countries often serve as models which limit productive possibilities when followed too rigidly.

B. Labor's Share in the Less Developed Countries

The second common characteristic of the less developed countries is the great supply of unskilled labor which resides largely in the agricultural sector. W. A. Lewis hypothesized that in such countries labor would be supplied to the modern sectors of the economy in unlimited amounts at the real wage rate existing in the non-modern sectors. He tended to think of a standard wage rate in the non-modern sectors as a given which was determined by various institutional factors. A more comprehensive model, however, requires us to view the wage rate as an endogenous variable determined by the level of technology and the rate of capital formation in the non-modern sectors and by the rate of growth occurring in the modern sector. Nevertheless, the important point is that real wages will be determined by a variety of factors which shape and define the standard of living in the traditional sector. These factors change at a slower pace than do the other economic variables. Without going into further detail, the Lewis formulation can be accepted within the framework of our analysis.

Generally speaking, in the less developed countries the relative cost-output ratio for capital is above that for labor. Accordingly, one would expect that more labor-intensive methods of production would be used in order to take advantage of the abundance of relatively cheap labor. However, the experience of Japan suggests that the methods of production used in the modern sectors of the economy have been imported from the advanced countries and are capital-intensive. The production functions introduced from abroad no doubt provide the less developed countries with the best means for rapidly "catching up" with the developed nations. Nevertheless, the introduction of capital-intensive modes of production into such countries serves only to lower labor's share. In other words, the introduction of modern technology causes a drop in labor's share in economies where low wage rates are tied to a traditional sector with a labor surplus.

Finally, the relationship between long-term cyclical trends and labor's share in Japan needs brief mention. In periods of economic growth, the modern sector experienced very rapid growth as a result of sizeable investments infused with foreign technology. Since labor is drawn out of the traditional sector at the wage rate prevailing in that sector, there is a considerable difference between the wages and the productivity of workers in the modern sector. On the other hand, this difference narrows when output falls, since wage rates are not elastic but are tied to the prevailing standard of living in the traditional sector. Accordingly, upswings in economic activity are associated with a decline in labor's share, whereas downswings are accompanied by a rise in labor's share.

5. Conclusions

This paper has given only the briefest of summaries. Although based upon empirical research, it presents hypotheses which will require much more rigorous scrutiny before being fully accepted as statements of fact. For example, it suggests that real wages in the traditional sector supplying labor are rather impervious to economic fluctuations. However, looking at the experience of Japan in the prewar period, we can see some minor difficulties. Real wages in agriculture have remained constant even during the economic upswings. Indeed, they even dropped a little in the early part of the period. In the downswings, however, they showed considerable resistance to the drop in monetary wages in the urban sector; indeed, real wages rose as a result of price deflation. This means that labor's share will move in the aforementioned way, but the movement will be more vigorous than it would were wages for unskilled labor constant. Likewise, it is hypothesized that the increase in labor's share during a downswing would be due to a drop in productivity or output in the modern sector while the going wage rate in the traditional sector remained unchanged. The above example, however, suggests that labor's share would rise even without such a drop in productivity. This is but one example of the need for additional research in this area.

A Short Bibliography

I. Estimates and analyses of long-term trends in labor's share in the Japanese economy:
  A. Umemura Mataji, *Chingin–Koyō–Nōgyō* [Wages, Employment and Agriculture] (Tokyo: Taimeidō, 1961).
  B. Ohkawa Kazushi, "Changes in National Income Distribution by Factor Share," in *The Distribution of National Income*, ed. by J. Marchal and B. Ducros (New York: Macmillan, 1968), pp. 177–185.

II. International comparisons of labor's share:
  C. Shinohara Miyohei, "Kōgyō ni Okeru Bumpairitsu" [Labor's Share in Manufacturing], in *Nihon Keizai no Bunseki* [An Analysis of the Japanese Economy], ed. by Tsuru Shigeto and Ohkawa Kazushi, vol. I (Tokyo: Keisō Shobō, 1953), pp. 167–195.
  D. Simon Kuznets, *Modern Economic Growth: Rate, Structure and Spread* (New Haven and London: Yale University Press, 1966). The Japanese translation is *Kindai Keizai Seichō no Bunseki*, trans. by Shinoya Yūichi, vol. I (Tokyo: Tōyō Keizai Shimpō Sha, 1968).

III. A similar explanation of Japan's low labor's share:
  E. Tsujimura Kōtarō, "Koyō Kōzō to Shotoku Bumpairitsu" [The Employment Structure and Labor's Share], in *Sengo Nihon no Keizai Seichō*, ed. by Komiya Ryūtarō (Tokyo: Iwanami Shoten, 1963), pp. 103–128. An English-language translation of this book has been published: Komiya Ryūtarō (ed.), *Postwar Economic Growth in Japan*, trans. by Robert S. Ozaki (Berkeley: University of California Press, 1966).

IV. Other related items mentioned in this paper:
  F. Ohkawa Kazushi and Henry Rosovsky, *Japanese Economic Growth: Trend Acceleration in the Twentieth Century* (Stanford:

Stanford University Press, 1973), Chapter Two.

G. R. S. Eckaus, "The Factor-Proportions Problem in Underdeveloped Areas," *American Economic Review* (vol. 45, no. 4: September 1955), pp. 539–565.

Index

age, as determinant of salary, 206–7
agricultural households. *See* households
agriculture and forestry: as source of
industrial workers, 38–39, 257, 263;
labor force participation of women
in, 28–29; productivity in, 19; work
force retention rate in, 10–11
Arisawa Hiromi, 46, 47, 49, 55, 128,
130

Bank of Japan, 229
base-up formula, 158, 199
basic pay (*kihonkyū*), 160, 161, 164–
67, 171–72
Basic Survey of the Wage Structure
(Chingin Kōzō Kihon Tōkei Chōsa),
101, 203, 213
Baumol, W. J., 101
Bernouille-Laplace function, 63, 64
blue-collar workers, 178, 210
bonus, semiannual, 148, 155, 175, 201,
256
breadwinner. *See* primary earner
budget survey, household, 55
Bureau of Labor Statistics (U.S.A.), 55
Bureau of Statistics, 129
business cycle, 5–18, 76, 129

capital: formation of, 82; rate of utilization of, 76, 79, 82; stock of, 76, 82
capital-labor ratio, 76, 79
career employment. *See* lifetime employment
Chamberlain, Neil W., 239
chemical industry, 225
civil service, 121
coefficient of dispersion, 190
collective bargaining, 181–82, 216–35,
252

commuting, time spent, 134
consumer prices, 125, 159, 230. *See
also* inflation
Council on Industrial Structure (Sangyō Kōzō Shingikai), 68, 83

death rate among workers, 22
Denison, E. F., 240
Densangata (electrical industry) wage
package, 111, 156, 157
depression (1930s), 6–7, 17, 18
DLA (Douglas-Long-Arisawa) effect,
52, 60, 64
Dōmei (labor confederation), 158, 236
Dōrō (Dōryokusha Rōdō Kumiai), 248
Douglas, Paul H., 46, 47, 49, 50, 51,
52, 55, 128, 130

early retirement. *See* retirement
earnings profile, 86
Eckhaus, R. S., 269
Economic Advisory Council, Subcommittee on the Labor Force, 133
economic development, 262, 268
Economic Planning Agency, 152, 189
Economic Research Institute, 189
economic theory: Keynesian, 41, 71;
Marxist, 257, 262; "modern", 262
education, as determinant of wages,
208. *See also* tertiary education
electrical goods industry, 225
employees, increase in number of, 32–
40, 257. *See also* households, employee; mid-career employee; permanent employee
employment: levels of in prewar economy, 8; guarantee of, 121; opportunities for, 54
Employment Insurance Account, 138,
139

273